MACROFINANCE

the financial system
and the economy

FRANK J. JONES

*San Jose State University
and SRI International*

Winthrop Publishers, Inc.
Cambridge, Massachusetts

To Mom and Dad

Library of Congress Cataloging in Publication Data

Jones, Frank Joseph.
   Macrofinance.

   Includes bibliographies and index.
   1. Finance.   2. Business enterprises—Finance.
3. International finance.   I. Title.
HG173.J66   332   77–15800
ISBN 0–87626–543–3

Cover design by David Ford

© 1978 by Winthrop Publishers, Inc.
   17 Dunster Street, Cambridge, Massachusetts 02138

10 9 8 7 6 5 4 3 2 1

CONTENTS

part III   the domestic financial system: interest rates, financial institutions, and financial markets

part IV   the international financial system

part V   the financial behavior of the corporate business sector

PREFACE

This book is designed to provide a broad and basic description of the financial system and the parts of the economy that are closely related to the financial system. In particular, the book is designed to describe the financial and economic environments of the business firm.

The original intent of the book was for use in the introductory corporate finance course as a supplement to a traditional corporate finance text because such texts do not typically include sufficient coverage of the financial and economic environments of the financial manager. For this purpose, Chapter 11, which discusses recent changes in corporate financial behavior over business cycles, serves as a transition from this book to the corporate finance text.

However, the book's broad coverage also makes it useful for other courses. Since the book covers the methods of determining and forecasting interest rates, the financial institutions, the financial markets, and the international financial system, it can be used as the principal text in a financial markets and institutions course. The book's extensive coverage of the monetary system, monetary policy, and domestic and international banking enable it to be used in a course on money and banking. The book could also be used in a principles of macroeconomics course to provide an alternative treatment of macroeconomic theory and policy and a more thorough treatment of the financial aspects of macroeconomics, including interest rate determination, than macroeconomics texts usually provide.

The book is also intended for corporate financial managers who wish to gain a better understanding of their financial and economic environments so they can more effectively manage their firms' financial activities. Finally, the book should appeal to general readers, whether nonfinancial managers, investors, or informed citizens, who wish to get a better appreciation for the workings of the financial and economic systems.

There are several aspects of this book, and biases of the author in presenting this material, that give it such potential broad use and appeal. First, there is unquestionably a strong conceptual framework (often called theory) that provides a basis for understanding the financial and economic systems and the relationships among them. Many treatments of the financial system are primarily descriptive and provide little conceptual framework for understanding the financial system. This the author finds unacceptable. To simply describe each part of the financial and economic systems in isolation does not provide a basis for understanding the interactions among these systems. This book stresses the conceptual framework of the financial and economic systems.

Often, however, when conceptual frameworks or theories are presented, they are done so in terms of abstract, usually mathematical, models that can be comprehended only by readers with considerable backgrounds in mathematics and the specific area that is being modelled. This book, however, presents the conceptual framework of the financial and economic systems in a nontechnical, descriptive manner. Instead of a complex, mathematical model of the macroeconomy, a simple, diagrammatic model is used to explain the relations between economic policies and economic goals. The conceptual basis of the financial system is treated with clear, concise descriptions of basic relationships rather than with involved equations. In all parts, a basic understanding of the relationships, rather than the techniques and manipulations, is stressed.

It is also a bias of the author that concepts and relationships should not only be presented, but also illustrated and that the illustrations should be based on current, applicable data. Data are used extensively in this book to illustrate concepts and the relationships among various parts of the financial and economic systems. The flow of funds data made available by the Board of Governors of the Federal Reserve System provide a very valuable source of financial and economic data that has been, in the author's estimation, greatly underutilized. The flow of funds data are an integral part of this book. They are used to provide an overview of the financial system, to show the nature of various types of financial institutions, and to show who are the issuers and purchasers of various types of securities. And, most importantly, the flow of funds data are used to show the relationships among various parts of the financial and economic systems. The financial system is very competitive and responds quickly to changes in financial and economic conditions. The frequent, substantial shifts among financial institutions and securities are illustrated with the flow of funds data, thus showing the thorough integration of the financial markets, the financial institutions, and the economic system.

In summary, the characteristics this book embodies are that: 1) it stresses the conceptual interrelationships among various parts of the financial and economic systems; 2) it uses data to illustrate these interrelationships and shows the rapid, large shifts in the financial system in response to changing conditions; 3) practical applications of all concepts are given; 4) it is very current in its presentation of data, examples, and concepts; 5) its coverage of the financial and economic system is very comprehensive; and, 6) it is nontechnical—the concepts introduced are explained and used in a way that is comprehensible to the general reader.

Part I of this book, which includes Chapters 1 and 2, provides an overview of the economic and financial systems and of the coverage of the remainder of the book. Part II, Chapters 3 through 6, treats the goals and policies of the economic system both in a conceptual and in an applied way and discusses a model that shows how the goals and policies are related.

Part III, Chapters 7 through 9, treats the domestic financial system, including the role of the interest rate, how it is determined and how it can be forecast, and the individual financial institutions and markets and their relationships. Part IV, Chapter 10, discusses the international financial system. Part V, Chapter 11, is basically an applied chapter on corporate financial behavior over time. It shows the corporations' financial responses to both business cycles and long-run changes.

If this book is used as a supplement in a corporate finance course, Part II, Chapters 3 through 6, could be eliminated to save time, particularly if the students have had a good introductory course in the principles of macroeconomics. Part V, Chapter 11, could be treated either before the corporate finance text is begun or after the treatment of financial analysis and financial ratios. Similarly, Parts III and IV could be covered at either the beginning or the end of the corporate finance course.

For use in a financial institutions and markets course or in a money and banking course, the material in the book could be covered in the order in which it occurs. For a money and banking course, the material on the non-bank-related financial markets could be omitted and supplementary material on commercial banks substituted. For use in a principles of macroeconomics course, Parts II and possibly V could be omitted.

Numerous people have assisted in the preparation of this manuscript. I would like to thank Professor T. Gregory Morton of the University of Connecticut for many perceptive and helpful comments and my colleague Rob Sanderson for many discussions involving the topics covered in this book. I would also like to thank Mark Weisler for his invaluable assistance in the preparation of the manuscript and Chuck Murphy, finance editor at Winthrop Publishers, Inc., for his editorial advice and support.

I would also like to thank my son, Ryan, for the many long hours he spent keeping me company at his desk next to mine. Finally, primarily because this book was written mainly during "spare time," I would like to thank my wife, Roni, for her general support and her tolerance of a view of my back. Without Roni and Ryan, it would not have been possible.

I hope the readers will also be tolerant of the remaining deficiencies and mistakes in this, the first edition of the book. I would appreciate comments from readers on both its form and substance.

INTRODUCTION TO THE ECONOMIC AND FINANCIAL SYSTEMS

I

introduction

1

The purpose of this book is to present an overview of the current financial and economic systems in the United States. An understanding of these systems is essential for business managers, investors, and well-informed citizens. And such an understanding is particularly critical for the financial managers of firms. While the perspective taken in this book is that of the business financial manager, the discussion of the financial and economic systems is sufficiently broad to be applicable to the needs of other readers.

To operate efficiently, businesses need managers who have different specialties: marketing, production, personnel, and finance. This book examines the role of financial managers. In performing their specific functions within the firm, managers operate within an environment that is external to the firm but that affects their operations within the firm. This book discusses the economic and financial environments of business firms, and investigates how this environment affects business managers' performances. By having a better understanding of their environment, financial managers should be able to more effectively perform their functions within the firm.

The traditional role of financial managers has been to raise the funds required by their firms. When their firms needed more funds than they generated internally, financial managers arranged to obtain additional funds by borrowing from commercial banks, issuing stocks, bonds, or commercial paper, or in other ways.

In the last several years, however, the role of financial managers has broadened. Since the 1950s, financial managers have become more involved in the overall management of the firm. Instead of simply being told the level of funds required by the firm and proceeding to raise it from external sources, financial managers now participate in *anticipating* the financial needs of the firm, *acquiring* the funds it is anticipated the firm will need, and *allocating* the funds to specific assets in the firm. These three functions are called the 3 A's of the financial manager. Anticipating the firm's financial needs requires a forecast of the firm's sales and what new assets the firm will require to generate these sales. The level of funds that must be raised depends on the level of assets needed; the composition of these funds (for example, whether they should be long-term bonds or short-term bank borrowing) depends on the type of assets needed. The funds raised are then used to purchase the specific assets the firm anticipates it will need. These three functions of the financial manager encompass the firm's activities.

Financial managers are not unconstrained in their attempts to achieve their goals. Their behavior and their firm's performance depend to a significant extent on circumstances that are beyond the firm's capacity to control. Whether the economy is in a recession or a strong expansion affects the sales of the firm and hence its need to increase its plant and equipment, inventories, and accounts receivable. The level of prices on the stock market, bond rates, and the cost and availability of bank credit affect the ability of firms to raise external funds and the composition of these funds.

Since the behavior and success of financial managers are affected and constrained by the environment in which the firm operates, it becomes imperative for them to investigate this environment. The environment consists of three parts: the financial system, the economic system, and the social system. The *financial system* comprises the set of institutions, markets, and relationships that is involved in borrowing and lending funds and that affects the volume and cost of credit. Specifically, the financial system includes commercial banks, savings and loan institutions, life insurance companies, the stock and bond markets, investment bankers, and many other institutions and markets in the private sector. In addition, government institutions such as the Federal Reserve System and the U.S. Treasury are components of the financial system.

The financial system in turn is part of a larger environment, the *economic system*. The economic system consists of all individuals and institutions participating in exchanges that involve goods or services and money. It is composed of business, labor, consumers, and various levels of government and governmental agencies. The foreign sector also affects the domestic economy.

The economy is in turn a component of the *social system*. The social system has many economic and noneconomic goals. A society designs and influences its economic system to achieve these goals. Among the economic and social goals in the United States are high employment, stable prices, economic growth, an equitable distribution of income, and preservation of free enterprise. Figure 1–1 depicts the financial, economic, and social components of the environment.

The role of financial managers in the firm has become much more demanding in recent years. As noted above, they have assumed a much

Economic and Social Goals

1. High employment
2. Low inflation
3. Economic growth
4. Balance of payments equilibrium
5. Others

Economic System

1. Business
2. Labor
3. Consumers
4. Government

Financial System (selected parts)

1. Private
   Commercial banks
   Savings and loan associations
   Life insurance companies
   Investment banks
   Stock markets
2. Government
   Federal Reserve System
   Federal Home Loan Bank System
   Securities and Exchange Commission
   U.S. Treasury

Financial Manager

1. Anticipate level and composition of funds needed
2. Raise funds to finance these assets
3. Allocate funds to specific assets

FIGURE 1–1   THE ENVIRONMENTS OF THE FINANCIAL MANAGER

broader purview and responsibility within the firm, becoming involved in anticipating the need for funds and in the allocation of funds to assets as well as in actually acquiring the funds. But even their traditional role of acquiring funds has become more challenging because the external environment in which they operate has become much more dynamic in the last decade. As is discussed throughout this book, several factors are responsible for this increased dynamism: the more active use of monetary policy to achieve economic and social goals; high rates of inflation; increased sophistication in asset and liability management by nonfinancial corporations and financial institutions; availability of new securities; and the increased impact of international financial events on the domestic scene due primarily to freely fluctuating international exchange rates and the multinational firm.

This increased dynamism manifests itself in large variations in interest rates, variations in the availability of credit through various specific channels such as the stock and bond markets and commercial banks, and the availability of new securities for borrowing and lending such as certificates of deposit, Eurobonds, and cap loans. Changing rates of inflation can also affect corporate profits due to inventory valuation and fixed asset depreciation methods. And the recent recessions of 1970 and 1974 have caused large variations in sales. To perform their functions successfully, financial managers must be able to understand, interpret, and even anticipate changes in the firm's environment.

This book describes those parts of the financial, economic, and social environment shown in Figure 1–1 that have the greatest effects on the functions of financial managers. Part I provides a general discussion of the economic and financial system. The remainder of the book follows the plan of Figure 1–1, from the outside (broad goals) to the inside (more specific). Part II begins with the goals of the economic system and then discusses the use of economic policy to achieve these goals. Part III concerns the financial system in more detail, with emphasis on those parts that affect financial managers. It begins with a discussion of the determination of interest rates, the link between the economic and financial systems. Part IV examines the international financial system, discussing the environment of the multinational firm. Finally, Part V provides the link between the environment of financial managers and their activities within the firm by showing how the environment has affected financial decisions in the firm in recent years.

the economic
and financial
systems: an overview

2

the economic system

For the purpose of exposition, the economy is initially divided, somewhat artificially, into two sectors. The first sector–the *business sector*—produces goods and services. The second sector—the *household sector*—purchases these goods and services from the business sector and provides to the business the inputs needed to produce them, mainly managerial, clerical, and manual labor skills. (A third sector, the *government*, is also introduced.) Figure 2–1 depicts this simplified two-sector economy.

The upper loop shows goods and services being produced by the business sector and purchased by the household sector; the goods and services are exchanged for dollar payments. But business must employ inputs or factors of production to produce the outputs they sell. These inputs are supplied by the household sector. For their labor inputs, they receive a wage or salary from business. Households also supply funds, or financial capital, to businesses by buying their bonds and stocks for which they receive interest coupons and dividends, respectively. Business uses these funds (and funds supplied in other ways) to buy plants and equipment which are also inputs in the production process. Consequently, dollars, in the form of wages, salaries, interest, and dividends,

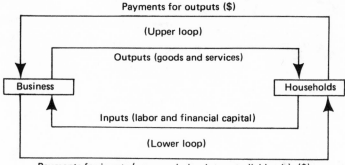

FIGURE 2–1   CIRCULAR FLOW OF EXPENDITURES IN THE ECONOMY

flow from business to households thus completing the circular flow of the dollars.

To summarize, business uses labor and funds from households, for which it pays wages, salaries, interest, and dividends, to produce goods and services which it then sells to households. Households use their wages, salaries, interest, and dividends to pay for the purchase of these goods and services. There is, therefore, a circular flow of funds or expenditures in the economy.

the economic system expanded

Figure 2–1's depiction of the economy, however, is unrealistic. One obvious oversimplification is that households do not spend all of their income on goods and services. They actually save some of their income. In addition, firms do not sell all their output to households; some produce plant and equipment, called investment goods, which they sell to other business firms. For example, in 1976 U.S. households earned, after taxes, $1,181.8 billion but spent only $1,078.6 billion on goods and services, leaving savings of $77.8 billion.[1] And, firms sold $241.2 billion of investment goods to other firms.

A more realistic economy is depicted in Figure 2–2. Business firms, to produce or supply goods and services (P), employ labor and financial capital from households, thus generating income (Y) for households.

---

[1] Due to the accounting system used, consumption plus savings does not equal income. Two other small categories, "interest paid by consumers" and "personal transfer payments to foreigners" are alternative uses of income. These categories are not considered herein.

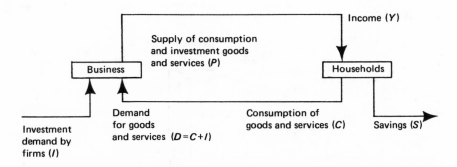

FIGURE 2–2   ALTERNATE VIEW OF CIRCULAR FLOW OF EXPENDITURES IN
THE ECONOMY

Households use this income, in part, to finance their consumption expenditures (C). The remainder they save (S). Business will continue to supply only those goods and services that it can sell; that is, only those for which there is a demand (D). There are two types of demand: the demand for goods and services by households, called consumption (C), and the demand for plant and equipment by other firms, called investment (I). In this model C and I represent the total demand for business firms' output.

Two obvious simplifications remain in Figure 2–2. First, not all income generated from the production of goods and services by firms accrues to households. Some of the income accrues to the firms themselves; it is called *profits*. However, a portion of these profits is paid as dividends to households. The remainder, called *retained earnings*, is kept by business and is used to finance their investment expenditures. Retained earnings, then, is income accruing to business.

A second simplification in Figure 2–2 is that an important sector of the economy, the government sector, is omitted. The government sector receives income taxes from households (T_H) and profits taxes from business (T_B) and uses these tax revenues to finance its purchase of goods and services (G), such as jet airplanes and highway construction. If the government spends more than it receives in total taxes $(T_H + T_B)$, it is said to have a *budget deficit*. If it receives more in taxes than it spends, its budget is said to be in *surplus*.

Figure 2–3 illustrates an economy with these two further additions. In this economy, business produces goods and services, generating income both for itself and for households. Both pay taxes to the government on their income. The government uses these taxes to finance its purchases from business. Households use some of their income to purchase business output, and save the remainder. Firms use their retained earnings to finance their purchases from other firms. The total demand for firms' output, then, is the sum of the demands from households, other firms, and the government: total demand equals $C + I + G$.

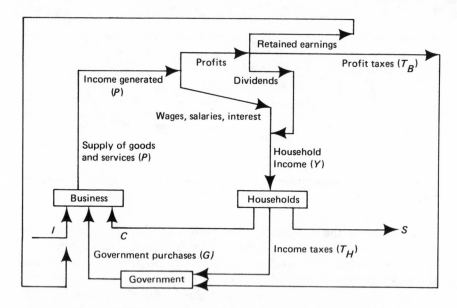

FIGURE 2-3 EXPANDED CIRCULAR FLOW OF EXPENDITURES IN THE ECONOMY

One very important question about this model of the economy is what determines whether business will produce a high level of output, thus employing all the available labor, or a very low level of output leaving many laborers unemployed. This question is addressed in Chapter 4.

Another question concerns the relation between the revenues and the expenditures of the three sectors in the economy. The terms *deficit* and *surplus* are commonly used with reference to the budget of the United States government. Budgets for the households and business sectors can also be considered. The data given above show that households earn more than they spend; households are therefore surplus units. Conversely, in 1976, business had retained earnings of $48.5 billion and investment expenditures of $241.2 billion; business is a deficit sector, spending more than it earns.

the financial system—conceptually

To focus on the essentials, reconsider the economy shown in Figure 2-2. Households are surplus units and earn more than they spend. Business firms are deficit units; they spend more than they earn and borrow to finance their deficit. What do households do with their savings? Where do businesses borrow the funds that allow them to spend more than they earn? The answer to both of these questions is the *financial system*. The function of the financial system is to accept the excess of surplus units and lend it to deficit units that wish to borrow. The financial system is the channel or conduit through which the savings of surplus sectors flow to the deficit sectors that wish to borrow.[2] Figure 2–2 can be modified as shown in Figure 2–4 to show the role of the financial system. The financial system is pictured as the repository of the savings of households and the source of the borrowing of business firms.

Figure 2–1 showed that goods and services are supplied to households in exchange for money and that labor is supplied to business in exchange for money. Is there any exchange through the financial system? Money obviously flows from the saver, the household, to the borrower, the business. Business is incurring debt. As a manifestation of this debt we can view business as providing IOU's to the lender. An IOU is simply a promise to repay the loan on a certain date. A more formal word than IOU for this promise is *security*. In some cases the IOU or security is actually a piece of paper which is exchanged; in others, it is a signed contract or verbal agreement. Several characteristics of these securities or IOU's are discussed below.

Through the financial system, funds flow from savers to borrowers; securities, indications of indebtedness, flow from borrowers to savers. What factors affect the amount savers are willing to save and borrowers

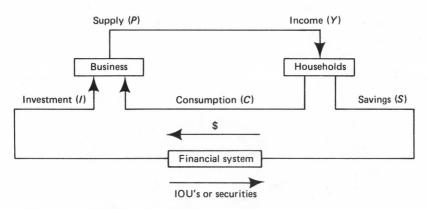

FIGURE 2-4 CIRCULAR FLOW OF EXPENDITURES IN THE ECONOMY, INCLUDING THE FINANCIAL SYSTEM

---

[2] Depicting all households as surplus sectors, none of whom borrow, and all business firms as deficit sectors is another simplification. Not all households earn more than they spend—some spend more than they earn and are deficit units. Some business firms also generate more retained earnings than they invest and are surplus units. However, households taken together earn more than they spend. And businesses, aggregated, spend more than they earn.

willing to lend? To answer this question, again refer to Figure 2–1 and consider what factors affect the quantity of goods demanded by consumers and supplied by firms. The major factor determining both the level of demand by consumers and the level of supply by firms is the *price* of the goods. In economic terms, these relationships are usually expressed in terms of demand and supply curves, as shown in Figure 2–5. As the price of a good increases, consumers will buy less of the good and producers will supply more. In competition, the quantity Q_o of the good will be sold at a price P_o. Similarly, in the lower loop of Figure 2–1 the wage rate affects the quantity of labor supplied by households and demanded by firms.

What variable affects the level of savings and borrowing in the financial system in the way prices affect the goods market and wages affect the labor market? It is obviously the *interest rate* (*i*). (Other factors that affect savings, such as income, are discussed in Chapter 4.) The interest rate is the stimulus or incentive for households to save. As the interest rate increases, the reward for savings is greater so the level of savings should increase. More is said about this relationship below. The interest rate is also the cost of borrowing. As borrowing becomes more costly, firms borrow less to finance their investment expenditures. These relations are shown in Figure 2–6. The observed interest rate will be i_o, at which point savings, the supply of funds into the financial system, equals borrowing, the demand for funds. The level of funds borrowed and lent will be Q_o.

The financial system provides a channel that facilitates the flow of funds from savers who wish to earn a return on their savings to borrowers who wish to spend more than they earn. The interest rate is the variable that regulates the flow of funds through the financial system.

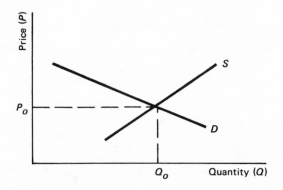

FIGURE 2–5 DEMAND AND SUPPLY OF GOODS

Introduction to the Economic and Financial Systems

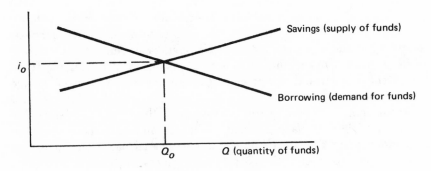

FIGURE 2-6 DEMAND AND SUPPLY OF FUNDS

the financial system—empirically

The financial system is the complex of institutions and markets that facilitates the flow of funds from surplus units to deficit units. Some of its major components are shown in Figure 2–7.

Two major modes exist to transfer funds from savers to borrowers. The first is by a direct transfer. For example, when a household buys a new issue of a corporate bond, the household is in essence lending directly to the corporation and receiving the bond as a security or IOU. Subsequent trading of the bond marked does not provide any new funds to the corporation but simply changes the identity of the creditor of the corporation. Similarly, the purchase of a new issue of corporate stock is a direct transfer of funds. In this case, however, the supplier of funds is an owner of the corporation, not a creditor.

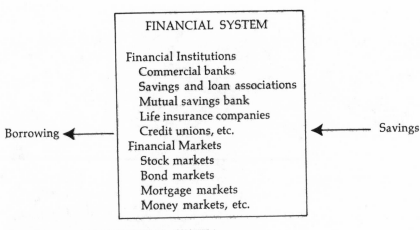

FIGURE 2-7 THE FINANCIAL SYSTEM

In the second mode, the funds are transferred from the saver to the ultimate borrower indirectly through an intermediary. When a household puts funds into a commercial bank savings account, the commercial bank may then relend these funds to a business which uses the funds to purchase plant and equipment. The household's addition to its savings account enables the bank to lend to the business. However, the funds do not flow directly from the saver to the ultimate investor, but through an intermediary in finance, the commercial bank. Business is not indebted to the saver but to the commercial bank; savers have a claim on the commercial bank, not the business.

The first mode of transfer, directly from the saver to the ultimate investor, is called *direct finance*. The second mode, through a financial intermediary, is called *indirect finance*. The nature of the distinction can be made more explicit by examining the balance sheets of the parties involved in the two modes. In Part I of Table 2–1, a household buys a $100 bond from a business. This bond represents a $100 asset to the household and a $100 liability to the business. The business owes the money directly to the saver. This is direct finance. In Part II the household puts $100 into its commercial bank savings account. The household deposit enables the bank to make a $100 loan to a business (commercial

TABLE 2–1*

I.   Direct Finance

Household		Business	
A	L + NW	A	L + NW
+100 (Bond)			+100 (Bond)

II.   Indirect Finance

Household		Commercial Bank		Business	
A	L + NW	A	L + NW	A	L + NW
+100 (Savings account)		+100 (Savings account)			
		+100 (Business loan)			+100 (Business loan from bank)

* A denotes assets; L liabilities; and NW net worth.

bank reserve requirements are ignored here). However, the business does not owe the saver but the commercial bank, which in turn owes the saver. This is indirect finance through a financial intermediary.

As indicated in Figure 2–7, in addition to commercial banks, several other types of financial institutions or financial intermediaries facilitate indirect finance. These include savings and loan associations, mutual savings banks, life insurance companies and so on. Chapter 8 examines financial institutions in detail.

securities and their characteristics

A security is an IOU or a promise to repay a debt. Savers buy securities; borrowers sell or issue securities. Securities have many different characteristics. An economy could function with only one uniform type of security. Why then the multiplicity of securities? There are many types of securities for the same reason that there are many types of automobiles and restaurants. Different buyers desire different characteristics in automobiles and restaurants and both buyers and sellers of securities desire to buy and issue securities, respectively, with different characteristics. The characteristics of automobiles and restaurants are obvious. What are the important characteristics of securities?

RETURN

Depending upon the nature of the security, the return can be called the interest rate, the coupon, or the dividend. The return represents the reward to the purchaser of the security, the saver, and the cost to the issuer of the security, the borrower. If $100 is lent, this amount plus a $6 return will have to be repaid in one year if the agreed rate of return is 6 percent. Obviously, the lender wants to earn a high return and the borrower wants to pay a low return. The actual return agreed upon is determined by the supply and demand for the security as shown in Figure 2–8. On some types of securities, there may also be a capital gain or loss that represents part of the return to the security's purchaser.

Several other characteristics of a security may affect its supply and demand, and hence its return.

RISK

The buyer of a security experiences two distinct types of risk. First, the borrower may become financially unable to pay the interest on the loan or to repay the entire loan when due. For example, if the bor-

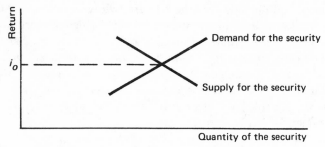

FIGURE 2–8   DEMAND AND SUPPLY OF SECURITIES

rower goes bankrupt the lender may not be able to recoup the funds lent. This type of risk is called *credit risk*. All securities have some degree of credit risk.

The second type of risk is called *market risk*. The price of some securities is fixed; it does not vary. For example, when you put $100 in your commercial bank savings account, you get back one year later $100 plus one year's interest. The bank cannot say that they had a bad year and hence can repay only $80. Such securities are *fixed-price securities*; they have no market risk.

Not all securities have fixed prices, however. If you buy a corporate stock or a bond for $100, the value of the stock or bond one year later when you are ready to sell it will not necessarily be $100. Its value will depend on the assessment by the stock or bond market of the worth of the security (which is in turn determined by the supply and demand for the security) and can be either more or less than $100. Securities whose principal values change according to supply and demand are called *variable-priced securities* and are said to have market risk. Market risk refers to the potential change in the value or price of a variable-priced security over time. Commercial bank savings accounts have no market risk; corporate stocks have considerable market risk.

In addition to high returns, buyers of securities normally prefer no or low risk. As an inducement to buy a security with a high risk, either credit or market, the buyer must receive a higher return for accepting the risk. Normally, high return and high risk go together in a security.

MATURITY

The maturity of a security refers to the period of time between when the initial lender supplies the funds to the borrower and when the borrower must repay the amount of the loan. A three-year bank loan and a twenty-year corporate bond have maturities of three and twenty years, respectively, when issued. Normally, the borrower must make interest payments in the interim. Some securities never mature; that is, the borrower never has to buy back the security. Corporate stock is an example of this type of security. Essentially, it has an infinite maturity. Conversely, those who deposit funds in a commercial bank savings account (the depositor, in effect, lends funds to the bank) can withdraw their funds, effectively, any time they choose. This type of security essentially has a continuous maturity—it matures at the discretion of the lender.

Many lenders prefer short maturity securities so they can be assured of getting the agreed upon amount of money back after a short period of time so that they can spend it on consumption or reinvest it. Borrowers often prefer long maturities because it may take a long period of time to generate a sufficient return from the investment to repay the loan.

The maturity of a security also has an important relationship to its market risk, as is discussed later in this chapter.

MARKETABILITY

It may not be necessary for holders of a security to wait until the security's maturity to dispose of the security and recoup their funds. They do have to wait until maturity to recoup their funds from the original borrower, but before maturity they may be able to sell the security to a third party.[3] The exchange of securities before their maturity is conducted through financial markets. Chapter 10 examines the various types of financial markets. Different financial markets, however, vary considerably in the facility with which securities can be exchanged through them. The important aspects of this exchange are the time it takes to exchange the security and the cost of the exchange. The cost of the exchange is the amount over the current market value of the security the buyer must pay to acquire it or the amount less than the current market value the seller receives to dispose of it.

The *marketability* of a security refers to the cost and the time of exchanging a security. For example, a share of a stock listed on the New York Stock Exchange can be exchanged very quickly during trading hours. The stock is sold at its market value but the broker charges a commission for conducting the sale—this represents the cost to the seller of the exchange. Since it takes very little time and some cost to sell the stock, the stock is quite "marketable," but not perfectly so. Real

---

[3] This can be done if the security is legally negotiable; that is, if the security is transferable from one person to another with the title passing to the transferee. For example, stocks and bonds are negotiable, commercial bank savings accounts are not.

estate is much less marketable. After an appraiser assesses the approximate market value of a property, it may take weeks before a buyer is found who will pay this price. And if the property is sold by an agent, the agent's cost may be substantial. On the basis of both time and cost, real estate is less marketable than a stock.

The exchange values of marketable securities are determined by the forces of supply and demand and may change frequently. Marketable securities are thus necessarily variable-priced securities; that is, their value is not fixed. The value of a marketable security with a fixed maturity is known for only one future date, its maturity date. At all other times the value of a fixed maturity security is uncertain. The value of a security with an infinite maturity, such as common stock, is uncertain at all times in the future.

Not all securities have markets; that is, not all securities can be sold to third parties. Commercial bank savings accounts are not marketable. But since depositors can withdraw their funds at any time, there is no need to sell the account to a third party. Commercial bank loans to businesses are not marketable—the bank must wait until the maturity of the loan before getting its funds back. Nonmarketable securities are fixed-price securities. For example, the value of a savings account is known to be the amount deposited, plus accrued interest. A business receiving a bank loan must repay the amount borrowed plus interest.

The mode of exchange of a security being newly issued by the borrower is often different from the subsequent exchanges of a security among investors. For example, a business selling its newly issued bonds uses a different market from that used by the purchaser of the bond who then wishes to sell it to a third party. When the bond is being initially sold by the business it is called primary security and it is said to be sold on a *primary market*. Subsequent sales of the bond are conducted on secondary markets, and in these exchanges the bond is called a *secondary security*. The primary and secondary markets for various securities are discussed in Chapter 9.

MISCELLANEOUS CHARACTERISTICS

Several other properties of securities are less essential for purposes of this discussion and are simply identified here.

An important difference exists between being an owner of a company and a creditor. The owner has a vote in formulating corporate policy and a share in profits and losses. The creditor normally has no vote in formulating corporate policy and receives a fixed payment periodically, independent of the level of profits. A stockholder is an owner and a bondholder, a creditor.

Some securities are secured by assets, which means that the lender has claim to the assets if the borrower does not pay the interest or principal on the loan. Such provisions reduce the credit risk of a security. For example, a mortgage lender holds title to the mortgaged property until the mortgage loan is repaid.

Corporate bonds have many other characteristics such as convertibility and callability which are discussed in Chapter 9.

LIQUIDITY

Liquidity is defined in terms of properties already discussed. Before defining liquidity, however, the relationship between market risk and maturity must be investigated. This relationship is direct: a marketable security with a longer maturity has greater market risk; that is, its price fluctuates more.

This relationship can be demonstrated by the following example. Consider a series of bonds of varying maturities which were issued at a time when the interest rate on bonds of all maturities was 6 percent.[4] At this interest rate, in order to issue a bond for $1000 (the amount paid for the bond initially by the lender and the amount repaid by the borrower at maturity) the issuer of the bond must agree to pay $60 per year to the buyer of the bond. This represents a 6 percent annual return on the $1000 investment. This amount must be paid every year until the bond matures, regardless of changes in the level of interest rates during the period. This payment is called the *coupon* of the bond.

Assume that after these bonds are issued, the interest rate on bonds of all maturities increases to 7 percent. Newly issued bonds with $1000 maturity values will then have to pay a coupon of $70 per year. Consequently, a previously issued bond which pays $60 per year and is worth $1000 at maturity will be worth less to a bondholder than one of the same maturity and maturity value which pays $70 per year. The $60 coupon bonds will sell for less than the $70 coupon bonds. But by how much less? It depends on the maturity of the bond. The second column of Table 2–2 shows how the price of a bond which pays a coupon of $60 per year when the prevailing interest rate is 7 percent varies with the maturity of the bond.

When interest rates rise from 6 percent to 7 percent, the price of a

---

[4] When a bond is issued two aspects of the bond must be stated in the bond contract. First is the maturity of the bond. Second is the fixed annual payment that must be paid by the issuer to the bondholder. This annual payment, called the coupon, remains fixed throughout the life of the bond independent of subsequent changes in the interest rates. In practice, bond coupons are paid in two semiannual installments. But, for simplicity, a single annual payment is assumed herein. Other characteristics of the bond may also be stated in the contract.

TABLE 2–2 PRICE VERSUS MATURITY FOR A $1000 MATURITY BOND WHICH PAYS $60 PER YEAR* AT PREVAILING INTEREST RATES OF 7 PERCENT AND 5 PERCENT

Maturity	Bond Price (at 7 percent)	Bond Price (at 5 percent)
½ year	$995.20	$1004.90
1 year	990.50	1009.60
5 year	958.40	1043.80
10 year	928.90	1077.90
20 year	893.20	1125.50
50 year	861.70	1183.10
100 year	857.30	1198.60
no maturity	857.10	1200.00

* Actually $30 every six months.

long maturity bond decreases much more than does the price of a short maturity bond. A holder of a one-half year maturity bond realizes a capital loss of only $4.80 (from $1000 to $995.20) while the holder of a twenty-year maturity bond realizes a capital loss of $106.80 (from $1000 to $893.20). The longer the maturity of the bond, the greater is the capital loss experienced by the bondholder.

If the interest rate had declined from the initial 6 percent to 5 percent, newly issued bonds would be paying only $50 per year and the previously issued bonds paying $60 would be more valuable than newly issued bonds. The bond prices in this case for varying maturities are shown in the third column of Table 2–2. The bond price increases with the maturity of the bond.

If the interest rates on a series of bonds of varying maturities change equally, the price of the longer maturity bond will change more and in the opposite direction of the change in the interest rate. The potential capital gain or loss is greater for longer maturity bonds.

Two important conclusions are now obvious. First, long maturity bonds have greater market risk than short maturity bonds. Second, an inverse relationship exists between interest rates and bond prices; that is, as interest rates increase, bond prices decrease and vice versa. The reason for the latter was indicated above.

What is the explanation for the effect of the bond maturity on its price variability or market risk? An intuitive rather than a mathematical explanation is given here. There are two types of return from holding a bond: an annual coupon payment and a possible capital gain or loss. The total return on a bond is the sum of these two. The coupon return can be expressed as a percentage return by dividing the dollar amount of the coupon by the current price of the bond. In bond jargon, this is called the *current yield* or *coupon yield*. For example, a bond which is purchased for $960 and which pays a coupon of $48 per year will have a current yield of $48/$960 = .05, or 5 percent. The current yield is an annual return since the coupon is paid every year.

In addition to the current yield there is a possible capital gain or loss at maturity. If a bond with a $1000 maturity value is purchased for $1000, there will be no capital gain or loss at the maturity of the bond. If it is purchased for $960 there will be a $40 gain at maturity; for $1040, a $40 capital loss. The percentage amount of this capital gain or loss is the dollar amount divided by the price paid for the bond: $40/$960 = .042, or 4.2 percent for the example above. Unlike the current yield, however, this yield occurs only once, at maturity. However, this yield can be expressed as an average annual return over the life of the bond; that is, the capital gain or loss can be amortized. For example, the $40 capital gain at maturity can be assumed to accrue at $4 per year for a ten-year maturity bond. The total return on the bond is then the sum of the current yield and the amortized capital gain. This is $48 + $4 divided by $960, or 5.4 percent in the example above.[5] The total return on a bond held to maturity is called its *yield to maturity*.[6]

Of course, the yield to maturity is the actual return only if the bond is held to maturity. If the bond is sold before maturity at a price not equal to the maturity value of the bond, the actual yield on the bond will differ from the yield to maturity.

What does this discussion have to do with the relationship between the variability of bond prices, bond maturities, and changes in interest rates? Consider a one-year bond and a twenty-year bond, each with a maturity value of $1000 and each paying a coupon of $50 per year. If each were purchased initially for $1000, the current yield on each would be 5 percent and there would be no capital gain or loss at maturity so the yield to maturity would also be 5 percent. Assume now that the interest rates on both of these securities increased to 6 percent. Newly issued bonds would pay $60 per year and consequently the $50 coupon bonds would be worth less than their original $1000. How much less? Each would sell at a price such that its total yield or yield to maturity was the same 6 percent now prevailing on newly issued bonds.

If the price of each declined equally, the current yield on each would be the same, $50 divided by the new price. The purchaser of the bonds at this lower price would also reap a capital gain if he held them to maturity. However, the capital gain at maturity on the one-year bond

---

[5] The method shown here involves an approximation. The exact method is not considered in this book.

[6] In practice, investors do not regard coupon returns and capital gains returns as equivalent because they are taxed differently.

would accrue all in one year while the same capital gain on the twenty-year bond would be allocated over twenty years, and so the annual or amortized capital gain of the twenty-year bond would be much less. Thus, although the two bonds would have identical current yields if both prices declined equally, the amortized capital gain would be greater on the one-year bond, and so the one-year bond would have a greater yield to maturity. But the prevailing interest rate on each was assumed to be 6 percent, and so this difference could not persist. It is clear that in order to have the yield to maturity on both bonds be 6 percent the price of the twenty-year maturity bond would have to decline much more than that of the one-year bond. The total capital loss of the twenty-year bond would be greater, but its annual amortized capital loss would be approximately the same as for the one-year bond. The longer the maturity, the greater is the necessary initial change in *dollar* value of the bond to give an equal *annual percentage* change in the value of the bond. This is the essence of the relationship between maturity and bond price variability.

If two bonds of different maturities experience equal interest rate changes, the longer maturity bond experiences the greater price change. But the assumption in this statement must be considered. Do interest rates on bonds of different maturities change equally? No! Normally, as discussed in Chapter 7, interest rates on short maturity bonds change more than on long maturity bonds. Interest rate changes have a greater impact on long maturity bonds but short-term interest rates change more. These effects work in opposite directions on the variability of bond prices for short and long maturities. The former effect is stronger, however, and long maturity bond prices fluctuate more than short maturity bond prices. Market risk is, consequently, greater for longer maturity bonds.

Liquidity can now be defined. In general, liquidity refers to the ease of converting an asset into a known amount of money. If a security can be converted quickly and inexpensively into a known amount of money, it is liquid. In terms of the properties discussed above, liquidity refers to the characteristics of minimum risk, both credit and market risk, and maximum marketability. The riskier and the less marketable an asset is, the less liquid it is.

Money is perfect liquidity—it *is* a known amount of money. Commercial bank savings accounts are very liquid. They have no market risk and little, if any, credit risk. And they can be converted into money at zero monetary cost in the time it takes to get to the bank. U.S. Treasury bills, a short-term liability of the U.S. government, have little market and credit risk and some cost of exchange, but are still quite liquid. Long maturity marketable securities, such as U.S. Treasury bonds, and corporate bonds, have more market risk and greater costs of transfer and are consequently less liquid. Real estate is not highly marketable and consequently is not liquid.

A security that is highly liquid is called a *near-money*. Savings accounts at commercial banks, savings and loan institutions, and mutual savings banks and also some short-term marketable securities such as U.S. Treasury bills are consequently near-monies.

an overview of the money and capital markets

Not all securities have markets on which they can be traded; that is, sold to someone other than the initial borrower. For example, as discussed earlier, markets for commercial bank time deposits are unnecessary and there are no markets for commercial bank business loans. This section considers only those securities that can be exchanged or marketed. For securities for which markets exist, the holder of a security can recoup his funds not by having the borrower repay him, but by selling the security to a third party.

Marketable securities are divided into two categories according to their maturities. Somewhat arbitrarily, a security with a maturity of one year or less is said to be a money market security and is exchanged on the so-called *money markets*. A security with a maturity of more than one year is called a capital market security and is exchanged on the *capital markets*. Money market instruments (they should actually be called near-money market instruments) are more liquid than capital market instruments because, due to their shorter maturities, they have less market risk. The nature of these markets is discussed in Chapter 9.

Lenders prefer securities that have the characteristics of low risk and high marketability: that is, high liquidity. They also desire a high return, both current yield and capital gains. To be induced to accept less liquid securities, lenders must receive a higher rate of return; to get more liquid securities, they will accept a lower rate of return. So an inverse relationship between the liquidity and the return of an asset is normally observed; high-return assets have low liquidities, and vice versa. Figure 2–9 shows the normal relations among the returns and the components of liquidity for several categories of assets.

The specific capital market securities are: U.S. Treasury bonds, and notes; long-term federal agency securities; state and local government securities (municipals); mortgages; corporate bonds; and, corporate stocks (equities). The domestic money market instruments are: U.S. Treasury bills; short-term federal agency securities; short-term

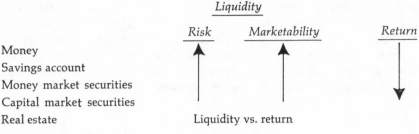

Liquidity vs. return

(Arrows point in direction of increasing desirability)

FIGURE 2–9   LIQUIDITY AND RETURN OF VARIOUS ASSETS

municipals; commercial paper; bankers' acceptances; certificates of deposits; and federal funds. They are discussed in detail in Chapter 9.

the flow of funds in the financial system

Throughout this chapter, households have been assumed to be the only supplier of funds to the financial system, and business the only borrower of funds. This assumption is an oversimplification. Actually, households borrow funds as well as supply them, and business supplies funds as well as borrows. In addition, the federal government and state and local governments also supply and borrow funds, as do commercial banks and other financial intermediaries.

This section shows data on the volume and the form of the funds supplied to and received from the financial system by the major sectors of the U.S. economy. In Table 2–3, the two columns shown for each sector, A (Assets) and L (Liabilities), provide a financial balance sheet for that sector. These financial balance sheets differ from total balance sheets in two important respects. First, no real assets are shown. For example, in the business sector there is no entry for their plant and equipment, and in the household sector there is no entry for housing. Only financial assets are shown. Second, equity funds are not shown with liabilities as a source of funds. Funds raised by selling stock and accumulated retained earnings are not shown on the liability side for business, commercial banks, and private nonbank finance—only true liabilities are shown. The asset value of common stock, however, is shown on the asset side of households and other owners.

Table 2–3 shows that the household sector is the major surplus

Introduction to the Economic and Financial Systems

sector; its financial assets exceed its liabilities by the greatest amount. It has large amounts of financial assets in the form of checking accounts and currency, savings accounts at commercial banks, savings accounts at other savings institutions, life insurance and pension fund reserves, corporate stock and U.S. government, state and local, and corporate bonds. The largest liabilities of the household sector are in the form of home mortgages and consumer credit.

The business sector is a deficit sector—its financial liabilities exceed its financial assets. Its largest financial asset is trade credit which is not a discretionary investment in the way that savings accounts are but is an aspect of selling its product. Its major liabilities are bonds, bank loans, and mortgages. Its equity funds are not shown.

Two other deficit sectors are the U.S. government and state and local governments. Both spend more than they earn, financing the deficit by borrowing. Both borrow mainly by issuing bonds.

The two financial sectors shown, commercial banks and private nonbank finance, have financial assets approximately equal to their liabilities. This is the nature of a financial intermediary. They borrow from some, incurring liabilities, and lend to others acquiring financial assets.

The household sector is a surplus sector, although it has substantial liabilities. The business sector and the two government sectors are deficit sectors, although each has some financial assets. The household sector lends some funds directly to these three deficit sectors by acquiring their securities. But the two financial intermediary sectors also borrow from all the sectors by accepting their deposits and lend to all sectors by funding mortgages or consumer credit or buying their securities. All sectors are both suppliers of funds to the financial system and demanders of funds from the financial system. But the types of their financial assets and liabilities and the balance among them differ considerably.

Part II elaborates on the economic system introduced here. Part III extends the discussion of the domestic financial system.

TABLE 2.3 FINANCIAL ASSETS AND LIABILITIES, December 31, 1975
(Amounts outstanding in billions of dollars)
(A) All sectors

Sector	Private domestic nonfinancial sectors								Rest of the world	
	Households		Business		State and local governments		Total			
Transaction category	A	L	A	L	A	L	A	L	A	L
1 Total financial assets	2496.9		629.0		139.2		3265.0		247.7	
2 Total liabilities		782.8		1109.3		240.3		2132.4		271.0
3 Gold									38.1	
4 S.D.R.'s									8.9	
5 I.M.F. position										2.2
6 Official foreign exchange										.1
7 Treasury currency										
8 Demand dep. and currency	165.6		67.4		14.3		247.3		14.0	
9 Private domestic	165.6		67.4		14.3		247.3			
10 U.S. Government										
11 Foreign									14.0	
12 Time and savings accounts	776.2		22.4		48.1		846.7		20.9	
13 At commercial banks	350.7		22.4		48.1		421.1		20.9	
14 At savings institutions	425.6						425.6			
15 Life insurance reserves	164.6						164.6			
16 Pension fund reserves	368.6						368.6			
17 Interbank claims										
18 Corporate equities	630.5						630.5		26.7	
19 Credit market instruments	346.8	753.5	85.5	834.4	70.1	229.6	502.4	1817.5	77.5	94.2
20 U.S. Treasury secs.	114.3		14.3		30.6		159.2		66.5	
21 Federal agency secs.	9.1		3.2		22.3		34.6			
22 State and local govt. secs.	74.2		4.5	6.7	4.4	223.8	83.1	230.5		
23 Corp. and fgn. bonds	65.9			254.3			65.9	254.3	2.6	25.6
24 Mortgages	72.7	508.2		286.8	12.8		85.6	795.0		
25 Consumer credit		197.3	30.9				30.9	197.3		
26 Bank loans n.e.c.		16.5		198.2				214.7		21.8
27 Pvt. short-term paper	10.5		32.6	17.8			43.1	17.8	8.4	11.1
28 Other loans		31.5		70.6		5.8		107.9		35.7
29 Security credit	4.0	13.7					4.0	13.7	.4	.3
30 Trade credit		7.9	283.3	234.8		10.7	283.3	253.4	11.6	14.2
31 Taxes payable				13.4	6.6		6.6	13.4		
32 Miscellaneous	40.5	7.7	170.5	26.7			211.1	34.5	49.5	160.0

A = Assets
L = Liabilities

Source: Flow of Funds Data, Board of Governors of the Federal Reserve System.

Introduction to the Economic and Financial Systems

U.S. Government		Financial sectors — Total		Sponsored agencies and mortgage pools		Monetary authority		Commercial banking		Private nonbank finance		All sectors		Floats and discrepancies
A	L	A	L	A	L	A	L	A	L	A	L	A	L	A
122.4	510.8	2407.1	2291.7	127.1	124.9	124.7	124.7	373.6	826.5	1281.6	1215.6	6042.1	5205.9	37.3
		11.6				11.6						49.7		
2.3												11.2		
2.2		*				*						2.2	2.2	
		.1				.1						.1	.1	
	8.7	10.6				10.6						10.6	8.7	−1.9
11.2		17.8	325.0	.3			82.5	.9	242.5	16.7		290.3	325.0	34.7
		17.8	300.1	.3			74.3	.9	225.8	16.7		265.2	300.1	35.0
11.2			10.9				7.8		3.1			11.2	10.9	−.3
			14.0				.5		13.5			14.0	14.0	
.6		16.4	884.6						455.6	16.4	429.0	884.6	884.6	
.6		13.0	455.6						455.6	13.0		455.6	455.6	
		3.4	429.0							3.4	429.0	429.0	429.0	
	7.7		156.9								156.9	164.6	164.6	
	41.9		326.7								326.7	368.6	368.6	
		58.6	58.6			3.9	38.3	54.7	20.3			58.6	58.6	
		197.4	42.2					.9		196.5	42.2	854.7	42.2	
88.2	416.3	1958.6	268.7	125.7	114.5	95.3		745.4	33.9	992.4	120.3	2626.7	2626.7	
	437.3	211.6		2.9		87.9		85.4		35.3		437.3	437.3	
7.0	7.9	79.2	112.9	.4	112.9	6.2		34.5		38.0		120.8	120.8	
		147.4						102.8		44.6		230.5	230.5	
		218.7	37.3					8.6	4.5	240.2	32.8	317.2	317.2	
13.5	4.4	704.2	7.2	87.5				136.5		480.3	7.2	803.3	803.3	
		166.4						90.3		76.1		197.3	197.3	
		277.0	40.5					277.0	10.5		29.9	277.0	277.0	
		28.7	51.4	3.0		1.1		10.3	18.9	14.4	32.5	80.3	80.3	
67.7		95.3	19.4	31.8	1.6					63.5	17.8	163.0	163.0	
		24.6	15.0					14.6		10.1	15.0	29.0	29.0	
6.4	5.2	7.7								7.7		308.9	272.8	−36.2
5.3			2.7						.6		2.1	12.0	16.0	4.1
6.1	1.2	103.6	211.3	1.2	10.5	3.2	3.8	57.1	73.6	42.0	123.5	370.3	406.9	36.6

questions

1. Distinguish between direct and indirect finance. Identify the debtors and creditors in each case.

2. An investor buys a new issue of a twenty-year bond at a time when the interest rate is 6 percent. The interest rate on this bond quickly increases to 7 percent and continues at that rate. At what price could the investor sell the bond shortly after its purchase? Ten years later?

3. An investor purchases a bond which pays an $80 coupon for $1030. The bond has ten years until maturity. What is the current yield (coupon yield) on this bond? What is the approximate yield to maturity?

4. Using Table 2–3, determine which sectors are surplus sectors and which are deficit sectors and the amounts of their surplus or deficit. Who are the major holders and issuers of corporate bonds and mortgages? Indicate the amounts.

5. Discuss the components of liquidity for demand deposits, Treasury bills, Treasury bonds, and real estate.

6. Discuss the role of the financial system in the economy.

selected references to part I

Henning, Charles N., Pigott, William, and Scott, Robert Haney. *Financial Markets and the Economy.* Englewood Cliffs, N.J.: Prentice-Hall, Inc., 1975.

Polakoff, Murray E. et al. *Financial Institutions and Markets.* Boston: Houghton Mifflin Co., 1970.

Robinson, Roland I. and Wrightsman, Dwayne. *Financial Markets, The Accumulation and Allocation of Wealth.* New York: McGraw-Hill Book Company, 1974.

THE ECONOMIC SYSTEM: GOALS, POLICIES, AND RELATIONSHIPS

the economic
system:
goals
and policies

3

An economic system consists of those institutions and practices in a society that determine the economic variables of the society. The economic variables are distinguished from other types of variables (social and political, for example) in that they are usually expressed in dollar values. For example, incomes, costs, and prices are all expressed in dollars and are economic variables. The institutions that interact to determine these and other economic variables can be separated into the business, consumer, labor, and government sectors of the economy. While all societies or countries have such sectors, they relate in very different ways in different countries. For example, the role of the government sector is much more predominant in determining economic variables in the Soviet Union than it is in the United States. The basis for this book is the current mode of interaction of these sectors in the United States.

Any economic system is expected to satisfy certain societal goals. The production of the maximum level of goods and services which can be achieved by fully utilizing its economic resources, both capital and labor, is an important goal for any society. Rapid growth in the capacity to produce goods and services is a related goal. Societies also desire stable prices (that is, no or low inflation). Another goal is for a balance of international payment—that is, a balance between the outflow of domestic currency to other countries and the inflow of foreign currency. Finally, countries typically have a specific view of the proper balance between the relative roles of the public sector (the government) and the private sector in the economy, and also on the proper distribution of income among various individuals in society. Different societies, however, have very different ideas about what is the ideal balance between the private and public sectors and the ideal distribution of income.

Economic tools or policies are means the government uses to achieve these goals. If the government does not think the economy is adequately achieving its goals, it uses these tools or policies to alter economic activity to better achieve them. The most common such policies are called *fiscal policy* and *monetary policy*. Fiscal policy refers to policies that affect the government budget. The government budget is determined by its revenues and its expenditures in the same way that a family budget is determined by family revenues and expenditures. U.S. federal revenues are derived mainly from tax collections. Fiscal policy, then, uses changes in federal taxation and expenditures to achieve economic goals. Monetary policy involves changes in the economy's money supply. The methods used to effect changes in the money supply are discussed later in this chapter. In addition to fiscal and monetary policies, some governments, at some times, use controls on price and wage levels to achieve their goals. Wage-price controls are also discussed in Chapter 5.

Economic policy can be viewed as the use of economic tools to affect the economic system in a way that achieves the economic goals, as shown in Figure 3–1. Stabilization policy, in particular, refers to the use of fiscal and monetary policies to achieve high employment and stable prices.

A casual awareness of current events makes it clear that the United States usually is not fully achieving its economic goals. One can infer from this observation that there are some limitations on the use and effectiveness of economic policy. Economic policies do not rapidly and perfectly achieve all the economic goals. And often when a policy improves the performance of the economy with respect to one goal, the economy does worse relative to another. Scholars and policy-makers of

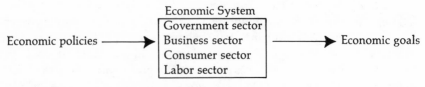

FIGURE 3–1   THE ECONOMIC SYSTEM

The Economic System: Goals, Policies, and Relationships

different political and economic persuasions have differing views on the effectiveness of using economic policies to achieve the goals, particularly the goals of high employment, stable prices, and rapid growth. Two prominent views are discussed in Chapter 6.

A brief discussion of the economic goals and policies is given in the next two sections of this chapter. In Chapter 4, a conceptual framework for relating the policies and the goals is presented. The goals and policies are discussed in more detail in Chapters 5 and 6, respectively.

economic goals

HIGH EMPLOYMENT

The following is an excerpt from the Employment Act of 1946 (PL 304–79th Congress):

Declaration of Policy

The Congress hereby declares that it is the continuing policy and responsibility of the Federal Government to use all practicable means consistent with its needs and obligations and other essential considerations of national policy, with the assistance and cooperation of industry, agriculture, labor, and State and local governments, to coordinate and utilize all its plans, functions, and resources for the purpose of creating and maintaining, in a manner calculated to foster and promote free competitive enterprise and the general welfare, conditions under which there will be afforded useful employment opportunities, including self-employment, for those able, willing, and seeking to work, *and to promote maximum employment, production, and purchasing power.* . . . (Italics added.)

With this act, the federal government assumed legal responsibility for promoting maximum employment. Note, however, that the bill refers to "maximum employment," not "full employment," and that no operational definition of maximum employment is provided. Economic policies have failed to achieve consistently the overall goals of the Employment Act of 1946.

The costs of failing to achieve full employment are clear. In personal terms, failure means that some potential workers are working less and earning less than they could be. In social terms, the cost of unemployment is that less than the maximum level of goods and services is being produced. Economists use a rule of thumb called *Okun's Law* to relate the unemployment rate to lost production. Okun's Law says that for each 1 percent of unemployment (over the normally accepted minimum rate of 4 percent) the actual production of goods and services is an additional 3 percent less than its maximum level.

PRICE STABILITY

Maintaining stable prices (that is, preventing inflation) is an important policy goal in the United States. The rate of inflation is measured by increases in the average price of different "bundles" of goods and services. The consumer price index is the average price of the goods and services purchased by urban wage earners and clerical workers for day-to-day living. The wholesale price index measures the average price of goods, such as steel, rubber, or glass, which are used as inputs in the production process. Finally, the GNP price deflator measures the average price of all the final goods and services produced in the economy and purchased by consumers, businesses, or governments.

Discussions of the evils or costs of inflation often generate more emotional than substantive arguments. What are the real costs of inflation? It could be argued that normally, but not always, inflationary periods are also periods of high employment and so inflation should be welcomed. Inflation causes some problems, however. First, inflation may have some arbitrary effects on the distribution of income, harming those whose incomes are fixed relative to those whose incomes are responsive to price changes. For example, the former includes the elderly living on fixed pension payments or life insurance annuities; the latter includes labor union members whose contracts have cost-of-living clauses. Inflation also increases the effective federal tax rate of both individuals and corporations, thus reducing their disposable income.

Second, inflation may lead to inefficient or wasteful activities. Individuals and firms may spend time and money attempting to immunize themselves from inflation rather than producing output. In the hyperinflation of post–World War I Germany, workers were paid twice a day so they could spend their income before its value further eroded. Accumulating wealth in real assets (such as real estate, art, and antiques) rather than financial assets (such as stocks and bonds) may be a manifestation of this phenomenon in the United States.

Third, it is often claimed that inflation has a destabilizing effect on the economy. Some say inflation is self-propelling and that a low level of inflation leads subsequently to hyperinflation. Others claim that inflation breeds recessionary forces. The evidence on either of these effects of inflation is not conclusive.

Finally, inflation affects the balance of payments, tending to make the balance of payments deficit greater.

ECONOMIC GROWTH

Economic growth refers to an increase in the national production of goods and services. A country's total production of final goods and services is defined as its *gross national product*. The significance of the word *final* in this definition is that intermediate goods (that is, goods that are subsequently converted into other goods), such as steel, are not counted as part of the gross national product *per se* but only when they are embodied in a final and usable product such as an automobile or a building. Gross national product consists of *consumption* goods and services claimed by households (such as automobiles, refrigerators, clothing, food, and haircuts), *investment* goods claimed by business (mainly plant, equipment, and inventories), and goods and services claimed by *governments*.

A country's gross national product can increase for two basic reasons. First, it can increase because the size of the country's labor force increases due to population increases. For example, if a country's labor force increased by 3 percent, its GNP would also increase by about 3 percent. However, even after a 3 percent increase in the number of workers and in total production, average workers could consume no more because they produced no more. That is, per-capita production, and consequently the per-capita claim on output, have remained constant. And a national and personal goal is not only to increase total production but to increase per-capita production (and per-capita claim on output).

Second, GNP and also per-capita GNP can increase because of an increase in labor productivity which is defined as the level of output per worker. Labor productivity must increase for the average worker's claim on output to increase. Labor productivity can increase for two reasons. One reason might be that the average worker, using the same capital equipment, may become more efficient due to better education or training, a better diet, or a better arrangement of the workers. Or, labor productivity may increase because the average worker is given more or better tools, machinery, or capital equipment with which to work. For example, a worker can excavate more holes for building foundations with a bulldozer than with a shovel.

A major reason for the recent increase in labor productivity in the United States has been the increase in its capital stock, the stock of plant and equipment. The capital stock can increase only if business "invests" in new plant and equipment. Consequently, business investment is an important cause of economic growth.

This point illustrates an important economic dilemma. A country's productive resources—labor and capital—can be used entirely to produce consumption goods. This would maximize the current consumption by its citizens. But in this case no new capital goods are produced, so its capital stock would not grow. Thus, the production of consumption goods would not increase. However, if a country's current productive resources were used primarily for the production of capital goods, current consumption would be lower, but the country's capital stock and its future productive capacity would increase. The choice, then, is ultimately between current and future consumption.

BALANCE OF PAYMENTS EQUILIBRIUM

The balance of payments of the United States measures the difference between the outflow of dollars because of the United States purchase of foreign goods and services or U.S. investment overseas, and the inflow of foreign currencies (or dollar value thereof) because of foreign purchases of U.S. goods and services or foreign investments in the United States. The balance of payments issue is discussed in detail in Chapter 10.

If considered individually, a country could easily state its preferences with respect to the first four economic goals. Full employment, stable prices, and rapid growth are the preferred states.[1] A balance between the outflow of domestic currency and inflow of foreign currency is also usually preferred.[2] While it may be difficult to achieve these goals, at least there is agreement as to what should be attained. With respect to the next two goals, however, there is not even wide agreement as to what the ideal situation is.

DISTRIBUTION OF INCOME

A country's distribution of income refers to the proportion of income which accrues to high-income individuals relative to that which accrues to low-income individuals. For example, if the richest 10 percent of individuals earned 50 percent of the country's income and the poorest 10 percent earned 1 percent, then the country would have a very uneven distribution of income. If the richest 10 percent earned 15 percent of the country's income while the poorest 10 percent earned 8 percent, the distribution of income would be much more even.

Opinions on what is the "best" distribution of income vary considerably. Some claim that in the interests of justice, an equitable distribution of income is best. Others claim that if everyone earns the same,

---

[1] Recently, however, the goal of growth has come under attack because of its accompanying environmental problems.

[2] However, countries have at times shown a preference for both surpluses and deficits in their balance of payments accounts.

there is little incentive to work hard and produce more; therefore, an uneven distribution of income is best because it provides an incentive for hard work. While a wide divergence of opinion is heard in the United States concerning the ideal distribution of income, policies that partially but not completely remove income disparities have traditionally been used.

The tax system is the major policy for equalizing the income distribution. A progressive income tax system imposes a higher tax rate on high-income than on low-income individuals, thus making after-tax income more equal than before-tax income. In addition, inheritance taxes prevent wealthy individuals from passing all of their wealth to their heirs. The other major policy for redistributing income is transfer payments. Transfer payments are government payments to individuals for which the individual provides the government nothing in return. Welfare payments and unemployment compensation are examples of transfer payments. Government payments to civil servants, however, are not transfer payments since the civil servants provide their services to the government in return. Transfer payments usually accrue to low-income individuals who are temporarily unemployed, retired, or disabled.

BALANCE BETWEEN PUBLIC AND PRIVATE SECTORS

Goods and services can be produced by facilities operated and owned by either the government or private individuals or firms. In a pure capitalistic economy all goods and services are produced by the private sector. In a pure socialistic economy, they are all produced by the public sector. The United States is called a "mixed" economy because some of the goods and services are produced by the public sector, others by the private sector. For example, national defense, mail delivery, and most education is produced by the public sector, but automobiles, food, and houses are produced by the private sector.

Some people assert that the government should produce fewer goods and services; others claim the government should produce more. Despite these differences, there is a national consensus that production should be dominated by the private sector. Table 3–1 shows the fractions of total GNP that the federal and the state and local governments have purchased in recent years.

TRADEOFFS

As has been pointed out, there is a consensus on what should be attained with respect to the first four economic goals. Primarily for this reason, when the economy is not satisfactorily achieving these goals, policy changes are implemented. However, frequently when policy

TABLE 3–1 PERCENTAGE OF TOTAL GNP

	1966	1969	1972	1975	1976
Federal purchases	11.5%	11.3%	8.7%	8.2%	7.9%
State and local purchases	11.9	12.5	12.9	14.1	13.7
Total government	23.4	23.8	21.6	22.3	21.6

changes cause the economy to improve relative to one goal, it worsens relative to another: that is, there are *tradeoffs*. The most widely discussed tradeoff is between full employment and price stability. Policies that reduce unemployment tend to be inflationary, and vice versa. The forces behind this relationship are considered in Chapter 5.

economic policies

FISCAL POLICY

Fiscal policy refers to the federal budget, which depends on federal revenues and expenditures. Federal revenues derive mainly from the personal income tax and the corporate profits tax. Major federal expenditures are for national defense, transfer payments (such as social security and unemployment compensation), and salaries of civil servants. Government spending and taxation are the elements of fiscal policy. Other aspects of fiscal policy are discussed in Chapters 4 and 6.

MONETARY POLICY

Monetary policy is concerned with controlling the money supply. Three questions related to monetary policy arise: 1) What is the money supply? 2) How is the money supply changed? and 3) How do changes in the money supply affect the economy? The first two questions are addressed here; the last question is addressed in Chapters 4, 6, and 7.

Money is defined as whatever is commonly accepted as a medium of exchange—whatever can be used to settle accounts or pay bills. In the United States money, then, is coin, currency, and checks. Checks and checking accounts are also called demand deposits. During March, 1977, the U.S. money stock consisted of $82.4 billion of coin and currency and $233.7 of demand deposits for a total of $316.1 billion.

How is the money supply changed? The government does not ask individuals to burn currency to decrease the money supply nor does it drop currency from airplanes to increase the money supply. A more subtle method is used to change the supply of money.

The money supply is changed by the interaction of a government authority with the system of commercial banks in the country. To show how these interactions cause changes in the money supply, some background on the government authority and the system of commercial banks is necessary.

The governmental authority responsible for implementing changes in the money supply is the Federal Reserve System (often called the Fed), which is the "central bank" of the United States. All developed countries have central banks whose dual function is to control the country's money supply and regulate its commercial banks. The Fed is a banker's bank in that it accepts (and indeed requires) deposits from commercial banks and makes loans to commercial banks. The Fed is discussed in detail in Chapter 6.

Commercial banks have many functions but what is unique about commercial banks is their authority to accept deposits in the form of checking accounts or demand deposits.[3] Commercial banks also accept savings accounts, but so do savings and loan associations, mutual savings banks, and credit unions. In this chapter it is assumed that commercial banks accept only demand deposits. A more realistic and complete commercial banking sector is discussed in Chapter 8. When funds are deposited in a checking account, the bank incurs a liability in that it must refund the deposit on demand by the depositor (this is the origin of the term *demand deposit*).

What do commercial banks do with the acquired funds? To make a profit, they lend some of the funds, charging the borrower interest. The loans have a fixed maturity (most bank loans have a maturity of less than one year). Consequently, if the bank lent all its deposited funds, and their depositors wished to withdraw their deposited funds, the bank would not be able to honor the withdrawal request. To prevent this, banks do not lend out all their deposits but keep some in the form of cash so they can honor withdrawal requests. Bank cash is called *reserves*.

Reserves provide no interest return to banks but they do provide liquidity so banks can honor withdrawal requests. Bank loans provide an interest return but banks cannot recoup their funds from the loan until the maturity of the loan. Banks can also use their funds in another way, which provides them with an interest return but which also allows them to recoup their funds at any time. This use is the purchase of Treasury securities (called Treasuries), bills, notes, and bonds, which they can resell at any time on the secondary markets. Bank purchases of Treasury securities are called *investments* and are distinguished from bank *loans*. Treasury bills are often called banks' *secondary reserves* because of

---

[3] Recently, as will be discussed in Chapter 8, other types of financial institutions have begun to offer deposits very similar to demand deposits.

their liquidity. However, the return to banks on Treasury securities is less than the return on their loans to business.

Bank assets, therefore, are cash or reserves, Treasuries, and loans. Consider a bank that receives all its funds in the form of demand deposits and with these makes some loans, purchases some Treasuries, and keeps the remainder in the form of reserves. The balance sheet for such a bank which has $100 of deposits and keeps 20 percent of these deposits in the form of reserves and 20 percent in Treasuries is shown in Table 3–2. Consider this balance sheet to be the balance sheet of all the commercial banks in the country added together—that is, the balance sheet of the commercial banking sector.

With this background, the interactions between the Fed and the commercial banking sector which determine the money supply can be considered. The Fed sets a minimum level of reserves which banks must hold to back their demand deposits. This minimum is usually expressed as a percentage of each dollar of deposits which must be kept in the form of reserves, and is called the *reserve requirement*. A reserve requirement of 20 percent means that for each dollar of deposits the bank must have 20¢ worth of reserves. And banks usually prefer to keep only minimally more than the required level of reserves because they earn no interest on reserves. Reserves in excess of the level of required reserves are called *excess reserves*.

Banks accept the demand deposits of the household and business sectors and in turn make loans to these sectors. The deposits represent an asset to the household and business sectors; the loans represent a liability. The balance sheet of the household and business sectors combined, assuming they also hold $30 of currency, is shown in Table 3–3.

The money supply of an economy, which consists of the commercial banking, household, and business sectors shown in Tables 3–2 and 3–3 is composed of $100 of demand deposits and $30 of currency for a total money supply of $130. Note particularly that cash held by the public is part of the money supply, but that cash held by commercial banks (reserves) is not considered as part of the money supply.

How does the Fed change the money supply? The Fed increases the

TABLE 3–2 COMMERCIAL BANKING SECTOR

Balance Sheet			
Assets (A)		Liabilities (L)	
Reserves (R)	$ 20		
Treasuries (T)	$ 20	Demand Deposits (DD)	$100
Loans (L)	$ 60		
Total Assets:	$100	Total Liabilities:	$100

The Economic System: Goals, Policies, and Relationships

TABLE 3-3 HOUSEHOLD AND BUSINESS SECTORS

Balance Sheet

A		L	
Demand Deposits (DD)	$100	Bank Loans (L)	$60
Currency (C)	$ 30		
Total Assets:	$130	Total Liabilities:	$60

money supply by increasing the level of excess reserves in the banking system. This is accomplished by buying Treasury securities from the banking system. For example, assume that the Fed buys $10 worth of Treasury securities from the banking sector of Table 3-2. The Fed accomplishes this by informing banks that they are going to buy a specified quantity of Treasury securities. Banks that want to sell Treasury securities then submit bids to the Fed indicating the prices at which they will sell them. The Fed then buys the desired quantity of securities from the banks that submit the lowest bids. The Fed essentially conducts an auction process in purchasing the securities. The purchase or sale of Treasury securities by the Fed in this manner is called an *open market operation*. The immediate effect of this $10 purchase of Treasury securities by the Fed is shown in Table 3-4. On the bank balance sheet there is a $10 decrease in Treasuries and a $10 increase in reserves, since the Fed pays $10 in cash for the Treasuries.

Banks still have $100 of demand deposits, the balance sheet of the household and business sectors remains as in Table 3-3, and the money supply remains at $130. But banks now have more than the required level of reserves. To support $100 demand deposits, they are required to keep $20 in reserves. But they have $30 in reserves and hence have excess reserves of $10. Since banks do not like to hold substantial excess reserves (because no interest is earned on them), how do banks eliminate these excess reserves? They do so by making loans to the household and business sectors. And the borrowers usually keep the receipts of their loans in their checking accounts. Through this mechanism, it can be seen that the creation of excess reserves in the banking sector leads to an in-

TABLE 3-4 COMMERCIAL BANKING SECTOR

Balance Sheet

A		L	
R:	$30	DD:	$100
T:	$10		
L:	$60		

crease in loans and demand deposits. And since demand deposits are part of the money supply, the money supply increases.

By how much will the money supply increase? Banks were initially content when their reserves of $20 represented the required 20 percent of their demand deposits. But with $30 of reserves, demand deposits must be $150 for the $30 of reserves to represent 20 percent of the demand deposits. If banks have $150 of deposits, $30 of reserves, and $10 of Treasuries, they must have $110 of loans for their balance sheet to balance. In this case banks once again have no excess reserves. The new balance sheets for the banking sector and the business and household sectors are shown in Table 3–5.

With $150 of demand deposits and $30 of currency, the money supply is now $180. A $10 purchase of Treasuries has led to a $50 increase in the money supply from $130 to $180. The increase has been entirely in the form of demand deposits. Each dollar increase in bank reserves due to open market operations has led to a five-fold increase in the money supply. Note that the reciprocal of the reserve requirement, one divided by 0.2, is also 5. This equality is not fortuitous.

The relationship between the changes in reserves and the money supply can be formalized. Denote the reserve requirement (as a percentage) by r. This means that the level of required reserves, R, must equal (r) (DD):

$$R = (r) \text{ (DD)} \tag{1}$$

For example, in Figure 3–2, with DD = $100 and $r = .20$, the level of required reserves is calculated to be $20. From equation (1) it is seen that a level R of reserves can support a level DD = R/r of demand deposits. For example, with r equal to 20 percent or 0.2, $1 of reserves can support $1/0.2 = $5 of demand deposits. Consequently, if reserves change by an amount R due to open market operations, the change in demand deposits will be

$$\Delta DD = \frac{\Delta R}{r} \tag{2}$$

TABLE 3–5

A) COMMERCIAL BANKING SECTOR

Balance Sheet

Assets		Liabilities	
R:	$ 30	DD:	$150
T:	$ 10		
L:	$110		

B) HOUSEHOLD AND BUSINESS SECTOR

Balance Sheet

Assets		Liabilities	
DD:	$150	L:	$110
C:	$ 30		

And if the currency holdings of the household and business sector remain the same, the change in the money supply will be the same as the change in demand deposits:

$$\Delta M_S = \frac{\Delta R}{r} \qquad (3)$$

where M_S denotes the money supply and ΔM_S denotes the change in the money supply.

Between the initial situation described in Tables 3–2 and 3–3 and the final state of Table 3–5, the Fed conducted an open market purchase of $10 of securities from commercial banks, banks increased their loans by $50, and bank demand deposits and the money supply both increased by $50.

A remaining issue concerns the mechanism for getting from the initial situation of Tables 3–2 and 3–3 to the final situation in Table 3–5. (See Table 3–6[a] for a replication of Tables 3–2 and 3–3.) After the open market operation (Table 3–6[b]), banks have excess reserves (denoted by X) of $10. Banks, to eliminate these excess reserves, make $10 in loans. The loan is made by crediting the borrower's checking account by $10. The borrower may then spend $10 by writing a check to a third party. If the third party deposits the check in a different bank, his bank will gain $10 in deposits and reserves and the lending bank will lose $10 in deposits and reserves. But, after the loan is made, the reserves and deposits of the banking system as a whole remain the same. As the funds are spent, different depositors may own the funds. And different depositors may deposit the funds in different banks. But for the banking system as a whole the total level of deposits and reserves remain the same.

This situation is described in part (c) of the table. The money supply is $140. However, with $110 of deposits, banks need only $22 of reserves. They have $30, and so they have $8 of excess reserves. To eliminate this excess they lend $8 by crediting the borrower's checking account balance. (Once again the borrower may spend the funds and the recipient may deposit the funds in a different bank.) As a result, loans increase to $78, demand deposits to $118, and the money supply to $148 as shown in part (d) of the table. Banks still have excess reserves of $6.4. They continue to increase their loans as long as they have excess reserves. And only when the situation is as described in part (e) will their level of excess reserves be zero. Then, banks lend no more, loans remain at $110, and the money supply at $180.

The process shown in Table 3–6 shows how, once the Fed creates excess reserves through open market purchases of Treasury securities, the banking sector interacts with the household and business sectors to increase loans and the money supply.

TABLE 3–6

| | COMMERCIAL BANKING SECTOR | | HOUSEHOLD AND BUSINESS SECTORS | |

(a)

	Balance Sheets		Balance Sheets	
Initial situation	A	L	A	L
	R: $20	DD: $100	DD: $100	L: $60
$M_S = \$130$	T: $20		C: $ 30	
$X = 0$	L: $60			

(b)

	A	L	A	L
After open market operation	R: $30	DD: $100	No change	
$M_S = \$130$	T: $10			
$X = 10$	L: $60			

(c)

	A	L	A	L
After banks lend $10	R: $30	DD: $110	DD: $110	L: $70
$M_S = \$140$	T: $10		C: $ 30	
$X = 8$	L: $70			

(d)

	A	L	A	L
After banks lend additional $8	R: $30	DD: $118	DD: $118	L: $78
$M_S = \$148$	T: $10		C: $ 30	
$X = 6.4$	L: $78			

(e)

	A	L	A	L
Final situation	R: $ 30	DD: $150	DD: $150	L: $110
$M_S = \$180$	T: $ 10		C: $ 30	
$X = 0$	L: $110			

If the Fed had sold $10 of Treasury securities to banks rather than bought them, bank reserves would have decreased by $10 and the money supply would have decreased by $50 to $80. Once again, a $10 change in bank reserves would have caused a $50 change in the money supply. In this case the changes are decreases. A demonstration of this is left as an exercise for the reader.

Two assumptions were implicit in the process of Table 3–6. First, it was assumed that banks did not wish to hold any excess reserves and always made loans until their excess reserves were zero. How are banks able to increase their loans? The variable they control which affects the volume of loans is the interest rate on bank loans. If banks wish to increase their loans they lower their interest rate. This phenomenon accounts for the decline in interest rates when the money supply increases. However, if banks do not increase their loans as much as they legally can and instead hold excess reserves, the money supply will increase by less than the maximum amount, $\Delta R/r$.

The second assumption made in the process of Table 3–6 is that the household and business sectors do not increase their currency holdings. If, for example, after the $10 bank loan in part (c) the borrower withdraws $10 from the bank and keeps it in the form of currency, then the balance sheets become as shown in Table 3–7. Banks cannot lend more because they have reserves equal to 20 percent of deposits. In this case, the money supply increases by only $10 due to increased currency holdings, rather than $50 due to increased demand deposits as is the case when currency holdings are not increased.

If the Fed increases reserves by an amount R, the maximum increase in the money supply that can occur is R/r, and this will occur only if banks hold no excess reserves and households and businesses do not increase their currency holdings. If banks hold excess reserves X, and the household and business sectors increase their currency holdings by ΔC, the increase in the money supply will be

$$\Delta M_S = \frac{R - X - \Delta C}{r} + \Delta C \tag{4}$$

The derivation of this formula will be left for the reader.

To repeat, increases in the money supply tend to cause decreases in the interest rate since banks are induced to lower interest rates in order to lend out their excess reserves. An increase in the money supply also tends to cause an increase in the demand for goods and services because the increased borrowing is often used to finance purchases of

TABLE 3–7

COMMERCIAL BANKING SECTOR		HOUSEHOLD AND BUSINESS SECTOR	
A	L	A	L
R: $20	DD: $100	DD: $100	L: $70
T: $10		C: $ 40	
L: $70			

goods and services. An increase in the money supply tends to cause a decrease in the interest rate and an increase in the demand for goods and services. Increases in the money supply thus constitute expansionary monetary policy; decreases are contractionary.

The use of fiscal and monetary policies is explored in more detail in Chapters 4 and 6.

questions

1. Consider a commercial banking system with reserves of $40, demand deposits of $200, and loans of $140. Assume that reserve requirements are 20 percent.
   a. What is the level of excess reserves?
   b. By how much could the money supply change if the Fed sold $5 of Treasury bills to banks?
   c. By how much could the money supply change if the Fed decreased reserve requirements to 15 percent?

2. Assume the banking system of question (1) but assume that reserve requirements are 15 percent.
   a. What is the level of excess reserves?
   b. By how much would the money supply increase if the banking system had no excess reserves?
   c. With no excess reserves, by how much would the money supply change if the Fed purchased $20 of Treasury bills and businesses increased their cash balances by $5?

3. Discuss the mechanism by which the money supply increases after the Fed purchases Treasury bills from the banking system.

a model
of the economy

4

Chapter 3 discusses the goals of the economic system and the policies that can be used to achieve these goals. This chapter shows the relationships between the policies and the goals—that is, how changes in the policies effect changes in the goals. A model of the economy is developed and used for this purpose.

A *model* is a conceptual framework for showing interrelationships among variables. In developing models, there is a tradeoff between realism and simplicity. A realistic model would consider every variable that affected every other variable. To thoroughly explain one variable, it might be realistic to show the tens or hundreds of other variables that influence it, but it would not be very simple to construct or use such a model. Conversely, it would be much simpler to ignore all but the two most important variables that affect another variable. But this might not be realistic because it does not explain the variable very accurately. In constructing practical models, the conflicting objectives of realism and simplicity must be reconciled. In this chapter, a relatively simple model that has several important elements of reality is developed.

A model can be expressed either by a set of equations or by a diagram. For example, Figure 2–2 of Chapter 2 shows a diagrammatic model of an economy. The relationships among variables are shown by arrows. In Figure 2–2 household consumption expenditures (C) are shown to depend on the income households earn (Y). A model in equation form would represent each relationship in the model as an equation; for example, the consumption expenditure relation might be:

$$C = (\$.90)Y \tag{1}$$

which says that each dollar of income leads to 90¢ in expenditures.

The main advantage of models in equation form is that they are more exact. A diagrammatic model shows that as income increases, consumption will increase, but it does not tell by how much consumption will increase. A model in equation form shows the exact relationship—in equation (1) consumption increases by 90¢ for every dollar increase in income.

Modern models of the economy are usually in equation form and some include hundreds of equations in an attempt to be realistic. The present treatment uses a relatively simple, diagrammatic model which demonstrates the basic interrelationships without obscuring them with mathematics.

model of the economy

Figure 2–3 provides a point of departure in the development of this model, and is the basis for Figure 4–1. What is not shown in Figure 2–3, however, is the financial system. As discussed in Chapter 2, the financial system channels funds from surplus sectors to deficit sectors. The financial system is included in Figure 4–1; the household sector is the major surplus sector and its savings flow into the financial system. The business sector is a deficit sector. It invests I but generates only RE of funds and must borrow $(I - RE)$. Finally, the government deficit is expressed as $G - (T_b + T_h)$ and it must borrow this amount (if this number is negative the government budget is in surplus and the government supplies funds to the financial system). The business and government sectors borrow from the financial system to finance their deficits. There is one other source of funds. In Chapter 3 it is shown that an increase in reserves supplied by the Fed permits banks to increase their loans and causes an increase in the money supply. Consequently, increases in reserves and the money supply represent an inflow of funds to the financial system.

Figure 4–1 is a diagrammatic model of the economy which is used to explain the relationship among the economic policies and goals. Two important parts of this model are identified as enclosures "A" and "B." These enclosed sections are referred to in the following paragraphs.

Consider the relationship of the goals of full employment and

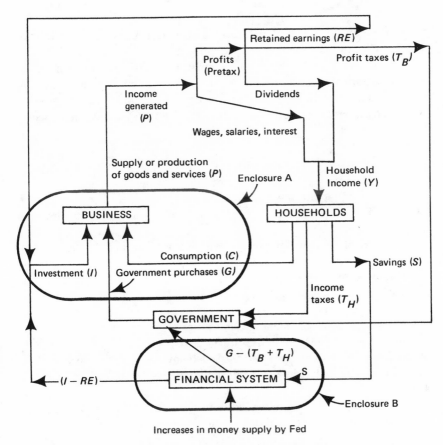

FIGURE 4-1   DIAGRAMMATIC MODEL OF THE ECONOMY

price stability and fiscal and monetary policies in the context of this model. This relationship can be considered by referring to enclosure A in the figure. The key to the level of employment is the supply or production of goods and services (P). To increase the supply of goods and services, business must hire more laborers. At a sufficiently high level of supply or production, all available workers will be employed—this is the full employment level of supply. At a lower level of supply, there will be unemployment because business will need fewer workers to produce a lower level of output.

What determines the level of supply at which business actually operates? Over a long period of time business will produce only what it can sell; that is, it will supply only that for which there is a demand. For a short period of time, however, business may produce more than it sells and add the excess to its inventories, or produce less than it sells, supplying the deficiency out of inventories. But over an extended period of time, it will produce exactly what it can sell.

Businesses' sales, which is the demand for their output, consists of three components: sales to households or consumption demand (C); sales to other businesses or investment demand (I); and sales to government (G). A series of propositions relating demand, supply, and income can be developed:

1. Demand consists of three components: C, I, and G.

2. Over an extended period of time, the level of supply or production will equal the level of demand.

3. The level of supply (or production) determines the level of employment.

4. As shown in Chapter 2 and also in Figure 4–1, the level of supply (or production) generates an *equal amount* of income, which accrues to business as profits or to households as wages, salaries, and interest.

Since the level of demand determines the level of supply and employment, an obvious remaining question is, what determines the level of demand? This question is addressed below. First, however, consider the relationship between the goals and policies by referring to Figure 4–1.

Production, over an extended period of time, will equal $C + I + G$, the level of demand, and will determine the level of employment. Denote the level of production that requires all the available workers and is, therefore, consistent with full employment by P_F. Consequently, if the level of demand equals P_F $(C + I + G = P_F)$, full employment will prevail. If, however, the level of demand is less than P_F $(C + I + G < P_F)$, there will be unemployment. Finally, the level of demand could be greater than P_F, the maximum production possible $(C + I + G > P_F)$. If producers are operating at maximum capacity and there is still excess demand for their output, they will raise the prices of their output. In this case, demand is greater than full employment supply and inflation results.

Three possible cases have been developed:

	Condition	Effects
Case 1.	$C + I + G < P_F$:	unemployment, no inflation.
Case 2.	$C + I + G = P_F$:	no unemployment, no inflation.
Case 3.	$C + I + G > P_F$:	inflation, no unemployment.

Achieving the goals of full employment and no inflation depends on a balance between the demand for goods and the full employment level of supply. If they are equal, both goals will be achieved simultaneously. If demand is less than P_F, there will be unemployment; if demand is greater than P_F, there will be inflation. Chapter 5 demonstrates that this description of the economy is oversimplified and that in reality Case 2 may not be feasible.

It might appear extremely fortuitous for the balance between full employment supply and demand to occur automatically. Forces that affect this balance are considered later in this chapter. First, however, consider how fiscal and monetary policies can be used to affect the equality between demand $(C + I + G)$ and full employment supply (P_F)—that is, to achieve Case 2—if initially either Cases 1 or 3 prevailed.

the use of fiscal and monetary policies

Consider Case 1, the problem of unemployment, as the initial situation. How can fiscal and monetary policies be used to achieve full employment? The problem in Case 1 is one of inadequate demand; demand is less than full employment supply. The solution requires stimulating demand. Consider first how fiscal spending and taxation can be used to stimulate demand. Since government spending (G) is itself a form of demand, an increase in government spending increases aggregate demand directly and therefore reduces unemployment. How can taxation be used to reduce unemployment? Figure 4–1 shows that for households their income (Y) is their source of funds, and taxes (T_H), savings (S), and consumption (C) are their uses of funds. A reduction in taxes increases the level of their income that can be used for both savings and consumption. In particular, the increase in consumption (C) increases total demand $(C + I + G)$, and tends to reduce unemployment. So a decrease in personal income taxes increases aggregate demand and reduces unemployment. Similarly, by referring to profits in Figure 4–1 one can see that a reduction in profit taxes (T_B) leaves more business income for both dividends and retained earnings. An increase in dividends increases personal income and therefore increases consumption. An increase in retained earnings provides business with more funds that can be used for investment, another form of demand. Reductions in business taxes also tend to increase aggregate demand.

Fiscal policy can therefore stimulate demand and reduce unemployment by either increased spending or reduced taxation. The role of monetary policy is somewhat more subtle. Monetary policy's effect on aggregate demand is through its effect on the financial system. This effect is illustrated in Enclosure B of Figure 4–1. Deficit sectors can purchase more goods and services only if they can borrow funds through the financial system to finance the purchases. In Chapter 2, it was shown that monetary policy operates through open market operations to change bank reserves which then lead to changes in bank loans and the money supply. Banks change their lending interest rate to influence their volume of loans. If the Fed purchases Treasury securities, bank reserves increase and this causes both the money supply and bank loans to increase. A decrease in the interest rates accompanies these changes. The increased bank loans are used to finance the purchase of goods and services, specifically the demand for plant and equipment by business, the demand for houses, automobiles, and many other goods by households, and government demand. An increase in money supply thus tends to stimulate the demand for goods and services and reduce unemployment.

In Case 3, an excess demand for goods and services causes inflation. Policies are therefore needed to reduce demand. Demand can be reduced by the opposite of the policies used in Case 1 to stimulate demand. A reduction in government spending, an increase in taxation, or a reduction in the money supply are all methods that can be used to reduce inflation. The uses of the various policies to solve the problems of Cases 1 and 3 are summarized in Table 4–1.[1]

TABLE 4–1 ECONOMIC PROBLEMS AND POLICIES

	Unemployment (Case 1)	Inflation (Case 3)
Fiscal policy	Increase G Reduce T	Reduce G Increase T
Monetary policy	Increase M	Reduce M

At this point, there seems to be no problem in fully achieving the macroeconomic goals by using fiscal and monetary policies. Various conceptual and practical issues are introduced in Chapters 5 and 6 which show that it may be much more difficult than here indicated.

what determines the level of aggregate demand?

Since the level of supply in the economy determines national production and the level of employment, and the level of supply in turn depends on the level of aggregate demand, the question of what de-

---

[1] Fiscal or monetary policies that tend to reduce aggregate demand are called *contractionary* or *tight* policies. Policies that tend to increase aggregate demand are called *expansionary, loose,* or *stimulative* policies.

termines the level of aggregate demand is crucial to an understanding of the determinants of national economic conditions. Both fiscal and monetary policies affect the level of demand. But what relationships in the private economy affect the level of aggregate demand? To answer the question of what determines aggregate demand, the three components of demand—consumption, investment, and government spending—must be considered individually.

Consumption demand is composed of the demand for durable goods (such as automobiles, refrigerators, furniture), nondurable goods (food and clothing), and services (medical care, transportation services, and the like). The factor that has the greatest impact on the level of consumption is income. Consumption increases if income increases and vice versa. Households tend to consume about 93 percent of their disposable (after-tax) income, saving the other 7 percent. While income is the most important determinant of consumption expenditures, other factors also contribute. Wealth may affect consumption. Individuals with the same incomes, but unequal wealth will engage in different levels of consumption. Those with more wealth will tend to consume a larger share of their income, either because they feel more financially secure and therefore save less, or because their wealth can be liquidated to finance consumption in excess of their income. The interest rate may also affect consumption. A lower interest rate makes consumers more likely to borrow to finance the purchases of automobiles, furniture, and other goods normally purchased with credit. In addition, decreases in the interest rate cause bond prices (and the prices of some other financial assets) to increase, household wealth to increase, and consumption to increase because of this. Consumer expectations also affect consumption. For example, if consumers expect a recession and fear losing their jobs they tend to consume less and save more.

Investment demand consists of additions to inventory; the demand for residential housing (this type of investment is due mainly to the household sector, not the business sector); and the business demand for plant and equipment. Different factors explain each type of investment demand. Inventory demand is a very small part of total investment demand but is important because of its volatility. Inventories are a buffer between production and sales. If production exceeds sales, inventories increase; if sales exceed production, inventories decrease. So as sales begin to increase, inventories decrease until production can be increased to match the sales. When sales initially decline, inventories increase until production can be reduced. Inventory demand depends on business expectations of future sales. Often these expectations are based on present conditions, and these expectations change only after actual conditions change. Inventory demand, consequently, tends to be destabilizing to the economy. For example, when other forms of demand decrease, inventories build up, and inventory demand then decreases also.

The demand for residential housing depends upon demographic factors such as new household formation and also on economic factors such as the available supply of mortgage money. The latter depends on deposit flows into savings and loan institutions and mutual savings banks, two major mortgage lenders. Deposit flows into these institutions and their effect on the housing market are considered in Chapter 8.

Business fixed investment—that is, the demand for plant and equipment—is an important component of investment not only because it is the largest component of total investment demand but also because it leads to an increase in the capital stock, which is a major factor in determining economic growth. Several factors affect business fixed investment demand. The first factor is the projected increase in real sales (that is, sales adjusted for price increases). If sales are projected to increase quickly, business will increase its stock of plant and equipment to be able to increase production and satisfy the increased sales demand. Second, if capacity utilization (the percentage of its total capital stock in use) is low, business can increase production without adding to its capital stock. Alternatively, if capacity utilization is high, output can be increased only by increasing its capital stock. The "trigger point" is considered to be at a capacity utilization of about 87 percent. Above this point, business investment demand increases if sales are projected to increase; below it, increased production is based on increases in the utilization of its capital stock. This trigger point is the desired operating rate of business. To operate at higher rates business has to use semiobsolete plant and equipment with high operating costs and would have inadequate "down-time" for the maintenance of its capital.

Two other factors that affect business fixed investment demand are the backlog of orders and the level of inventories. If its backlog of orders for its product is high or its level of inventories is low, business is more likely to increase its demand for plant and equipment to satisfy its orders or to replenish its inventories, respectively.

Business funds are needed to finance its plant and equipment purchases. A portion of these funds is raised internally in the form of profits that are not paid out as dividends (called *retained earnings*), and capital consumption allowances or depreciation, which also generate funds for the firm. Increases in the level of internal funds make possible increases in investment demand. Variations in profits are the main cause of variations in internal funds. However, as indicated in Chapter 2, business usually invests in excess of its internal funds and so external funds must be used. Most of these funds are borrowed. In addition to the availability, the cost of external funds—the interest rate—is also important. At high rates of interest, the cost of the borrowed funds may exceed the profit rate of the capital to be purchased and business will not borrow and invest. Consequently, as the availability of external funds decreases or their costs increase, business investment demand tends to decrease. The ways in which businesses raise their funds are considered in detail in Chapter 11.

Total government demand is composed of the demand by the federal government and by the state and local governments. Federal purchases tend to be quite different from state and local purchases. The many economic, political, social, and demographic factors which affect government demand are too numerous and complex to be discussed here.

circular flow relations

The discussion of the last section began with an orientation toward what factors affect aggregate demand, particularly private (that is nongovernment) demand. To summarize the findings, income is the most important determinant. Personal income is the most important determinant of consumption expenditures, and business income (specifically retained earnings) is an important determinant of business investment demand. The proposition "income affects demand" results from this discussion.

This proposition can be added (as proposition 3) to two propositions developed above (propositions 2 and 4, renumbered 1 and 2 here, respectively):

1. Over an extended period of time, the level of supply or production will equal the level of demand.
2. The level of supply generates an equal amount of income.
3. Income is a major determinant of the level of demand.

Writing these propositions in summary form emphasizes their interrelations:

1. Demand determines supply.
2. Supply generates an equal amount of income.
3. Income is used to finance demand.

Note the complete circularity in these propositions. The circularity can also be seen in the flow diagram in Figure 4–2, which is basically Figure 4–1 simplified by excluding the government and financial sectors. The main point of interest here is whether a full employment situation is likely to be achieved and maintained automatically (if it is maintained it is called a *full employment equilibrium*) or whether the use of government stabilization policies is necessary to achieve and sustain full employment.

A Model of the Economy   55

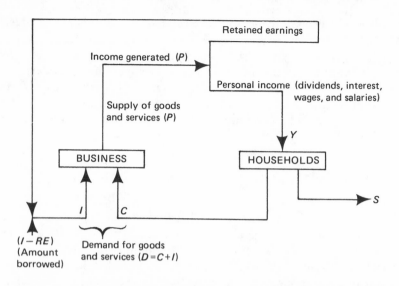

FIGURE 4–2 A SIMPLIFIED DIAGRAMMATIC MODEL OF THE ECONOMY

Assume that, with the model of Figure 4–2, the business sector begins producing a full employment level of output P_F. An equal amount of income will be generated and divided between retained earnings (RE) and personal income (Y). (There is no government and hence no taxes in the model of Figure 4–2.) That is, $P_F = RE + Y$. With their income Y households save an amount S and consume the remainder C. Business uses all of its income RE and an additional borrowed amount $I - RE$ to finance its total investment demand I.

Will the initial full employment situation be sustained; that is, will business continue to produce the full employment level of supply? It will only if it can sell all it produces, if there is a level of demand equal to the full employment level of supply. Total demand is consumption plus investment demand, $C + I$ (again, there is no government sector in this model). Is $C + I = P_F$? If so, business will continue to produce its maximum amount and full employment will prevail. If $C + I$ is less than P_F, business will accumulate inventories if it continues to produce its full employment level of supply. Consequently, it will cut back production, lay off workers, and unemployment will result.

The relationship between total demand $C + I$ and full employment supply P_F is critical in determining the level of employment. The conditions necessary for equality between $C + I$ and P_F will be algebraically derived and then interpreted. Figure 4–1 shows that full employment supply generates an equal amount of income:

$$P_F = Y + RE \qquad (2)$$

In addition, personal income is allocated to savings and consumption:

$$Y = C + S \tag{3}$$

Substituting equation (3) in equation (2) gives:

$$P_F = C + S + RE \tag{4}$$

Under what conditions does total demand $C + I$ equal full employment supply P_F? That is, under what conditions does the following hold true?

$$P_F = C + I \tag{5}$$

Since equation (4) is necessarily true, it is seen by comparing equations (4) and (5) that equation (5) can also be true only if:

$$S + RE = I \tag{6}[2]$$

But note that S is the quantity of savings of the household sector and RE is the savings of the business sector. For the economy to sustain full employment equilibrium, total savings, household and business, must be equal to the level of investment the business sector engages in from an initial full employment situation.

The rationale for this condition is obvious. Since the supply of goods and services generates an equal amount of income, for total demand to equal the supply the generated income must manifest itself completely as demand. Since the savings of households, S, is a part of their income which does not lead to demand, business must engage in a level of demand I which exceeds its income RE by this amount: that is, $I - RE = S$, or $I = S + RE$.

It might at first seem fortuitous for this condition to be met. Since total savings depends on the behavior of many households and total investment on the behavior of many firms, it seems extremely unlikely that $S + RE$ will equal I. But the role of the financial system is crucial in achieving equality between savings $(S + RE)$ and investment (I), or alternatively between household savings (S) and business borrowing $(I - RE)$. Its role, as discussed in Chapter 2, is to channel the savings of surplus sectors to borrowers or deficit sectors. The financial system makes the savings of households available to business borrowers. And

---

[2] This equation can be rearranged to give $S = I - RE$. Since RE is business savings and I is business investment, the difference $I - RE$ is the amount business must borrow to finance its investment. Consequently, $S = I - RE$ says that household savings equals business borrowing.

if, from an initial full employment situation, all household savings are channeled into business borrowing and investment, full employment will be achieved and maintained. If savings increase, interest rates will decline and stimulate borrowing and investment, thus sustaining full employment.

The circular flow description of the economy considered here shows that there are forces which give a tendency toward full employment equilibrium. One force is the income-generating effect of supply and the tendency for income to be used for expenditures. Another force is the role of the financial system to channel income of surplus sectors which is not spent on goods and services to other sectors which borrow and spend the funds. Are these forces strong enough to assure full employment at all times? If so, the economy would sustain a full employment equilibrium without the use of fiscal and monetary policies. If not, the use of these policies may be necessary to achieve full employment equilibrium.

Several factors may interfere with the forces tending toward full employment. First, certain factors may prevent the interest rate from declining even when there is an excess supply of funds. Second, investment demand may not increase in response to decreases in the interest rates. In both of these cases the financial system tends to accumulate funds that are not spent on goods and services. This would be particularly likely if capacity utilization were low. Finally, there may be long lags between: 1) the production of goods and services and the generation of income; 2) when additional income is earned and consumption demand increases; and 3) an increase in demand and the business decision to increase production. These three lags would not prevent achieving full employment but would increase the time needed to achieve it.

While some forces give the economy a tendency to sustain a full employment level of activity, there are also reasons for suspecting that these forces are not strong enough to keep the economy at full employment without the use of fiscal and monetary policies. Currently in the economics profession opinion is divided about the strength of these forces and consequently about the need for fiscal and monetary policies. Chapter 6 explores this division of opinion.

generalization of these results

The crucial relation is between the level of supply (P in general, P_F for the full employment level of supply) and the level of demand, $C + I$ in the model of Figure 4–2. The initial level of supply and consequently employment will be sustained only if there is an equal amount of demand: if $P = C + I$. If demand is less than the initial level of supply $(C + I < P)$, then business will reduce its supply and employment. If demand is greater than supply $(C + I > P)$, then business will increase its level of supply by hiring more workers if the economy was not initially at full employment, and increase the prices of its output if the economy was initially at full employment.

The critical comparison, then, is between P and $C + I$. And the desired level of supply, of course, is P_F, the full employment level of supply. In the last section it was shown by using the circular flow relations that the relation $P = C + I$ is equivalent to the relation $S + RE = I$ (or $S = I - RE$). That is, demand will be equal to the initial level of supply only if total savings in the economy $S + RE$ equals total investment. If $P > C + I$, or equivalently if $S + RE > I$, then the excess supply, or, equivalently, the excess savings, will lead to a reduction in employment. If $P < C + I$, or equivalently if $S + RE < I$, then the excess demand, or equivalently the excess investment, will lead to an increase in employment if possible, and inflation if employment cannot be increased. Of course, as discussed before in this chapter, fiscal and monetary policies can be used to reduce either unemployment or inflation. Table 4–2 summarizes the various possible relations between supply and demand, the effect of the relations, and the appropriate policy response.

summary

This chapter can be summarized by referring to three basic propositions: 1) demand determines supply; 2) supply generates an equal amount of income; and 3) income is used to finance demand.

The level of supply determines the level of employment in the economy because labor is used in the production process. Over an extended period of time, business will not continue to increase or decrease its inventory levels and consequently will supply only the level of output that can be sold, the level for which there is a demand. However, the supply process generates an equal amount of income in the form of wages, salaries, interest payments, and dividends to households and retained earnings to business. And income is predominately used to finance demand: household income is used to finance consumption demand and business income is used to finance investment demand. However, not all income for all sectors is used for demand. The household sector does not use all of its income for consumption expenditures but saves a portion of it. However, the business sector usually spends in excess of its income on investment demand. The role of the financial

TABLE 4–2 SUMMARY OF ECONOMIC CONDITIONS AND POLICY RESPONSES

Initial Supply Condition	Level of Demand	Results	Policy Response*
Initially at full employment, P_F	$C + I > P_F$ ($I > S + RE$)	Inflation	Reduce aggregate demand by fiscal policy or monetary policy
	$C + I = P_F$ ($I = S + RE$)	Full employment equilibrium with no inflation	No policy change necessary
	$C + I < P_F$ ($I < S + RE$)	Reduction in employment	Increase aggregate demand by fiscal policy or monetary policy
Initially at employment P less than full employment ($P < P_F$)	$C + I > P$ ($I > S + RE$)	Increase in employment	Two options: 1. No policy change and let employment increase at its own pace 2. Accelerate the increase in employment by increasing aggregate demand by fiscal policy or monetary policy
	$C + I = P$ ($I = S + RE$)	Equilibrium at less than full employment	Increase aggregate demand by fiscal policy or monetary policy
	$C + I < P$ ($I < S + RE$)	Reduction in employment	Increase aggregate demand by fiscal policy or monetary policy

* As discussed, aggregate demand is reduced by fiscal policy by increasing taxes (T) or decreasing government demand (G). Aggregate demand is reduced by monetary policy by decreasing the money supply. Aggregate demand is increased by using these policies in the opposite ways.

system is to channel the income not spent by the household sector to the business sector which does spend it. Thus, if business begins by producing a full employment level of supply P_F an equal amount of income is generated. If all this income is used for the purchase of goods and services (C and I) either directly or indirectly through the financial system, the level of demand will be equal to the initial level of supply, and the initial full employment level of supply will be sustained: a full employment equilibrium is in effect.

The Economic System: Goals, Policies, and Relationships

If not all the income generated by the initial level of supply manifests itself as demand, employment will decrease. In this case, demand can be stimulated by either fiscal or monetary policies. Conversely, if from an initial full employment level of supply, demand is even greater than supply (because the combined sectors in the economy desire to spend an amount greater than their incomes, financing the excess by borrowing), then inflation will result. In this case, fiscal and monetary policies could be used to reduce demand.

Because of the circular flow relationships (particularly the relationship that occurs when supply generates income used to finance demand) and the tendency for the financial system to channel funds from sectors that do not spend them to sectors that do, the economy tends to remain at full employment if it begins there. But other forces tend to keep the economy from reaching full employment or staying there if it does get there. If such forces dominate, fiscal and monetary policies are necessary to achieve and maintain full employment.

questions

1. Discuss the relations among production, income, and demand.

2. Discuss the relations between the level of demand and unemployment and inflation.

3. Discuss how monetary policy affects the level of aggregate demand. Discuss how this relates to the financial system.

4. Discuss how taxation and government spending affect the level of demand.

5. Discuss the main determinants of business investment demand and how monetary policy relates to this demand.

the premier goals:
high employment,
price stability,
and economic growth

5

Chapter 3 provides a general discussion of the six major macroeconomic goals. This chapter discusses the three goals of high employment, price stability, and economic growth in more detail. For each goal, there is a discussion of the problems which hinder the economy's achievement of the goal, the potential policy cure for each problem, and the ways of measuring how well the economy is achieving the goal.

unemployment

To interpret the relation between the published unemployment rate data and the social problems caused by unemployment it is necessary to understand the official definition of the unemployment rate. The official, well-publicized unemployment rate is determined from a monthly survey of 47,000 households conducted by the Bureau of Labor Statistics. Persons are classified as employed if they worked during a survey week (or if they were temporarily absent). Persons are classified as unemployed if they were not employed during the survey week *and* were available for work and had made a specific effort to find a job within the preceding four weeks. The civilian labor force is the sum of the employed and the unemployed according to these definitions. Note particularly that the unemployed who are no longer looking for work are not counted as either being unemployed or as being part of the labor force. The reported unemployment rate is the number of unemployed persons as a percentage of the civilian labor force. The significance of this definition is discussed below.

FRICTIONAL UNEMPLOYMENT

Some workers are temporarily unemployed either because they have voluntarily quit their jobs to search for a different job, or because they lost their job due to the closing of a plant, an employer's dissatisfaction with the worker's performance, or for other reasons. Such temporary unemployment is called *frictional unemployment*. Job mobility and the resulting frictional unemployment are essentially consequences of economic efficiency and through a better matching of workers and jobs, it helps promote economic growth. Consequently, frictional unemployment should not be regarded as a problem that should be cured and no policy cures are prescribed. And it is primarily because of frictional unemployment that an unemployment rate of about 4 percent is considered "full employment" for policy purposes. But, as is discussed below, the "full employment level of unemployment" varies with the composition of the labor force.

STRUCTURAL UNEMPLOYMENT

The structurally unemployed are those who do not have the skills that are in current demand by producers. Examples of structural unemployment are aerospace engineers during the late 1960s, due to a decline in government demand for aircraft, Appalachian miners during the 1950s and 1960s, due to a decline in the demand for coal, and teenagers who are new entrants into the labor force but have no salable skills. Structural unemployment is more permanent than the temporary frictional unemployment. And the structurally unemployed are not counted in the official unemployment statistics if, out of futility, they discontinue their job search. This is typically the case.

Policy cures for structural unemployment are of two types: job training and retraining, and encouraging geographic mobility. Various job training programs have been implemented to retain those whose skills are no longer needed by producers or to initially train those who have no skills. In addition, programs that provide information about jobs in other regions and tax incentives to migrate to these regions have been used to encourage the exodus of workers from regions of high unemployment.

CYCLICAL UNEMPLOYMENT

During recessions, or cyclical downturns, workers who have the skills needed by producers are often laid off because producers are selling less of their output, therefore producing less, and requiring fewer workers. Cyclical unemployment is the most volatile type of unemployment. In addition, the impact of cyclical unemployment is uneven across different types of workers. Cyclical unemployment affects workers in service industries much less than those in manufacturing. Within manufacturing, it affects white-collar or supervisory workers much less than it does blue-collar or production workers.

Conceptually, the policy cure for cyclical unemployment is clear. Fiscal and monetary policies can be used to increase aggregate demand and restore full employment.

THE UNEMPLOYMENT RATE: INTERPRETATIONS

The same objective unemployment rate figures do not convey the same message to all observers. The unemployment rate during 1976 was 7.7 percent. Some claim that the social problem of unemployment was much worse than this figure indicates; others claim it was not as bad.

Some observers, usually those of a liberal persuasion, assert that since many of the structurally unemployed are not officially counted as unemployed because they are not looking for a job, the official unemployment rate understates the actual unemployment rate. In addition, during recessions when unemployment increases, many of the skilled workers who are laid off recognize that no jobs are available. Consequently, they do not look for jobs and are not officially counted as unemployed. Liberals conclude, for this reason, that during recessions the increase in the official unemployment rate understates the actual increase.

Other observers, usually those of a conservative bent, assert that the social problem of unemployment is not as bad as the official unemployment rate indicates. They observe, as shown in Table 5–1, that the unemployment rate varies considerably by age and sex. Since many female workers are actually secondary earners in their families and many teenagers are not supporting families or even themselves, it is, they argue, less of a social problem for these groups to be unemployed than for adult males (their surrogate for heads-of-households) to be unemployed. And, they point out, the unemployment rate among adult males is lower than the official unemployment rate. They also believe that since the fractions of teenagers and females in the labor force has been in-

TABLE 5–1   SELECTED UNEMPLOYMENT RATES DURING 1976

All workers	7.7%
By sex and age:	
Both sexes, 16–19 years	19.0%
Men, 20 years and over	5.9%
Women, 20 years and over	7.4%
By color:	
White	7.0%
Negro and other races	13.1%
Other selected groups:	
Experienced wage and salary workers	7.3%
Household heads	5.1%
Married men	4.2%
Full-time workers	7.3%
Blue-collar workers	9.4%

Source: *Economic Report of the President, 1976* (Washington, D.C.: United States Government Printing Office, 1976), p. 199.

creasing during the last ten years, the level of unemployment which should be accepted as satisfactory is larger now than then. While an unemployment rate of 4 percent was a good policy goal for 1965, they assert, 5 percent or more is satisfactory today.

inflation

DEMAND-PULL INFLATION

As discussed in Chapter 4, when total demand is greater than the maximum output of goods and services which can be produced by business, inflation will result. If producers can sell at existing prices more than they can produce, they will increase prices. This demand-induced inflation is called *demand-pull inflation*. It occurs at, or close to, full employment.[1]

---

[1] Demand-pull inflation may occur somewhat before the economy reaches its absolute maximum output. As the output of the producing sector increases toward its maximum output it begins to use its less modern plant and equipment and hire new workers who do not have the skills of their original workers. Consequently, when production gets close to its maximum level, production costs increase for these reasons. Producers often increase prices to reflect these increased production costs. Thus, there are some demand-pull pressures somewhat before maximum output and full employment.

The policy cure for demand-pull inflation, as indicated in Chapter 4, involves the use of fiscal and monetary policies to reduce aggregate demand. Conceptually, no problems are involved.

COST-PUSH INFLATION

Demand-pull inflation occurs only at, or close to, full employment. The United States has often experienced significant price increases even with high levels of unemployment. Other causes of inflation are necessary to explain this situation. If asked to express two words which would characterize economics, the most frequent answers would be "demand" and "supply." Consequently, if demand-oriented inflation is possible, a supply-oriented inflation should also be expected. And there is one. Supply or production requires inputs, and changes in the costs of these inputs affect how the prices of the corresponding outputs will change. So the costs of inputs must be explored.

The two main inputs are labor and the capital stock. To a large extent the capital stock is purchased by funds supplied by the owners of the business. The return to the owners for their contributed funds is the profits of the business. The return to labor is their wages. In the production process, wages accrue to laborers and profits accrue to the owners of the business. The nation's income comprises mainly the wages and salaries that accrue to labor and the profits that accrue to business.

And in a real sense, the business sector and the labor sector compete for shares of the total income generated by the economy. Labor attempts to increase its share of total income by attempting to get higher wage rates and wages. But as wages increase, business costs increase and, if the prices of its output remain the same, business profits decrease. Business attempts to increase or restore their profits by increasing the prices of their output. And if prices increase with wages constant, profits will increase. However, with wages constant, the purchasing power of the wages decrease because of the price increase; "real" wages decrease. And labor usually responds to decreased real wages by attempting to get higher wages. This completes the circle.

Therefore, business and labor compete to increase their income shares by increasing prices and wages, respectively. And an increase in either tends to cause the other to increase: if labor gets a higher wage, business tends to increase its prices to restore its previous level of profits; and when prices increase, labor bargains for higher wages to restore the former purchasing power of its wages.[2] The type of inflation

---

[2] Due to increases in labor productivity (the quantity of output produced by each worker) over time, wages can increase somewhat without causing profits to decrease, even at the same price level. For example, if labor productivity increases

caused by wages and prices "leapfrogging" over each other is called *cost-push inflation* or often a *wage-price spiral*.

To determine the feasibility of a wage-price spiral, some basic economic factors must be considered. Since cost-push inflation is purported to exist in an economy operating at less than full employment, how can business increase prices and labor increase wages? If business is selling less output than it has capacity to produce, economic forces would seem to exert downward pressure on price as producers compete to sell more output. And if there are unemployed workers, there should be downward pressures on wages as unemployed workers agree to accept lower wages to get jobs. Cost-push inflation does not apply, however, to industries in which competitive pressures are great—that is, industries in which there are many small producers and purchasers of the output—but only to sectors where competitive forces are weak, which means industries in which there are a few large producers (oligopolies) or large, strong labor unions. In the latter case, producers can increase prices in a concerted fashion even though they are not selling as much as they have the capacity to produce. And labor unions can bargain for increased wages even though there are unemployed workers elsewhere in the economy or even in their own union.

Cost-push inflation can exist even with unemployed workers and unutilized capital stock because of concentrated business and labor. And cost-push inflation tends to be self-propelling: once it starts, it continues of its own accord. In recent years the phrase *inflationary psychology* has also been applied to self-propelling inflation. Wage increases are demanded by labor to adjust for past price increases or even in anticipation of future price increases. Prices are increased by business to adjust for past wage increases or in anticipation of future wage increases. Interest rates also increase in anticipation of inflation—this phenomenon is discussed in Chapter 7. Consumers and businesses accelerate their demands for consumption and investment goods so they can buy before the price increase. This adds demand pressures to cost-push inflation. Expectations of inflation become self-fulfilling and inflation continues of its own accord.

How does cost-push inflation begin? It could begin by either autonomous and excessive price increases by business or wage increases by labor. It could also begin with a large increase in the price of an important import, such as oil. Inflation could also begin as a demand-pull inflation and then after excess demand no longer existed, a cost-push

---

by 3 percent a year, business can afford to increase wages by 3 percent with no increase in prices and with no decrease in its profit rate. And if this profit rate applies to a larger volume of funds due to the funds invested during the year, the dollar level of profits will increase.

inflation could persist because of the inertia of prices and wages alternately increasing.

Conceptually, the cure for demand-pull inflation is clear. The cure for cost-push inflation is much less clear. Three different responses, if not cures, to cost-push inflation can be prescribed. The first response is based on the market mechanisms responsible for wage and price increases. The wage rate is determined in the market for labor. In a perfectly competitive labor market, wages increase if there is an excess demand for labor (that is, a demand for labor greater than the available supply) and decrease if there is an excess supply of labor (that is, unemployment). A basic assumption, however, in explaining cost-push inflation is that, due to bargaining strength, labor can bid up wage rates despite some unemployment. But if the level of unemployment became sufficiently high, even strong labor unions would reduce their wage demands. And wages in nonunionized sectors might increase even less, or perhaps decrease. Consequently, if the unemployment rate were high, the rate of increase in wages would decrease.

Correspondingly, prices are determined in the market for goods and services. With excess demand, prices increase—this is demand-pull inflation. If there is an excess supply of goods—that is, business is operating at less than full capacity utilization—prices would decrease in a competitive market. However, a basic assumption in cost-push inflation is the existence of concentration in some industries so the companies in these industries can increases prices despite having excess capacity. However, if excess capacity becomes substantial then even firms in concentrated industries would mitigate their price increases. And firms in competitive industries might decrease their prices. With a substantial excess supply of goods and services, firms would reduce their price increases.

So with a substantial excess supply of labor—high unemployment—and a substantial excess supply of goods and services—low capacity utilization—cost-push inflation will be reduced. However, these two characteristics describe a recession. So a recession can be called a policy cure for cost-push inflation, but it is hardly a desirable way to cure the problem. Nevertheless, most cost-push inflations in U.S. history have been reduced, if not cured, by recessions.

A second response to cost-push inflation has been various types of wage-price controls, sometimes called *income policies*. The basis for wage-price controls is the idea that if the world would stop for a short period of time and wages and prices stopped increasing during this period, then subsequently wages and prices would no longer have to leapfrog over one another. Wages could increase by an amount equal only to productivity increases, and prices could remain constant without hurting either labor's real wages or business' profits. The use of wage-price controls is an attempt to achieve this ideal situation by the temporary imposition of artificial ceilings on wages and prices. The belief is that the ceiling will temporarily prevent wages and prices from increasing. Once the wage and price increases have been stopped, the ceilings become unnecessary and can be removed.

However, some practical problems occur with wage-price controls. A complete description of the role of the market-oriented prices in the economy is beyond the scope of this presentation, although some examples can be given which indicate problems that can be caused by artificial price ceilings. Even though the economy as a whole may have excess supply, specific sectors of the economy may be experiencing excess demand. If prices are not allowed to increase in these sectors, the limited supply will be allocated through either illegal or noneconomic means. Long queues may form and only those at the head of the queue will be able to purchase the goods, or the goods may be sold only to friends of the producers. Often, goods will be sold on a "black market," sold illegally at a price higher than the ceiling.

Various types of misallocations can occur, particularly if some prices are controlled and others are not. For example, if the price of grain were not controlled (perhaps on the basis that the market for grain is competitive) but the price of cattle were, the price of cattle feed could increase enough so that cattle raisers would lose money by producing cattle and selling them at the ceiling price. Consequently, no cattle would be produced. During a recent episode of wage-price controls, export prices were exempted from controls. The world price for some U.S. produced goods became higher than the U.S. ceiling price. Consequently, domestic producers were exporting all their production at the higher prices. If a domestic firm wanted to purchase some of the goods, it had to import the goods at the higher world price. The absurdity that resulted was that after the U.S. goods were loaded on boats, the boat would proceed a short distance into the ocean, turn back and deliver the goods to a local purchaser, who could then legally pay the higher world price for the "import." Examples of the irrationalities of wage-price controls abound.

In addition, the administrative costs of enforcing wage-price controls may be substantial. An army of bureaucrats may be necessary to set ceilings, detect violations, and enforce wage-price rollbacks.

Finally, there is some question whether wage-price controls actually prevent inflation. Producers may respond to price controls by reducing quality or volume and selling at the same price or by other subtle means of effectively increasing prices. In addition, they claim, after the controls are removed, prices increase by as much as they would have during controls.

An overall evaluation of wage-price controls is difficult. Supporters admit that they cause misallocations of resources but claim that over a short period of time, these costs are minor relative to the benefits of reducing inflation. Opponents of controls claim that the misallocation costs are substantial and that in addition, wage-price controls do not cure inflation.

The third response to cost-push inflation depends on the rejection of the first two. If a recession is deemed an unacceptable way to cure inflation and wage-price controls are thought to cause too many economic misallocations and, in addition, may not be effective in controlling inflation, the remaining response is to learn to live with inflation. Supporters of this response have also supported methods to make the economy "neutral" with respect to inflation, methods that prevent any party from either gaining or losing due to inflation. The attempt to do this has been called *indexing*. According to this concept, many economic variables would be indexed or tied to a price index. Labor contracts with cost-of-living clauses and social security benefits which are tied to the consumer price index are already "indexed." A complete indexing system would tie all wages, salaries, transfer payments, interest rates, and even the tax system to price levels. Inflation becomes less objectionable if no one gains or loses because of it.

The best policy response to cost-push inflation is not obvious. None of the three possible choices is completely satisfactory. Policymakers have, at different times, selected each of these as the best of a bad lot.

RESOURCE SCARCITIES AND BOTTLENECKS

The discussion of demand-pull inflation implies that in that situation demand exceeds full employment supply uniformly across all sectors of the economy due to inadequate levels of productive resources, labor and capital, in all sectors. Recently, inflation has occurred for two different but related reasons, both of which relate to a specific sector of the economy.

One is caused not by a shortage of labor or capital but by a shortage of raw materials used in the production process. Raw material shortages can occur for many reasons. Beef prices rose because schools of anchovies, which were used as a protein source in cattle feed, migrated from their normal habitat off the west coast of South America. Wheat prices rose because of a combination of an increase in the worldwide demand for food and bad weather. Oil prices rose because of the formation of a cartel by oil-producing nations. Increases in the prices of these raw materials cause price increases in the products that use these resources as inputs. These price increases are then propagated to other product prices and wages due to cost-push inflation.

What is the policy cure for this type of inflation? Economic policies cannot prevent bad weather or anchovy migration, and the policies that could prevent cartelization are as much political as economic. Other than price controls, no standard economic policies exist that can prevent price rises in the sector that experiences the shortage. Nor could these policies prevent inflation in the prices of goods which use these resources as inputs. Preventing the propagation of price increases to other sectors requires the responses to cost-push inflation.

The second reason is that price increases in a specific sector occur because demand exceeds the supply that can be produced by the available capital and labor only in that specific sector. This could be due to an increase in demand greater than was projected and planned for. Consequently, the level of investment may have been too low or adequate levels of some specialized type of labor skills may not have been developed. This situation is a demand-induced inflation in a specific sector rather than uniformly over the economy. If the goods of this sector are used as inputs in other sectors, prices in these sectors will also increase because of cost increases. And these price increases could cause an economy-wide cost-push inflation. Supply shortages in the original shortage sector will eventually disappear as new capital is formed in response to the high profit rates which result from the price increases and as new workers gain the specialized skills because of the increased wages accruing to these skills. But the cost-push inflation could sustain

TABLE 5–2 ECONOMIC PROBLEMS AND THEIR CURES

Problem	Types	Cures
Unemployment	Frictional	None needed
	Structural	Job retraining; geographical mobility
	Cyclical	Stimulative fiscal and monetary policies
Inflation	Demand-pull	Contractionary fiscal and monetary policies
	Cost-push	1) Recession; 2) Wage-price controls; 3) Accept inflation and implement indexing
	Resource scarcities	None
	Bottlenecks	Better forecasting of demands and better planning of supply

itself. Again, the original price increases could not have been prevented by standard economic policies.

Better forecasting and planning could have, in both cases, prevented the inflation, however. The various types of unemployment and inflation and their cures are summarized in Table 5–2.

the tradeoff: price stability versus high employment

Considering the two major goals of economic policy individually, the choices are clearly for stable prices and full employment. This section considers whether these two goals can be pursued independently or whether policies taken to affect one goal also affect the other. The economic model of Chapter 4 gives the impression that both goals can be achieved simultaneously. The various combinations of inflation and unemployment that can be achieved in the context of this model are shown in Figure 5–1. Obviously, the preferred choice, point X, would be at the origin of this graph where there is no inflation or unemployment and which is achieved when demand equals full employment supply.

However, the model of Chapter 4 considered only demand-pull inflation and cyclical unemployment. In a world with only demand-pull inflation and cyclical unemployment, the delicate use of fiscal and monetary policies could cause demand to equal full employment supply and achieve both goals. This is not the case when, in addition, frictional unemployment, structural unemployment, and cost-push inflation are considered.

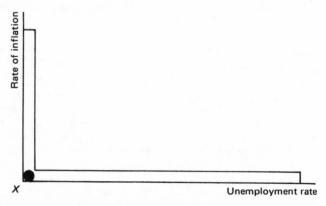

FIGURE 5–1 THE UNEMPLOYMENT-INFLATION TRADEOFF WITH ONLY DEMAND-PULL INFLATION AND CYCLICAL UNEMPLOYMENT

The Economic System: Goals, Policies, and Relationships

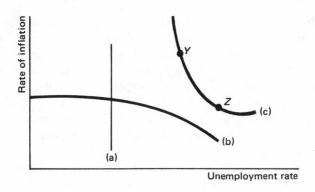

FIGURE 5–2 THE UNEMPLOYMENT-INFLATION TRADEOFF—A MORE REALISTIC VIEW

Frictional unemployment and structural unemployment occur at any level of demand and are essentially independent of the level of demand and the rate of inflation. Curve (a) in Figure 5–2 shows the tradeoff between inflation and unemployment in a world characterized by only frictional and structural unemployment—the rate of unemployment is independent of the rate of inflation.[3]

Cost-push inflation can occur even with unemployment. However, as discussed, as unemployment increases, cost-push inflation becomes more moderate. The tradeoff between inflation and unemployment in a world characterized only by cost-push inflation is shown by curve (b) in Figure 5–2.

In a world characterized by both frictional and structural unemployment and cost-push inflation, the total tradeoff between unemployment and inflation will be a combination of both curves (a) and (b); this combined curve is shown as curve (c). Curve (c) shows the choices of inflation rates and unemployment rates in a world that has structural unemployment and cost-push inflation in addition to cyclical unemployment and demand-pull inflation.

Curve (c) of the figure portrays much less optimistic prospects for policy than does the curve in Figure 5–1. The most significant aspect of curve (c) is that it does not go through the origin of the graph; that is, it is not possible to achieve stable prices and full unemployment simultaneously. Even worse, its curvature shows that as progress is made toward achieving one goal, the economy deviates farther from the other. For example, in proceeding from point Y to point Z on curve (c), the rate of inflation decreases but the unemployment rate increases.

---

[3] To the extent that structural unemployment is excluded from the measured unemployment rate, the actual rather than the measured rate of unemployment is being considered.

Such curves are called *Phillips curves* after the British economist, A. W. Phillips. In recent years, considerable controversy has arisen over the shape and even the existence of the Phillips curve. Two aspects of the relationship between inflation and unemployment are clear, however. First, no single stationary curve explains the relationship between inflation and unemployment for all time. This relationship changes as inflationary expectations change. And these anticipations depend on past inflation. In addition, although inflation and unemployment may both respond to the same policy, they may respond at different speeds. For example, unemployment will increase more rapidly than cost-push inflation will decline in response to contractionary policies. Second, there is undoubtedly some tradeoff, at least in the short run, between inflation and unemployment. For example, cost-push inflation will increase and unemployment decrease in response to recession-inducing policies.

economic growth

Economic growth is measured by the rate of change of real gross national product. The three major causes of economic growth are: (1) increases in the quantity and quality of the labor force; (2) technological change; and (3) increases in the capital stock.

Increases in the size of the labor force occur mainly because of population increases, although social changes such as the degree of female participation in the labor force may also affect its size. However, some government policies may impede growth in the labor force. Minimum wage laws may keep the young and the unskilled out of the labor force because employers do not regard them as sufficiently productive to warrant the minimum wage and are prevented by law from paying less. In addition, generous levels of welfare payments may induce some welfare recipients to remain out of the labor force. The quality of the labor force depends on the levels and types of education and job training. Government job training programs can affect economic growth through this channel.

The principal cause of technological change is business and government expenditures on research and development. The link between research and development expenditures and the actual technological change is imperfectly understood, as is the inducement for business research and development expenditures.

Increases in the capital stock are caused by business investment expenditures. Several governmental policies can be used to stimulate investment and increase the rate of economic growth These policies operate through the various determinants of investment demand that were discussed in Chapter 4. First, business investment is normally low if business is not using its currently owned capital stock; that is, if its capacity utilization is low. Thus, one policy that stimulates economic growth is maintaining a high level of employment and capacity utilization by fiscal and monetary policies. But, as noted in Chapter 4, inflation is harmful to business profits and hence to investment. So if fiscal and monetary policies are too stimulative, they will harm business investment. Therefore, a delicate balance of fiscal and monetary policies that maintains high employment without generating inflation will increase investment demand and the rate of economic growth.

One aspect of fiscal policy which relates to business investment is called *crowding out*. This concept is discussed in Chapter 6. Various government tax policies also affect business investment in plant and equipment. If the tax rate on corporate profits is high, business will have a lower level of after-tax profits and less internal funds to finance investment. This will reduce business investment. The federal government allows business to subtract from their taxes a percentage of certain types of their investment expenditures: this policy is called an *investment tax credit*. For example, with a 10 percent investment tax credit, if a business spends $80,000 on equipment, it can subtract $8,000 from its tax bill, making the effective price of the equipment $72,000. Because of the investment tax credit, business will engage in more investment because its effective purchase price becomes lower. *Rapid depreciation* of plant and equipment allows business to reduce its tax payments and increase its internally generated investment funds. In the last decade, the investment tax credit and rapid depreciation policies have been used frequently to encourage investment.

This chapter discusses the major economic goals. Chapter 6 elaborates on the major economic policies used to achieve these goals.

questions

1. Give two interpretations of the unemployment rate as an indicator of the social consequences of unemployed workers.

2. How can cost-push inflation exist despite the existence of unemployment? How do business, labor unions, and consumers contribute to cost-push inflation?

3. Give three responses to cost-push inflation and evaluate them.

4. Discuss how structural unemployment and cost-push inflation affect the Phillips Curve.

the application of fiscal and monetary policies

6

Chapter 3 provides a very general discussion of the economic goals and policies. Chapter 4 presents a model which showed the relationships between the goals and the policies. Chapter 5 considers three of the goals in detail. This chapter gives a detailed discussion of fiscal and monetary policies.

The first two sections of this chapter consider fiscal and monetary policies individually. Each section addresses three questions about the policy. First, what institution is responsible for implementing the policy? Second, what are the specific tools of this policy? Third, what measures can be used to interpret the stance or posture of the policy, to tell whether it is stimulative or contractionary? The third section considers the relative effectiveness of fiscal and monetary policies. The fourth section examines a current dispute about their relative effectiveness.

fiscal policy

EXECUTOR

Fiscal policy is implemented jointly by the president and the Congress. The Congress passes policies on taxation and appropriations (the authority for expenditures) and the president approves them.

TOOLS

Expenditures and taxes are the tools of fiscal policy. The main categories of expenditures are the government's purchases of goods and services, such as the purchase of jet airplanes, highway construction, payments to government employees, and expenditures for transfer payments. Transfer payments are government payments to persons who provide no goods or services in return to the government. Examples of transfer payments are welfare payments, unemployment compensation, and social security benefits.

The major types of federal government taxes are the personal income tax, the corporate profits tax, the capital gains tax, the inheritance tax, and the social security tax.

There are two types of automatic responses of fiscal policy to changes in the economy which tend to stabilize the economy. The first such response is through government unemployment compensation. When the economy weakens and unemployment increases, unemployment compensation payments increase and provide the unemployed with purchasing power which prevents demand (and production) from decreasing as much as it otherwise would. The second response is due to the progressive personal income tax system (in which the tax rate increases with the income level), which also tends to stabilize the economy. When the economy weakens, incomes decrease but this decrease in incomes puts households in a lower tax bracket so that their after-tax incomes, and demands, decrease less than their total incomes. Because of their automatic stabilizing effects, these components of fiscal policy—unemployment compensation and the progressive tax system—are called *automatic stabilizers*. Other changes in fiscal policy do not change automatically but only by deliberate actions by the Congress and the president. Such changes are called *discretionary fiscal policy*.

INDICATORS

The main indicator of fiscal policy is the surplus or deficit of the government budget. If government expenditures exceed tax revenues, the government is adding more funds to the economy than it is removing as taxes. This generates a budget deficit. If tax revenues exceed expenditures, the government is removing more in taxes than it is adding in expenditures. This generates a budget surplus. The official government budget is called the *unified budget*.

A large budget deficit is interpreted as a more stimulative fiscal policy, because the government is injecting more spending in the economy than it is extracting as taxes. A large surplus is regarded as contractionary because the government is withdrawing more in taxes from the economy than it is spending.

But there are some limitations to using this interpretation of the budget. The government can autonomously set some parts of the budget: for example, expenditures on goods and services and the tax *rates* for the personal income tax and the corporate income tax. However, other parts of the budget are not determined autonomously by the government but respond automatically to the level of economic activity. For example, when unemployment increases, government expenditures on unemployment compensation automatically increase. And the levels of personal income and corporate profits decrease, and so even with constant tax *rates,* the tax revenues of the government from these sources decrease. The government deficit tends to increase due to both increased expenditures and decreased tax revenues when unemployment increases.

To interpret the budget properly, a distinction must be made between the aspects that the government sets autonomously and the aspects that respond automatically to economic conditions. There could be a large budget deficit because the government has spent much on goods and services and has low tax revenues due to low tax rates. Or despite modest expenditures and high tax rates, there could be a large budget deficit because the economy was in a deep recession, causing expenditures on unemployment compensation to be high and tax revenues to be low.

To be able to compare the posture of two budgets, only the aspects that the government sets autonomously should be compared. To do this, the level of the budget surplus or deficit of the two budgets should be compared on the basis of the economy operating at the same unemployment rate for each budget. A hypothetical budget has been developed which determines for each budget what its surplus or deficit would be if the economy were operating at full employment. The actual budget is adjusted for its additional unemployment compensation expenditures and its reductions in tax revenues relative to full employment levels. In this way a budget surplus or deficit is calculated for the budget under full employment conditions. For this purpose 4 percent unemployment is considered full employment. This calculated, hypothetical budget is called the *full employment budget.* Data on the actual and full employment budgets for several years are given in Table 6–1.

Several facts can be observed from Table 6–1. In 1976, actual expenditures were $388.9 billion, whereas at full employment (4 percent unemployment) expenditures would have been $383.3 billion. The difference, $5.6 billion, is unemployment compensation paid by the government. Actual receipts were $330.3 billion, whereas at full employment receipts would have been $361.9 billion; the difference of $31.6 billion was a shortfall of tax revenues. Consequently, while the government actually ran a deficit of (and had to borrow) $58.6 billion, if the economy had operated at 4 percent unemployment they would have run a deficit of only $21.4 billion.

TABLE 6–1   ACTUAL AND FULL EMPLOYMENT BUDGETS ($ BILLION)

	1969	1970	1971	1972	1973	1974	1975	1976
Actual Budget								
Expenditures	188.4	204.2	220.6	244.7	265.0	299.7	357.8	388.9
Receipts	197.0	192.1	198.6	227.5	258.3	288.2	286.5	330.3
Surplus (+) or Deficit (−)	8.5	−12.1	−22.0	−17.3	−6.7	−11.5	−71.2	−58.6
Full Employment Budget								
Expenditures	189.0	203.7	219.3	243.8	265.0	298.7	350.3	383.3
Receipts	196.3	205.9	211.5	228.3	260.4	300.6	325.4	361.9
Surplus (+) or Deficit (−)	7.3	7.2	−7.8	−15.5	−4.6	1.9	−24.9	−21.4
Unemployment Rate	3.5	4.9	5.9	5.6	4.9	5.6	8.5	7.7

Source: *Federal Budget Trends*, Federal Reserve Bank of St. Louis.

The full employment budget can be used either to compare the posture of two budgets or to interpret the posture of an individual budget. For example, by considering the actual budget deficits of 1973 and 1974 one would conclude that 1974's budget was more stimulative because it had a larger deficit. However, by comparing the full employment budgets it is clear that 1973's budget was more stimulative because it had a full employment deficit while 1974 had a full employment surplus. The actual budget of 1974 showed a larger deficit because the unemployment rate was higher in 1974 and not because the discretionary part of the budget was stimulative. And, ironically, the tight budget of 1974, as reflected in the full employment budget, contributed to the high unemployment and hence to the actual budget deficit.

The actual budget deficit is important because it is that amount the government must actually borrow. But for interpreting the posture of fiscal policy, the full employment budget is more useful. It makes possible the interpretation of the stance of fiscal policy at full employment, which is a goal of fiscal policy. And it makes possible the comparison of the postures of two budgets by removing their differences because of different prevailing unemployment rates.

monetary policy

EXECUTOR

The Federal Reserve System, which is the nation's central bank, implements monetary policy in the United States. As indicated, the main function of a central bank is to regulate the money supply. The Federal

Reserve System is composed of the Board of Governors, located in Washington, D. C., and twelve regional Federal Reserve Banks dispersed throughout the country. The main functions of the regional banks are to regulate banks, assist in check processing, and provide other services to banks in their region.

The Board of Governors of the Federal Reserve System (the Fed) is the major implementor of monetary policy. The Fed consists of seven members who serve fourteen-year terms; a new member is appointed every two years. The chairman serves a four-year term. All the members and the chairman are selected by the president. However, the term of the chairman is not coterminous with the president's term.

The most unique aspect of the Fed is its political independence. In what way is the Fed independent? Why was the Fed given this independence?

The Fed's political independence is derived from two sources. First, the members' long terms make them immune to political pressures from presidents, members of Congress, or the public. Second, the Fed has an independent source of revenues which prevents Congress and the president from censuring the Fed by withholding funds. The revenue comes from interest payments on their large holdings of Treasury securities which they accumulate in conducting open market operations.

The Federal Reserve Act of 1913 instituted the Fed and gave it its independence. It was recognized that the Congress and the president had the authority to spend money. If the same institutions also had the authority to print money—that is, control the money supply—there could be a considerable inflationary bias in the economy because the institutions would print the money to finance their expenditures. So a distinct institution, the Fed, was empowered to control the money supply. And this institution was made independent of the Congress and the Executive so that it could refuse to print the money necessary to finance government expenditures. An independent Fed, therefore, provides an anti-inflationary force in the economy. Recurring criticisms of the Fed for being too concerned with preventing inflation at the cost of high unemployment confirm that the Fed does provide such a bias.

TOOLS

Monetary policy employs several tools. The most important of these, open market operations, is discussed in detail in Chapter 3. Open market operations are the purchase or sale by the Fed of Treasury securities from the banking sector.

The course of open market operations is determined by the Federal Open Market Committee (FOMC), which consists of the seven members of the Board of Governors and five of the twelve Federal

Reserve Bank presidents on a revolving basis, with the exception that the president of the Federal Reserve Bank of New York is always one of the five bank presidents. The committee meets once every three to four weeks to discuss economic and financial policy and to determine the course of open market operations.

The actual trading in Treasury securities is conducted by an official of the Federal Reserve Bank of New York called the Manager of the System Open Market Account (SOMA). He conducts open market operations in a manner intended to be consistent with the instructions given him by the FOMC at their last meeting. Often the members of the FOMC contact each other and the manager of the SOMA between meetings to alter the course of open market operations. Open market operations are conducted daily. Their course can be changed at the regular meetings of the FOMC or more frequently if needed.

The way in which open market operations are conducted is somewhat more intricate than discussed in Chapter 3, however. Several financial institutions in the country deal in (that is, buy and sell) Treasury securities. They are called *Treasury dealers*. To finance their holdings of these securities, the dealers borrow from commercial banks and use their Treasury security holdings as collateral on the loans. When the Fed wishes to buy Treasury securities, they contact all the dealers and get price bids on the securities dealers wish to sell. The Fed then buys the securities from the dealer who offers the lowest price. But when a dealer sells the securities to the Fed, the dealer loses its bank collateral and consequently must repay its bank loan with the receipts it receives from the Fed. The dealer is thus the intermediary between the Fed and the bank. When the Fed buys securities, the bank ends up with more reserves and fewer dealer loans which are secured by the Treasury securities as collateral. Changes in bank reserves are instrumental in changing the money supply, as discussed in Chapter 3.

Open market operations are the most frequently used tool of monetary policy. They can be conducted as often as needed in any magnitude, large or small, through well-developed bank and dealer markets with very little disruption to the economy.

The Fed can also change the money supply by changing reserve requirements.[1] For example, as discussed in Chapter 3, if the Fed reduced the reserve requirements from 25 percent to 20 percent, each dollar of reserves could support $5 of money supply instead of $4. A reduction in reserve requirements tends to increase the money supply. Changes in reserve requirements are used only infrequently, however, to change

---

[1] Actually, the Board of Governors rather than the FOMC has the authority to set reserve requirements.

the money supply. In addition to changing the money supply, such changes affect bank profits because banks earn no return on their reserve holdings. Consequently, an increase in reserve requirements reduces bank profits. The Fed prefers not to affect bank profits frequently and arbitrarily in controlling the money supply. Also, changes in reserve requirements are usually made in magnitudes that cause larger changes in the money supply than small open market operations. Finally, reserve requirement changes make necessary substantial adjustments in bank portfolios.

The third major policy tool of the Fed consists of setting the *discount rate*.[2] Banks that experience greater than expected run-offs in deposits may find themselves with less reserves than required. To meet their reserve requirements, they may borrow from the Fed. The interest rate the Fed charges on its loans to banks is called the discount rate. It is thought that at a high discount rate, banks are more likely to hold excess reserves so they are not as likely to experience unexpected deficiencies in reserves. An increase in the discount rate then is interpreted as tighter monetary policy. Changes in the discount rate occur more frequently than changes in reserve requirements but much less frequently than open market operations are conducted.

The Fed also has a host of other powers, legislated in the "alphabet" Regulations A through Z. The most important of these are Regulations G, U, T, and Regulation Q. Regulations G, U, and T give the Fed the power to set *margin requirements* on stock purchases. Margin requirements refer to the fraction of the investor's own funds that must be provided when borrowing the remainder for a stock purchase. Higher margin requirements are used to discourage excessive stock market speculation; lower requirements are intended to encourage stock purchases. Regulation Q allows the Fed to set maximum levels of interest rates that banks can pay on their deposits. Currently, banks are not allowed to pay any interest at all on demand deposits and no more than 5 percent on passbook savings accounts. The import of Regulation Q ceilings is discussed later in this chapter.

INDICATORS

Several alternate and competing measures are used to assess the posture of monetary policy both by the Fed in conducting monetary policy and by those trying to interpret the Fed's actions. The first measure is the rate of interest. As discussed above, if the Fed purchases Treasury securities, bank reserves increase and this permits banks to

---

[2] The discount rate is established by the regional Federal Reserve Bank for its district and reviewed by the Board of Governors.

make more loans which they attempt to do by lowering interest rates. Through this mechanism, open market purchases of Treasury securities tend to lower interest rates. More directly, Fed purchases of Treasury securities tend to drive their prices up and consequently their interest rates down, as discussed in Chapter 3. The sale of Treasury securities does the opposite.

Two specific interest rates are considered indicators of monetary policy. The first is the rate on Treasury bills. Since open market operations are usually conducted by buying and selling Treasury bills, this rate is thought to be particularly responsive to monetary policy. The second rate of interest is the Federal Funds rate, the rate on the borrowing and lending of funds among commercial banks. These loans are usually for a one-day period. When banks do not have an adequate level of reserves to meet their reserve requirement, they can borrow either from the Fed at the discount rate or from banks that have excess reserves. The market for interbank loans is called the Federal Funds market and the rate of interest on these loans is called the Federal Funds rate. This rate is very volatile and sensitive to the level of actual bank reserves relative to their requirements. Since open market operations affect the level of reserves, the Federal Funds rate is very responsive to open market operations.

Another measure of monetary policy relates the level of unborrowed reserves banks actually hold to the level of their required reserves. At any time some banks have excess reserves, which means more than required. Other banks do not have the required level of reserves—they have to borrow to meet their requirements. If for the banking system as a whole, the actual level of reserves is greater than the required reserves, the banking system is said to have *net free reserves*. If their level of unborrowed reserves is less than the required level, it is said to have *net borrowed reserves*—banks have borrowed from the Fed to make up this deficiency. The level of net free or borrowed reserves has often been used as a measure of the posture of monetary policy. Obviously, a higher level of net free reserves would be interpreted as reflecting a more expansionary monetary policy.

Another measure of the posture of monetary policy is the rate of change in the level of bank reserves. As the economy grows, the levels of bank deposits and bank loans grow. To support this growth, bank reserves must grow. The faster the rate of growth of reserves, the more expansionary is monetary policy. Growth in reserves permits or supports growth in the money supply. Consequently, the rate of growth of the money supply can also be used to interpret monetary policy. As discussed, the money supply is the sum of currency and demand deposits: this definition of the money supply is called M1. For reasons that are discussed below, a rate of growth of about 4 percent in the money supply is considered "neutral"; a higher rate of growth is considered expansionary and a lower rate of growth is considered contractionary.

Bank depositors can easily shift from demand deposits or checking accounts to interest-bearing deposits or savings deposits. Because of this easy substitutability, a second definition of the money supply, called M2, adds bank interest-bearing deposits (excluding certificates of deposits) to M1. And since savings deposits at savings and loan associations, mutual savings banks, and credit unions are very similar to savings deposits at commercial banks, a third definition of the money supply, M3, includes all these savings deposits. Other more inclusive measures of the money supply have also been defined. Rates of change of each of these measures of the money supply could be used to interpret monetary policy.

Do all of these measures receive equal attention by the Fed in formulating monetary policy? Until the last decade, the Fed concentrated on what they called "credit conditions," which could be translated as the level of short-term interest rates, mainly the Treasury bill rate, and the level of free reserves in the banking system. More recently they have given more importance to the "aggregates," reserves and the money supply, in the formulation of monetary policy. At present the Fed seems to consider mainly the Federal Funds rate and changes in the level of the money supply (or changes in the supplies of different measures of the money supply) in formulating monetary policy. They set targets for these measures at their FOMC meetings and attempt to meet these targets between meetings by using open market operations. Actually, the Fed sets ranges they attempt to achieve for each measure, rather than exact targets.

Table 6–2 shows the ranges for the Federal Funds rate, and the M1 and M2 measures of the money supply set by the FOMC during its meetings between December 1975 and December 1976. The FOMC then attempted to keep the Federal Funds rate, M1, and M2 within these ranges by using open market operations. Figures 6–1 and 6–2 indicate the Fed's success in keeping these measures within the prescribed ranges. Overall, the Fed did quite well. It was somewhat more successful in achieving its Federal Funds rate goals than its money supply goals, however. This is to be expected since continuous information on the Federal Funds rate is available and the Fed therefore can continuously act to change it if desired. But data on the money supply become available only weekly and are frequently revised even after that. It is, therefore, difficult to act frequently and accurately to keep these measures within their ranges.

As discussed below, some disagreement has occurred between those who favor interest rates and those who favor the money supply as the most important indicator of monetary policy. And basic differ-

TABLE 6-2 FOMC OPERATING RANGES 1975–1976 (SHORT RUN TOLERANCE RANGES

Date of Meeting	Federal Funds Rate	Period to which M1 and M2 Ranges Apply	Ranges Specified	
			M1	M2
December 16, 1975	4½–5½%	Dec.-Jan.	4–7%	7–10%
January 20, 1976	4¼–5	Jan.-Feb.	4–9	7–11½
February 17–18, 1976	4¼–5¼	Feb.-Mar.	5–9	9–13
March 15–16, 1976	4¼–5¼	Mar.-Apr.	4–8	7–11
April 20, 1976	4½–5¼	Apr.-May	4½–8½	8–12
May 18, 1976	5–5¾	May-June	4–7½	5– 9
June 22, 1976	5¼–5¾	June–July	3½–7½	6–10
July 19–20, 1976	4¾–5¾	July-Aug.	4–8	7½–11½
August 17, 1976	5–5½	Aug.-Sept.	4–8	7½–11½
September 21, 1976	4¾–5½	Sept.-Oct.	4–8	8–12
October 19, 1976	4½–5¼	Oct.-Nov.	5–9	9–13
November 16, 1976	4½–5¼	Nov.-Dec.	3–7	9½–13½
December 20–21, 1976	4¼–5	Dec.-Jan.	2½–6½	9–13

Source: *Review*, March 1977, Federal Reserve Board of St. Louis, p. 3.

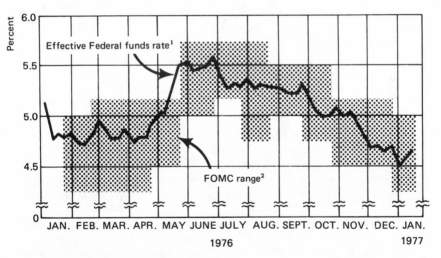

1 Weekly averages of daily rates.
2 At each regularly scheduled meeting during 1976 the FOMC established a range of tolerance for the Federal funds rate. These ranges are indicated for the first full week during which they were in effect.

FIGURE 6-1 FOMC RANGE FOR FEDERAL FUNDS RATE
Source: *Review*, March 1977, Federal Reserve Board of St. Louis, p. 10.

The Application of Fiscal and Monetary Policies   85

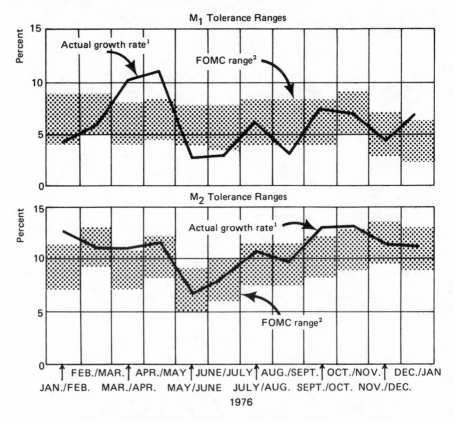

FIGURE 6–2   FOMC RANGES OF TOLERANCE FOR MONETARY AGGREGATES
Source: *Review*, March 1977, Federal Reserve Board of St. Louis, p. 11.

ences and inconsistencies between these two measures are apparent. For example, if the Fed concentrated on controlling interest rates, and interest rates began to increase due to an increased demand for loans, the Fed might increase reserves and the money supply substantially to prevent the increase in interest rates. The large increase in the money supply would be interpreted as expansionary money supply by those favoring the money supply as an indicator. The constant or ever-increasing interest rates would be interpreted as neutral or even tighter policy by those favoring interest rates as an indicator.

However, if the Fed used only the money supply as an indicator, it would not increase the money supply any faster due to an increase in the demand for loans. Consequently, interest rates would rise. Monetary policy would be interpreted as neutral by those who favored the money supply as an indicator and tight by those who favored interest rates. The Fed, currently watching both an interest rate and two money supply measures, can be confronted with this type of inconsistency between its measures. In this case, the Fed often changes the ranges on one of the measures. The dispute about the use of these two indicators is discussed below.

overall effectiveness of fiscal and monetary policies

Several criteria can be used to judge the relative effectiveness of fiscal and monetary policies.

LAGS

Once a policy change is needed, there may be a time lapse before the policy is actually enacted. This is called *inside lag*. There are two parts of the inside lag. The first is the time between when a policy change is needed and when the need for a change is recognized. This is called the *recognition lag*. The second is the time between when the change is recognized and when the change is enacted. This is called the *action lag*. After the policy change is enacted, there will be another time lapse before the policy change affects the intended economic variables, such as unemployment or inflation. This is called the *outside lag* (also called the *impact lag*). Figure 6–3 illustrates these lags. The length of these policy lags is important to the overall effectiveness of the policy.

◄――――― Inside Lag ―――――┃――――― Outside Lag ―――――►

Time policy change is needed	Time policy change is enacted	Time policy change affects economy (unemployment or inflation)

FIGURE 6–3   TYPES OF POLICY LAGS

The Application of Fiscal and Monetary Policies   **87**

The inside lag is institutional in nature: it depends on how long the institution responsible for the policy takes to act. The outside lag is economic in nature: it depends on how long the policy change takes to filter through the economy.

How long are the inside and outside lags for fiscal and monetary policies? The inside lag for monetary policy is very short. The Fed meets every three to four weeks to consider policy changes and can change policies even during that period. Because fiscal changes must be approved by both the Congress and the president, the inside lag of fiscal policy varies but can be quite long. For example, the tax cut of 1964 was proposed in 1962 and the tax surcharge of 1968 was proposed in 1966.

It is more difficult to assess the outside lag of monetary and fiscal policies. The effects of both policies do not occur suddenly, and are not concentrated at a point in time but occur gradually over a period of time. And during this period of time many other factors that affect the economy may occur. For these reasons, there is considerable dispute over the length of the outside lags of both policies. The majority opinion is, however, that the outside lag of monetary policy is longer than that of fiscal policy. And within fiscal policy, the lag of tax changes is longer than that of expenditure changes. Estimates for the outside lag of monetary policy range from six months to two years. For fiscal policies, the outside lag of tax changes is estimated to be about three months, and for spending even less. Figure 6–4 summarizes these lags.

On the basis of the total lag, the choice between fiscal and monetary policies is difficult. If fiscal policy could be implemented more quickly, it would be preferable on this basis.

Policy lags are more important than may be readily apparent. Consider an economy that at time t_1 is rapidly approaching full employment. A contractionary policy is enacted at this time to prevent the economy from overheating and generating inflation. Assume, however, that the policy has a long lag and that the policy does not affect the economy until time t_2, which is six months later. At t_2 the economy will experience a contractionary force. If the economy has overheated, the inflation will be mitigated and the stabilization policy will be effective. During the six-month period between t_1 and t_2, however, the expansion-

	Inside Lag	Outside Lag
Fiscal Policy	Long	Very Short—Spending Short—Taxing
Monetary Policy	Very Short	Long

FIGURE 6–4   LENGTHS OF POLICY LAGS

ary forces may disappear and contractionary forces develop (there may be, for example, a large decrease in the demand for consumer durables). In this case, the economy may be slipping into a recession when the contractionary forces are felt. The effect of the policy, then, is to exaggerate the recession. The policy destabilizes the economy rather than stabilizes it.

If a policy has a longer lag than the period which can be forecast in the future, the effect of the policy can be destabilizing. The art of forecasting is as yet very imperfect. Consequently, policies, particularly monetary policy, may be destabilizing.

POLITICS

Political forces relate somewhat to the inside lags of fiscal and monetary policies. Given the political process, it is normally quite easy to enact expansionary fiscal policies but very difficult to enact contractionary policy. Congress and the president much prefer increasing spending and reducing taxes rather than the opposite. For this reason, fiscal policy has been very useful in addressing recessions but much less useful in addressing inflations.

Monetary policy, then, normally must provide the contractive forces necessary to combat inflations. This is politically feasible because the members of the Board of Governors are not elected but are appointed for long terms. And it was to provide an anti-inflationary force in the economy that the Fed was given its political independence. So normally, but not always, fiscal policy has supplied most of the expansionary thrust during recessions and monetary policy most of the contractionary thrust during inflations.

Coordination between fiscal and monetary policies is important. Loose fiscal policy can, to some extent, force the hand of monetary policy. A loose fiscal policy may result in a large budget deficit which must be financed by borrowing from the public. This large demand for funds tends to make interest rates rise. The Fed then has two choices. It can continue to increase the money supply only moderately and let interest rates rise. Or it can increase the money supply substantially to mitigate the rise in interest rates. The latter, however, may be inflationary. The Fed can combat fiscal policy's inflationary policies only at the cost of higher interest rates. This is a difficult choice, particularly if inflation is a real concern.

UNIFORMITY OF IMPACT

A desirable stabilization policy should have a fairly uniform effect over the entire economy. For example, if the goal is to reduce the overall rate of spending in the economy by 5 percent, an ideal policy would reduce the spending of each sector by 5 percent. Are fiscal and monetary policies even in their impact?

Monetary policy has been quite uneven in its impact in recent years. And housing has been the sector most strongly influenced by monetary policy, helped when monetary policy is expansionary but seriously harmed when monetary policy is contractionary. Housing is strongly related to monetary policy because of the nature of the mortgage market. The major mortgage lenders in the economy are savings and loan institutions, mutual savings banks, and commercial banks. The first two types of institutions get most of their funds through consumer-type savings accounts; commercial banks also get a large share of funds from such deposits. Regulation Q ceilings, mentioned earlier, set ceilings on the interest rates commercial banks can pay on their deposits. Similar limitations exist on the interest rates that savings and loan institutions and mutual savings banks can pay on their deposits.

During times of contractionary monetary policy, interest rates rise above the maximum that these depository institutions can pay. Depositors can then earn a higher rate of interest on Treasury bills, commercial paper, and other securities than they can on deposits in these financial intermediaries. Consequently, some depositors withdraw funds from their deposits in these intermediaries and invest in marketable securities. This phenomenon is called *disintermediation:* withdrawing funds from financial intermediaries. Since these intermediaries make most of their loans to the mortgage market, when they lose deposits they must reduce their new mortgage commitments. This reduces the demand for new houses and housing construction is curtailed. This is the link between tight monetary policy and a weak housing market.

The housing market is hit hardest by tight monetary policy but it is not the only sector hit.

> This record would be more tolerable if monetary policy hit every sector of the economy with equal force. But it does not. In reducing the available supply of money, or increasing the cost of money, or some combination of both, the Fed tries to clamp economic activity by squeezing people out of the financial markets. It is the nature of these markets that the process hits those with the weakest claims on the money that is available. The housing market is invariably hit first, followed by state and local governments (which are often limited in what they can pay to borrow), small business and the stock market. The Fed's ultimate target may be consumer or capital spending, but consumer loans reward banks handsomely, and big corporate borrowers usually have long close ties to their banks. Both groups are the last to feel the razors of tight money, and policy has to be made very tight before either group feels the pinch at all.[3]

Monetary policy clearly has a very uneven impact.

---

[3] *Business Week*, October 6, 1973.

Fiscal policy can be very selective and uneven or very even depending on the specific policy. Government expenditures on a specific good affect the market for that good significantly but also have spillovers into other markets. Most tax policies have very even impacts. For most types of fiscal policy, its impact is more uniform than the impact of monetary policy.

the modern front: keynesians versus monetarists

A well-publicized and divisive dispute is currently taking place among modern economists about the relative effectiveness of and need for monetary and fiscal policies. One school of thought, called the *monetarists*, dates to Adam Smith's *Wealth of Nations*, which was published in 1776. Its recent bastion has been the University of Chicago, and the Nobel Prize–winning economist Milton Friedman is its leading spokesman. The other school, called the *Keynesian* school, dates to John Maynard Keynes's *General Theory of Employment, Interest and Money*, published in 1936. A leading proponent of this school is the Nobel Prize–winning economist Paul Samuelson. The two schools are contrasted by the series of propositions shown in Table 6–3.

Initially, the Keynesians and the monetarists have different basic orientations. The Keynesian school is demand oriented. It asserts that

TABLE 6–3 SUMMARY OF KEYNESIAN AND MONETARIST POSITIONS

Keynesian	*Monetarist*
Orientation: Demand Oriented	Orientation: Money Supply Oriented
1. Monetary policy is strong but its relation to the economy is variable.	1. Monetary policy is very strong and its relation to the economy is stable.
2. Fiscal policy is strong.	2. Fiscal policy is ineffectual.
3. While both monetary and fiscal policy have lags, the lags are not so long that the policies destabilize the economy.	3. The lags of monetary policy are very long and therefore the policies destabilize the economy.
4. The economy is basically unstable.	4. The economy is basically stable.
5. Therefore, use fiscal and monetary policies to stabilize the economy.	5. Therefore, neither fiscal nor monetary policies are needed and so they should not be used.
Inclination: Liberal or Activist	Inclination: Conservative or Passive

aggregate demand (consumption, investment, and government demands) is the driving force of the economy. If aggregate demand is too low, unemployment will result; if it is too high, there will be inflation. The circular flow diagram in Chapter 4 is demand oriented. Government policies affect the economy by affecting demand. Government spending affects demand directly; government taxation affects consumption or investment, depending on the type of tax changed. Monetary policy affects the interest rate and, therefore, investment demand.

The orientation of the monetarists focuses on the role of the money supply in the economy. The total expenditures on final goods and services in the economy during a year is measured by GNP in current prices, or nominal GNP. To separate the effects of rising prices from the effects of increases in real output, GNP can be expressed as the product of the price level, P, and real GNP or GNP measured in constant prices. Denote real GNP by Y. Nominal GNP can be expressed as $P \times Y$. So $P \times Y$ represents the total money expenditures in an economy during a year.

Does this mean that the money supply, M, must be equal to GNP? Of course not. Each dollar of the money supply may be spent on goods and services more than once during a year. Total money expenditures then will be M times the average number of times each dollar of the money supply is spent during a year. Denote the average number of times each dollar is spent during a year by V for the velocity of money. Then total dollar expenditures can be expressed both as $M \times V$ and as $P \times Y$. Therefore,

$$MV = PY$$

This equation is called the *quantity theory of money* and is the key to monetarism.

The data in Table 6–4 show the price level P, real gross national product Y, and their product, nominal GNP. More importantly, it shows that given P, Y, and M, the velocity of money can be calculated from $V = PY/M$. The calculated values of V are given in column 6 of the table.

What are the policy implications of the quantity theory of money? The policy implications can be derived from the monetarists' premise that the velocity of money is stable, if not constant. This means that V does not exhibit wide variations over time. With this premise, the quantity theory of money demonstrates that a 5 percent increase in the money supply causes a 5 percent increase in nominal GNP. What part of this increase is due to an increase in the price level and what part due to an increase in real GNP? The quantity theory gives no guidance on this important issue. Economic reasoning does provide some guidance, how-

TABLE 6-4 DATA RELATED TO QUANTITY THEORY OF MONEY

Year	Nominal Gross National Product (Billion Current Dollars)	Price Level (P) 1972 = 1.00	Real Gross National Product (Y) (Billion Dollars 1972 Prices)	Money Supply (M) (December Billion Dollars)	Velocity of Money (V)
1966	$ 753.0	0.77	981.0	175.7	4.29
1969	935.5	0.87	1,078.8	208.8	4.48
1973	1,306.3	1.06	1,235.0	270.5	4.83
1974	1,413.2	1.16	1,214.0	283.1	4.99
1975	1,516.3	1.27	1,191.7	294.8	5.14
1976	1,692.4	1.34	1,265.0	312.2	5.42

ever. If the economy was initially at full employment, Y could not increase, and so P would increase by 5 percent. If the economy was initially at a high level of unemployment, the increase in the money supply would probably not cause inflation. Consequently, P would remain constant and Y would increase by 5 percent. In intermediate situations, probably both P and Y would increase somewhat.

As indicated above, monetarists believe that the ideal annual increase in the money supply is about 4 percent. The quantity theory gives the reason for selecting this number. A policy goal is to keep the price level P constant. Real GNP, Y, increases by about 3.5 percent to 4 percent per year because of growth in the labor force and increases in labor productivity. Therefore, with stable prices, PY tends to increase by about 4 percent per year. Since V remains approximately constant, M should increase by about 4 percent.

Recently some monetarists have shown a preference for a different form of the quantity theory. They have observed, as shown in Figure 6–5, that since 1950, the velocity of the M2 definition of money ($V2 = $ GNP/M2) has been more stable than the velocity of the M1 definition of money ($V1 = $ GNP/M1). Consequently, they express the quantity theory in terms of M2 rather than M1, that is $M2 \times V2 = PY$. In addition, they have observed that there is a two-quarter lag in the effect of the money supply on GNP. Thus, changes in the money supply one quarter affect GNP two quarters later. Therefore, monetarists introduce a time dimension into the quantity theory: $M2_t \times V2 = (PY)_{t+2}$ where the subscripts t and $t + 2$ represent the time in quarters.

From these different orientations, it is clear why the Keynesian and monetarist schools prefer different indicators of monetary policy. Monetarists prefer the rate of increase of the money supply as the indicator with a 4 percent increase regarded as approximately neutral.

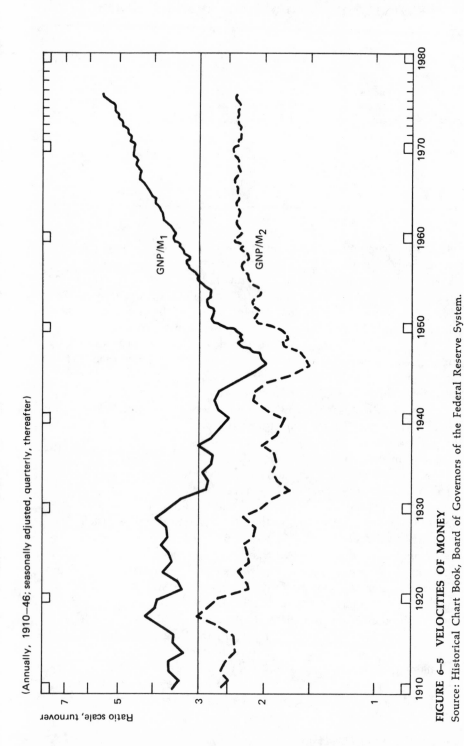

(Annually, 1910–46; seasonally adjusted, quarterly, thereafter)

Ratio scale, turnover

GNP/M₁

GNP/M₂

FIGURE 6–5 VELOCITIES OF MONEY

Source: Historical Chart Book, Board of Governors of the Federal Reserve System.

Keynesians have traditionally preferred the interest rate as the indicator because of the effect of interest rates on the demand for goods and services. But in recent years, Keynesians have become more eclectic and now believe that both interest rates and the rate of increase of the money supply should be used as indicators.

The Keynesian and monetarist orientations provide the basis for very different views of the economy and policy prescriptions for the economy. Keynesians believe that monetary policy affects the economy by changing the interest rate, then investment demand, and hence unemployment and inflation, as discussed in Chapter 4. But they assert that this relationship is not stable; at different times, identical changes in the money supply have different effects on nominal GNP. In monetarist parlance, Keynesians assert that the velocity of money is very variable.

Monetarists also believe that monetary policy has an effect on the economy. But they assert that the effect is not through a change in the interest rate but directly on all types of expenditures because, due to the stability of V, each additional dollar is spent V times. They also assert that because of the stability of V, the relationship between M and nominal GNP is stable. Although they do not believe, and Figures 6–3 and 6–5 verify, that V is not absolutely constant, they believe that the relationship between V and nominal GNP is more dependable than any other relationship in the economy.

Keynesians and monetarists agree that monetary policy has a strong effect on the economy. Their differences of opinion on the dependability of the relation between M and GNP revolves around the question, "How constant is constant?" with respect to V.

What do these two schools believe about fiscal policy? Keynesians believe that fiscal policy affects unemployment and inflation in the ways discussed in Chapter 4. The active use of fiscal policy was initially regarded as most innovative and perhaps revolutionary about Keynesianism. Keynes taught that to cure recessions the government should increase its spending or decrease taxes to increase aggregate demand even if these changes lead to a budget deficit. Deficit spending to cure recessions is still associated with Keynesianism. And this policy is often attacked by fiscal conservatives.

Monetarists, conversely, claim that fiscal policy has absolutely no effect as a stabilization tool. Consider their view of the use of government spending to reduce unemployment. The government can finance its increase in spending in three ways: (1) by increasing taxes; (2) by borrowing, that is, engaging in deficit spending; or (3) by printing the money. Actually, as discussed above, the Treasury cannot print money. But in two ways, however, the effect is the same as if the Treasury printed the money to finance its expenditures. The first occurs if the

Treasury sells its securities directly to the Fed. The second happens if the Treasury sells its securities to the public, but the Fed, in an attempt to keep interest rates from increasing, purchases the securities from the public. In either case, from the public's perception, it appears that the "government," composed of the Fed and the Treasury, has printed money to finance its expenditures.

The monetarists consider the effects of government spending financed by each of these three methods separately. They assert that there is no net effect on the economy if the expenditures are financed by taxes. They claim that if individuals are taxed, consumption expenditures decrease by the amount of the tax. Since governmental expenditures increase by the amount of the tax, total expenditures remain the same. If business were taxed to finance the government spending, business investment would decline by that amount instead.

If the government borrows to finance its expenditures, it must sell Treasury securities to the public. This tends to cause interest rates to rise and therefore investment to decrease. Monetarists assert that the rise in interest rates resulting from the sale of Treasury securities is sufficient to cause investment to decrease by the same amount that government spending increases (which is the amount borrowed by the government). There is consequently no net effect on total spending in the economy—business spending decreases by the same amount that government spending increases. This phenomenon, as has been discussed in Chapter 5, can be described as government spending *crowding out* business spending. A related way of viewing this is that there is a limited amount of loanable funds in the economy. When the government borrows more to finance its deficit, less is left for business to borrow to finance its investment. Thus, government borrowing *crowds out* business borrowing. These two types of crowding out are related very closely.

Monetarists believe that total spending in the economy remains constant if increases in government spending are financed by either increased taxes or borrowing. They do think, however, that government spending financed by printing money does affect total spending. But the increase in total spending is due to the increase in the money supply according to the quantity theory of money, not the increase in governmental spending. In this case, they assert that it is monetary policy and not fiscal policy that affects the economy.

Monetarists and Keynesians disagree on fiscal policy mainly concerning government spending financed by borrowing. With respect to spending financed by taxes, Keynesians claim there may be a small positive effect and the monetarists say no effect. Keynesians agree with monetarists that government spending financed by increases in the money supply has a strong effect, but they believe that there is a fiscal effect as well as a monetary effect. But concerning deficit spending, monetarists say there is no effect and Keynesians say there is a substantial positive effect. Keynesians agree that government borrowing causes interest rates to rise and investment to decrease somewhat. But they believe that the decrease in investment is less than the increase in government spending. Keynesians believe there is partial, not complete crowding out.

Keynesians believe that both monetary and fiscal policies affect the economy. They also believe that although both policies have outside lags, these lags are short enough that both policies can be used to stabilize the economy.

Keynesians also believe that the economy is basically unstable; if the economy is left to its own devices and no stabilization policies are implemented, the economy will experience substantial recessions and inflations. Thus, Keynesians' obvious conclusion is that both monetary and fiscal policies should be actively used to stabilize the economy.

Monetarists believe that monetary policy is very strong but that its lag is very long. Consequently, they believe using monetary policy would destabilize the economy, and should not be used. Instead, the money supply should be increased by approximately 4 percent every year to support economic growth. Fiscal policy has no effect on stabilizing the economy so its use for this purpose is irrelevant.

However, the monetarists believe that the economy is basically stable and that if fiscal and monetary policies are not used, the economy tends toward a noninflationary, full-employment condition of its own accord. Monetarists claim that the recessions and inflations that have been experienced by the United States have been caused by the improper use of monetary policy. If the money supply had been increased at an annual rate of about 4 percent every year, there would have been no recessions and inflations according to the monetarists. The monetarists' conclusion is, therefore, that neither monetary nor fiscal policy should be used as stabilization policies.

Since Keynesians prescribe the active use of fiscal and monetary policies, their economic activism is consistent with political liberalism. Political liberals usually have a Keynesian bent. Monetarists have a passive approach to economic policy—the government should use neither monetary nor fiscal policy. This approach is sometimes called laissez-faire—"hands-off" the private economy by the government. This passive approach is consistent with economic conservatism. Political conservatives often have a monetarist bent.

The gulf between the Keynesian and monetarist conceptions of the economy and their policy prescriptions is wide. This is particularly confusing for economic policy-makers, such as the president and Congress, who often get contradictory advice from equally expert advisors. A rapprochement has occurred in some areas, but the areas of dispute remain significant.

questions

1. From the data for 1975 in Table 6-1 calculate:
   a. the amount of tax revenue lost due to each 1 percent increase in the unemployment rate;
   b. the amount of unemployment compensation paid for each 1 percent increase in the unemployment rate; and
   c. the actual budget deficit in 1976 if the actual unemployment rate had been 10.0 percent.

2. Discuss *your* inclinations toward the Keynesian and monetarist schools of thought.

3. Assume that in 1977 the average price level is 1.00, real GNP is $800 billion, the money supply is $200 billion, and the velocity of money is 4.00. Assume that in 1978 *potential* real GNP is $840 billion.
   a. What would the money supply have to be in 1978 to achieve full employment if the velocity of money remained constant?
   b. What would the money supply have to be in 1978 to achieve full employment if the velocity of money increased to 4.1?
   c. If the velocity of money remained 4.0 in 1978 and the money supply increased to $220 billion, would there be unemployment or inflation? How much?

4. Discuss the difference between automatic and discretionary stabilizers. What are the fiscal stabilizers? Can you conceive of any monetary stabilizers or destabilizers?

5. Discuss the importance of the choice of an indicator of monetary policy by the Fed and how different indicators could lead to different results. How are the indicators used currently?

6. Discuss the factors that affect the overall effectiveness of fiscal policy and monetary policy.

selected references to part II

1. Bach, G. L. *Economics: An Introduction to Analysis and Policy,* 9th ed. Englewood Cliffs, N.J.: Prentice-Hall, Inc., 1977.
2. Economic Report of the President, U.S. Government Printing Office, Washington, D.C., Annually.
3. Kaufman, George G. *Money, the Financial System and the Economy,* 2nd ed. Chicago: Rand McNally, 1977.

4. McConnell, Campbell. *Economics*, 6th ed. New York: McGraw-Hill Book Company, 1975.

5. Ritter, Lawrence S. and Silber, William L. *Principles of Money, Banking, and Financial Markets*. New York: Basic Books, Inc., 1974.

6. Samuelson, Paul A. *Economics*, 10th ed. New York: McGraw-Hill Book Company, 1976.

THE DOMESTIC FINANCIAL SYSTEM: INTEREST RATES, FINANCIAL INSTITUTIONS, AND FINANCIAL MARKETS

the interest rate:
the link between
the economic
and financial systems

7

the role of the interest rate

The economy can be divided into the real and the financial sectors. The real sector is concerned with the use of physical resources—labor and capital—to produce goods and services, and the exchange of these goods and services. The financial sector is concerned with the lending and borrowing of funds, or, as discussed in Chapter 2, the exchange of IOU's or securities. Chapters 3 through 6 emphasize the real sector of the economy. Chapters 8 through 10 treat the financial sector. This chapter discusses the interest rate, which in addition to being the major variable in the financial sector, is the link between the real and the financial sectors.

The funds used to finance the purchase of goods and services can be derived from two sources. The first source is earned income, which for the household sector is derived mainly from wages and salaries, and for the business sector is derived from profits. The second source is borrowed funds. As discussed in Chapter 2, the interest rate is the main determinant of the level of funds that are borrowed and lent. The exchange of funds is in the domain of the financial sector. Since the interest rate significantly affects the level of borrowed funds and borrowed funds are used to finance the purchase of goods and services, the interest rate is the link between the real and financial sectors.

Borrowed funds are not equally important in the financing of all goods and services. Households almost always use borrowed funds to purchase housing, very often use borrowed funds to purchase automobiles and consumer durables, but usually do not use borrowed funds to purchase food. Borrowed funds are normally an important source of financing for business investment. State and local governments use borrowed funds to build schools, hospitals, highways, and other types of construction. Consequently, the financial sector has its greatest effect on the markets for housing, automobiles, durables, business investment, and state and local expenditures, as discussed in Chapter 6.

The financial system is in "equilibrium" when the demand for borrowed funds equals the supply of loanable funds. The interest rate is the variable that achieves this equality or equilibrium. To the lender the interest rate represents a reward for abstaining from consuming with the funds, and saving them instead. For example, if the rate of interest were 6 percent and an individual had $100 of disposable income, that person could either consume $100 today or save the money at 6 percent and consequently have $106 in a year to finance consumption. The choice, then, is between consuming $100 today and $106 one year hence. The $6 of added consumption is the reward for abstaining from consumption today and saving instead. As this reward, measured by the interest rate, increases, the supply of loanable funds should increase. This is reflected in the upward sloping supply curve of Figure 7–1. The slope of this curve depends on savers' preference for current consumption relative to their preference for future consumption.

The interest rate represents a cost to borrowers. At a 6 percent rate of interest, if $100 is borrowed today, $106 must be repaid in a year. How are borrowers able to pay this interest cost? Borrowing by business to finance the purchase of plant and equipment is a large use of borrowed funds. Consider the ability of business to pay the interest

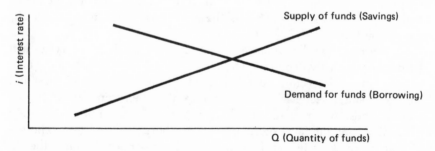

FIGURE 7–1 DEMAND AND SUPPLY OF FUNDS

cost to borrow for this purpose. Consider alternative modes of business production. Business could use a very labor-intensive mode of production, where it would use mainly labor to produce goods, then sell the goods and use its sales receipts to pay its labor. The need for borrowed funds would be small. Alternatively, business could use a capital-intensive mode of production, where it would use mainly plant and equipment along with little labor to produce goods. But the sales receipts necessary to pay for the capital are generated only gradually over the life of the plant and equipment. Borrowed funds are thus needed during the time over which the necessary sales receipts are generated.

But if goods are produced more efficiently—that is, at a lower cost—over the long run in the capital-intensive mode, business can afford to pay the interest cost on the borrowed funds and still earn higher profits. Business can afford to pay the interest cost because the borrowing allows it to purchase capital which makes it more efficient and more profitable.

But at higher rates of interest, fewer investments will be profitable and so the demand for loanable funds will decrease. This relation is reflected in the downward sloping demand curve in Figure 7–1. The slope of this curve depends on the increased profitability from capital-intensive modes of production.

The interest rate is responsible for achieving equality between the aggregate supply of funds and the aggregate demand for funds in the financial system. But the financial system is not one uniform market for funds. As discussed in Chapter 2, it is composed of several distinct financial institutions and markets. And, as is discussed in Chapters 8 and 9, specific sectors of the financial system specialize by attracting funds from specific types of savers and making funds available to specific types of borrowers.

The interest rate not only achieves equality between the total supply of funds and the total demand for funds but also achieves equality between the supply of and demand for funds in each specific sector. In the latter mode, the interest rate allocates funds to various sectors of the economy, that is, determines the level of funds flowing into mortgages, corporate bonds, consumer credit, and other sectors.

determinants of the interest rate

Interest rates exhibit considerable variability: at times they are high and at other times they are low. This section investigates the factors that affect the interest rate, and describes the three different frameworks or theories which attempt to explain the level of the interest rate.

Since the asset with the most liquidity is money and the economic term for preference is *demand,* the phrase *liquidity preference* can be translated as the *demand for money.*

How does liquidity preference or the demand for money relate to the interest rate? The demand for money depends on the rate of interest in two ways. Keynes called the first way the *speculative demand for money.* To illustrate the relationship between the speculative demand for money and the rate of interest, he considered a world with only two financial assets, money and bonds. The choice of which of these assets investors choose to hold depends on which yields the greater expected return. The return on money is zero—one dollar held in currency or demand deposits remains one dollar. However, two forms of returns on bonds exist: a coupon return and a potential capital gain or capital loss. If a capital loss on bonds is large enough to exceed the coupon return, the total return on bonds will be negative, and holding money, even at a zero return, would be preferable.

When are bonds likely to show a capital loss? As discussed in Chapter 2, the prices of bonds move in the opposite direction of the interest rates. If interest rates rise, the price of bonds decreases. Consequently, if interest rates are expected to rise sufficiently, bonds will be expected to show a capital loss and money would be preferred to bonds. The next question is, at what times are interest rates expected to rise? If interest rates are presently low, it is almost definitional to say that they are expected to rise.

In sum, if interest rates are presently low, they are expected to rise, a capital loss is expected on bonds, and it may be preferable to hold money rather than bonds. Thus, the demand for money will be high at low interest rates. Conversely, if interest rates are presently high, they are expected to decrease, so a capital gain on bonds is expected, and bonds are preferred to money.

The downward sloping curve in Figure 7–2 illustrates the relation between the speculative demand for money and the interest rate. The demand for money decreases as the present interest rate increases because the lower the present interest rate is, the more it is expected to rise, and the greater the expected capital loss is, the more likely investors are to hold money.

There is a second way to explain the relationship between the demand for money and the interest rate. The interest rate can be viewed as the return that is foregone by holding money rather than an interest-bearing asset. For example, at a 6 percent rate of interest investors forego earning $6 during a year if they hold $100 in currency or demand deposits instead of the interest-bearing asset. Consequently, the higher the rate of interest, the greater is the return foregone by holding money, and the less money is held. This relation also agrees with the curve shown in Figure 7–2.

The interest rate is determined in the liquidity preference theory of interest by the supply and demand for money. The supply of money is determined by the Fed: the Fed can set the money supply at any level. An arbitrary level of the supply of money, S_0, is shown with the demand for money in Figure 7–2. The level of the interest rate that results from this combination of supply and demand is i_0.

If the Fed increases the supply of money to S_1, the interest rate will decrease to i_1. Investors will be content to hold this larger supply of money only at the lower rate of interest. Initially they will purchase bonds with the increased money supply, driving bond prices up and interest rates down. At the lower interest rates, they will choose to hold money.

The liquidity preference theory of interest explains the level of the interest rate by the supply and demand for money. An increase in the supply or a decrease in the demand for money both cause interest rates to decline.

LOANABLE FUNDS

The loanable funds explanation of the interest rate depends on the supply and the demand for loanable funds, the funds that are borrowed and lent. The supply of loanable funds, the amount people with excess funds wish to lend, increases with the interest rate as shown by S_{LF} in

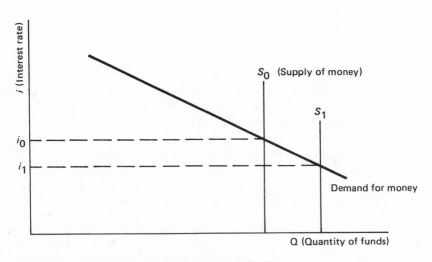

FIGURE 7–2 DEMAND AND SUPPLY OF MONEY

The Interest Rate

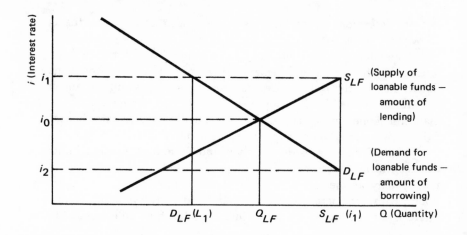

FIGURE 7-3   DEMAND AND SUPPLY OF LOANABLE FUNDS

Figure 7–3 because the interest rate is the return to lenders. The demand for loanable funds, the amount of desired borrowing, D_{LF}, in Figure 7–3, decreases as the interest rate rises because the interest rate is the cost to borrowers.

In Figure 7–3 the equilibrium level of the interest rate is i_0 and the quantity of funds lent and borrowed is Q_{LF}. If the interest rate were initially i_1, the supply of loanable funds, S_{LF} (i_1), would be greater than the demand for loanable funds, D_{LF} (i_1), and competitive pressures would force the interest rate down to i_0. If the interest rate were initially i_2, there would be an excess demand for funds and competitive pressures would force the interest rate up to i_0.

INFLATION AND THE REAL RATE OF INTEREST

A third explanation of the level of the interest rate relates the interest rate to inflation. Assume that savers deposit $100 in an account that pays an annual interest rate of 5 percent. At the end of the year the savers have $105, a 5 percent increase in dollars.

If there has been no inflation during the year, the savers also have 5 percent more purchasing power at the end of the year because they have claim to 5 percent more dollars and the price level is the same. If, however, the price level has gone up by 3 percent, they have claim to 5 percent more dollars but their purchasing power has increased by only 2 percent because of the price increase.[1]

---

[1] This calculation is based on an approximation. Initially, the saver had $100 and could buy 100 units which cost $1.00 each. At the end of the year the saver has $105 but due to the inflation each unit cost $1.03. The saver can then buy 105/1.03 = 101.94 units, an increase of 1.94 percent. Approximating this by 2 percent ignores the fact that the interest payments also depreciate in value due to inflation.

This example provides the basis for two definitions. The *nominal rate of interest* is defined as the percent increase *in the number of dollars* earned or paid over a period of time. The *real rate of interest* is defined as the percent increase in *purchasing power* over a period of time. Since in both cases the saver had 5 percent more dollars at the end of the year, the nominal rate of interest in each case is 5 percent. In the case with no inflation, the saver also had a 5 percent increase in purchasing power so the real rate of interest was also 5 percent. In the case with 3 percent inflation, however, the gain in purchasing power, the real rate of interest, was only 2 percent.

This example indicates the way to calculate the real rate of interest (denoted by i_R). It is equal to the nominal rate of interest (i_N) minus the rate of inflation (ΔP), that is [2]

$$i_R = i_N - \Delta P \tag{1}$$

or alternately

$$i_N = i_R + \Delta P \tag{2}$$

The nominal rate of interest is observable. The rate of inflation is based on observed prices. The real rate of interest is not observable and can only be calculated.

From the lender's viewpoint, the real rate of interest is the increase in purchasing power due to saving. Consider the real rate of interest from the business borrower's viewpoint. Obviously, the business borrower would not sacrifice purchasing power unless something was gained. The business borrowers, as discussed above, invest the borrowed funds in plant and equipment to increase their ability to produce goods and services by using capital instead of labor. Business would sacrifice no more in purchasing power than it could gain in producing goods and services by investing the borrowed funds in capital. The gain on investing in capital, called the *return to capital*, is the real rate of interest from the borrower's viewpoint. In equilibrium, the real rate of interest paid on the last dollar borrowed and invested by business will equal the real return on capital or the increase in its efficiency in producing goods and services.

The real rate of return is determined by two factors. One is the return to capital. If business gets a high return from borrowing and investing in capital, it will pay a higher real rate of return on borrowed funds. The second factor is the potential savers' preferences for consuming now rather than consuming in the future. If potential savers have a

---

[2] Again, this is an approximation because it ignores the depreciation of the interest payment due to inflation. The exact equation is $i_N = i_R + \Delta P + (\Delta P)(i_R)$.

great preference for consuming today, they can be induced to save only if the real rate of interest is high. This type of preference will tend to increase the real rate of interest.

If prices were stable, the nominal and real rates of interest would be equal. How does inflation affect the nominal rate of interest? Consider this question from both the lenders' and borrowers' viewpoints. Unless lenders were subject to a "dollar illusion" they are concerned with the real rate of interest on their savings, not the nominal rate. Consequently, they would tend to demand, or bargain for, increases in the nominal rate of interest equal to the increase in the rate of inflation to keep their real rate of interest constant. To the extent that their savings depended on the real rate of interest they would decrease their lending if the real rate of interest declined (that is, if inflation increased by more than the nominal rate of interest). This tends to make the real rate of interest return to its original level, with the nominal rate higher by an amount equal to the increase in the rate of inflation.

Is there a similar tendency on the borrowers' side for the nominal rate of interest to increase? Since the prices of the goods and services business sells increase during inflation, reported (before-tax) profits also increase during inflation, thus increasing the capacity of business to pay a higher nominal rate of interest. Consider the situation in which a business borrows $100 at the beginning of a year at a 5 percent rate of interest and uses these funds to produce $100 of inventory. Assume that the firm sells the inventory at the end of the year for $110 if there is no inflation during the year. It can then repay the $100 loan along with the $5 interest and have $5 remaining. This represents a 5 percent return on the amount borrowed.

If, however, the inflation rate was 5 percent during the year, the business could sell its inventories for approximately $115, or 5 percent, more than with no inflation. After it pays back the $105 principal and interest on the loan, it has $10 remaining, a 10 percent return on the amount borrowed. Business thus has the capacity to increase the nominal rate of interest it pays on the loan. If initially the nominal rate of interest remained 5 percent, there would be an increase in the demand for funds to produce and sell more inventories (assuming, of course, that there was a demand for the output). This increased demand for funds would tend to drive the nominal rate of interest up until it had adjusted for the increase in inflation.[3]

---

[3] This simple example ignores the fact that the inventories have to be replaced at higher costs. But, if the inflation continues, they can be sold at even higher prices. Plant and equipment also have to be replaced at higher prices. It also ignores the fact that taxes will have to be paid on these higher profits which tends to reduce the after-tax profits.

Conceptually, from both the lenders' and borrowers' viewpoints pressures exist which tend to make the nominal rate of interest increase by the amount of the inflation. Do interest rates really respond this way? Consider the evidence in Figure 7–4.[4] The figure shows that changes in the rate of inflation are reflected in the nominal rate of interest. Since the early sixties, changes in the rate of inflation have caused approximately equal changes in the interest rate. However, the relationship has not been exact. And when changes in the nominal interest rate do not exactly reflect changes in the rate of inflation, the real rate of interest changes.

There are two obvious explanations for changes in the real rate of interest. First, because the real rate of interest is the real return to capital, it should decrease during recessions because of a substantial amount of unused capital. Note that during the recessionary periods of 1970–1971 and 1974–1975 the drop in the nominal interest rate was much greater than that in the rate of inflation, and the real rate of interest decreased.

The second reason for changes in the real rate relates to *unexpected* changes in the rate of inflation. The nominal interest rate for a security should reflect the *expected* average rate of inflation over the maturity of the security. If the financial markets *expect* a higher rate of inflation in the future, nominal interest rates should increase to reflect these expectations. However, if inflation changes unexpectedly, the nominal rate of interest will not correctly reflect the change, and the real rate of interest will change in the opposite direction of the unexpected change in the rate of inflation. Figure 7–5 shows an example of such changes.

Between times T_0 and T_1, the nominal rate of interest is 8 percent, the rate of inflation 5 percent, and the real rate of interest 3 percent. Assume these are the normal levels.

Assume that at T_1, the rate of inflation *unexpectedly* increases to 6 percent. Since the change is unexpected, the nominal rate does not change and the real rate of interest decreases to 2 percent. Assume that by T_2, the financial markets recognize the change in the rate of inflation, and the nominal rate of interest increases to 9 percent, restoring the real rate of interest to 3 percent. At T_3 the rate of inflation *unexpectedly* decreases to its original level of 5 percent. Again, because the change is unexpected, the nominal rate remains at 9 percent, so the real rate increases

---

[4] While Figure 7–4 shows the current bond interest rate, the average rate of inflation over the previous three years, rather than the current rate of inflation, is shown. Since bond rates are long-term interest rates, the real rate over their maturity will be determined by the average rate of inflation over their maturity. The rate of the past three years is assumed to be indicative of the next three years.

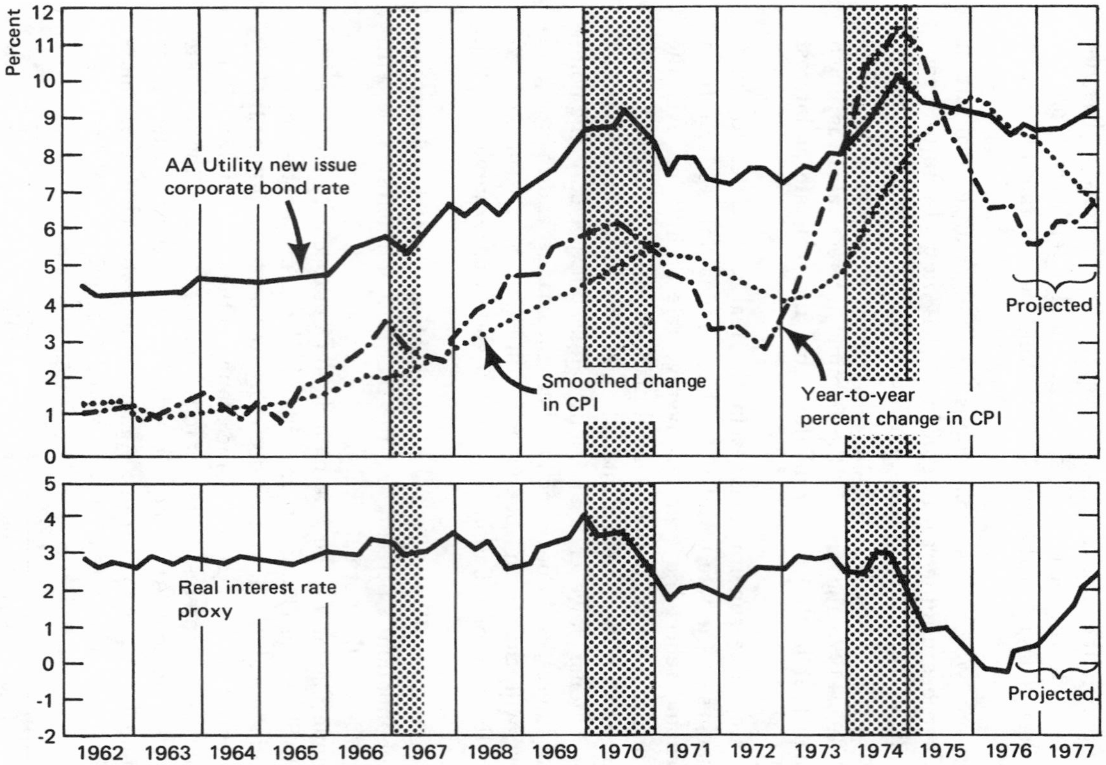

Note: Smoothed change in the CPI is a twelve-quarter moving average in quarter-to-quarter percent changes at compound annual rates of growth. Real interest rate proxy is the difference between the corporate bond rate and the smoothed changes in the CPI.

FIGURE 7–4 PRICES AND INTEREST RATES

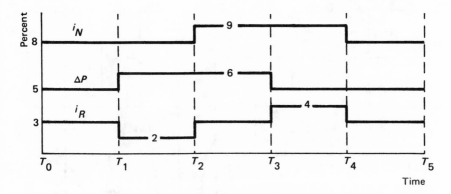

FIGURE 7-5 THE NOMINAL RATE OF INTEREST, THE REAL RATE OF INTEREST, AND INFLATION—THE TIMING OF CHANGES

to 4 percent. By T_4, the financial market recognizes the change in the rate of inflation, the nominal rate of interest decreases to 8 percent, and the real rate of interest decreases to its normal level of 3 percent. Once again, all is normal.

Such temporary disequilibria in the real rate of interest are difficult to observe in Figure 7–4. The financial markets adjust quickly and the curves shown in Figure 7–4 represent long-term interest rates and three-year averages of the rate of inflation. These disequilibria are more evident from the data on a short-term interest rate and a quarterly rate of inflation shown in Figure 7–6. Changes in the short-term real rate of interest occur frequently.

Three explanations of the interest rate have been given. The first two were shown to be equivalent. The inflationary expectations explanation of the interest rate will be shown to be complementary to the first two. Later in this chapter, methods of using each of these explanations of the interest rate to forecast interest rates will be discussed.

Monetary Policy and the Nominal Rate of Interest—A Second Look. In Chapter 4 and at the beginning of this chapter, it was shown that an increase in the money supply caused a decrease in the nominal rate of interest because of the liquidity effect. Yet if this increase in the money supply was large and persisted over a long period of time, an increase in inflation would result. An increase in inflation, as shown, causes an increase in the nominal rate of interest.

An increase in the money supply causes an immediate and short-lived decrease in the interest rate due to the liquidity effect. But if the money supply continues to increase at a substantial rate, the interest rate

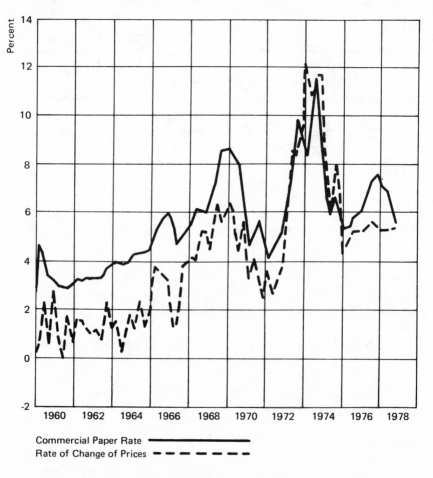

Commercial Paper Rate ————————
Rate of Change of Prices — — — — — — —

*The Rate of Change of Prices is the quarterly change in the Consumer Price Index
 expressed as an annual rate.

FIGURE 7–6 COMMERCIAL PAPER RATE AND CONSUMER PRICE INDEX*
Source: Based on Data from the Economic Report of the President.

will increase because of expectations of inflation or actual inflation
generated.

Increases in the money supply can cause short-run decreases and
long-run increases in the interest rate. It is consequently difficult to
interpret the posture of monetary policy by observing the interest rate.
An increase in the interest rate can be due to a recent tightening of
monetary policy or a loosening of monetary policy some time ago.

---

* The Rate of Change of Prices is the quarterly change in the Consumer Price Index
expressed as an annual rate.

structures of the interest rate

Heretofore in this chapter, "the" interest rate has been discussed. A general familiarity with the financial markets and a reading of Chapter 2 makes it clear that there is not one, but several, interest rates that differ not only in name but also in their level. This section considers three different structures of interest rates.

TAXABILITY STRUCTURE

The coupon payments of corporate bonds are subject to the federal personal income tax. Consequently, the after-tax rate on a corporate bond is less than the coupon rate by an amount determined by the bondholder's tax bracket. However, it is not legal for the federal government to tax the coupon payments of state and local government securities.[5] Municipal securities are tax-exempt and so their after-tax yield is the same as their before-tax yield. Since investors are concerned with after-tax yields, coupon rates on municipal securities are lower than the rates on similar corporate or federal securities because they are tax-exempt. For example, to an investor in the 50 percent tax bracket, a 4 percent municipal security has the same after-tax yield as an 8 percent corporate security. Interest rates differ because of the tax status of the security.

Another aspect of taxability also causes interest rates to differ. While coupon payments on corporate bonds are taxed at the personal income tax rate, capital gains are taxed at the capital gains tax rate (if the security is held one year or more). The capital gains tax rate is one-half the personal income tax rate. Consequently, the after-tax value of 1 percent of coupon return is worth less to an investor than 1 percent of capital gains. Recall that the yield to maturity includes both the coupon rate and the capital gains if held to maturity.

If, then, one security is selling at $1000 with an $80 coupon, its 8 percent yield to maturity is entirely due to the coupon return. If another security is initially selling for $900 with a $60 coupon for an 8 percent yield to maturity, its yield to maturity consists of 6.66 percent coupon return and the remainder due to capital gains. Since the *"discount security"* (a security selling at less than its maturity value of $1000) has a portion of its return due to capital gains, which has a lower tax rate, the after-tax return on the discount bond is greater than that of the bond

---

[5] State and local governments cannot tax the coupons on federal securities either but this exemption is not as important as the federal exemption because the income tax rates of state and local governments are generally lower than federal rates.

selling at "par" (the maturity value of $1000). Therefore, the price of the discount bond will be bid up and the yield to maturity at its actual trading price will be somewhat less than 8 percent.

Discount bonds normally sell at a rate somewhat lower than bonds selling at par or at a premium at a price greater than its maturity value because of the tax advantages.

CREDIT RISK

The two main characteristics of a security, as discussed in Chapter 2, are return and risk. Purchasers of securities prefer high returns and low risk. If a security has high risk, purchasers demand a high return to compensate for higher risks. Two types of risks were identified, credit risk and market risk. Interest rates on securities should increase as either of these types of risk increase. The next two structures of interest rates are explained as variations in the interest on securities due to variations in these two types of risk. This section discusses the relation between the rate of interest and the credit risk of a security.

A security's credit risk is a measure of the likelihood of the borrower being able to pay the interest and principal on the security when due. Federal securities have the lowest credit risk. Federal agencies are thought to have the next lowest credit risk because they are backed by the federal government. Corporate securities are rated below agencies in credit risk. The relative credit risks of corporate securities are rated by two private financial corporations—Moody's, and Standard & Poor's. Table 7–1 describes their rating categories.

Interest rates increase as the credit risk of a security increases. Consequently, the interest rate on a Treasury security is less than that on an Aaa Corporate which is less than on a C Corporate. Examples of the effect of credit risk on long-term interest rates are shown in Table 7–2 (for May 27, 1977).

The credit risk structure of interest rates explains variations in the interest rates of various securities of the same maturity by variations in the credit risk of the issues.

MATURITY

The second type of risk is the market risk. As discussed in Chapter 2, a security's market risk increases as its maturity increases. This section discusses the relationship between a securities' term to maturity and its interest rate, usually called the *term structure of interest rates*. A curve showing the relationship between the interest rate and the maturity on securities is called a *yield curve*. There are three different explanations of the relationship between the maturity of a security and its interest rate.

TABLE 7-1 BOND RATING CATEGORIES

Moody's	Standard & Poor's	Description
Aaa	AAA	Highest grade obligations. Highest degree of protection of interest and principal.
Aa	AA	High grade obligations. Differ only slightly from highest grade.
A	A	Upper medium grade obligations.
Baa	BBB	Medium grade category. Borderline between definitely sound obligations and those where the speculative element begins to predominate.
Ba	BB	Lower medium grade. Have some speculative elements. Future protection of interest and principal is not well assurred.
B	B	Speculative. Payment of interest cannot be assured under difficult economic circumstances.
Caa*	CCC	Outright speculation.
Ca*	CC	Outright speculation to a greater degree.
C*	C	Bonds on which no interest is being paid.
	DDD DD D	All in default. Rating is indicative of relative salvage value.

* The description applies to the Standard & Poor's, not the Moody's rating.
Sources: Moody's Investors Service, Inc. and Standard & Poor's Corporation.

TABLE 7-2 INTEREST RATES BY CREDIT RISK (MAY 27, 1977)

Type of Security	Interest Rate
Long-term Treasury Bonds	7.67%
Long-term Federal Agency Bonds	7.88
Aaa Corporate (Utility) Bonds	8.15
Aa Corporate (Utility) Bonds	8.35
A Corporate (Utility) Bonds	8.65

Liquidity Hypothesis. One aspect of a security's liquidity is its potential for capital loss or capital gain. This potential increases as the maturity of the security increases. The interest rate on a security should increase as its maturity increases to compensate for the increase in market risk. This explanation of the relationship between the interest rate and the maturity of a security is called the *liquidity hypothesis,* and is illustrated by the yield curve in Figure 7–7. The liquidity hypothesis

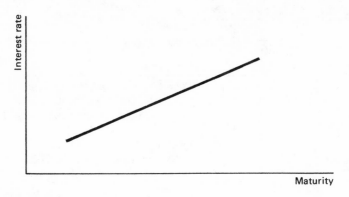

FIGURE 7-7 LIQUIDITY HYPOTHESIS EXPLANATION OF TERM STRUCTURE OF INTEREST RATES

does not purport to provide a complete explanation of the term structure of interest rates, but only to complement other explanations as discussed below.

Expectations Hypothesis. The expectations hypothesis is based on the notion that savers desire to maximize their interest return over the entire period they plan to hold a security, and borrowers desire to minimize their interest cost over the entire period they plan to have a security outstanding. Both lenders and borrowers base their choice of the maturity to purchase or issue, respectively, on this basis.

Consider a two-year time horizon. Lenders can purchase a one-year security at the beginning of the horizon and then after this security matures, purchase another security with a one-year maturity. Or they can purchase a two-year security at the beginning of the horizon and hold it until the end. Similarly, borrowers can issue two sequential one-year maturity securities, or initially issue a security of two-year maturity. How do lenders and borrowers choose between these two options? Their choice will depend on the present observed interest rates on securities with one-year and two-year maturities, and the rate of interest expected on one-year securities one year in the future, that is not currently observable. Lenders will choose either two sequential one-year securities or an initial two-year security depending on which gives a higher total return over the two-year period. Borrowers will choose the option that gives the lower return.

Assume, for example, the current one-year rate is 6 percent, the current two-year rate is 8.5 percent, and the one-year rate expected one year in the future is 8 percent. The effective interest rate over the two years if two sequential one-year securities are purchased or issued is the average of 6.0 percent and 8.0 percent, or 7.0 percent. The effective interest rate if the two-year security is purchased or issued is, obviously, 8.5 percent. Figure 7–8 illustrates this example.

Lenders would choose to purchase the two-year security to get the higher 8.5 percent return. Borrowers would choose to issue the two one-year securities to get the lower effective 7.0 percent rate. But if all the lenders chose the two-year market and all the borrowers chose the one-year markets, there would be an excess supply of funds in the two-year market tending to make the two-year rate decrease, and an excess demand for funds in the current one-year market tending to make the one-year rate increase.

How much would the two-year rate decrease and the one-year rate increase? The expectations hypothesis says the rates will continue to move until the effective rate of two sequential one-year securities equals the current two-year rate. Both lenders and borrowers would be indifferent to the two options and consequently the interest rate would not change further. In the example, if the one-year rate expected one year in the future remained 8 percent and the current two-year rate declined to 7.5 percent and the current one-year rate increased to 7.0 percent, the effective rate of two one-year securities would be 7.5 percent, the same as the two-year rate. At these rates, borrowers and lenders would be indifferent between the one- and two-year markets and so these rates would persist. The current observed interest rates are 7.0 percent for a one-year maturity and 7.5 percent for a two-year maturity according to the expectations hypothesis.[6]

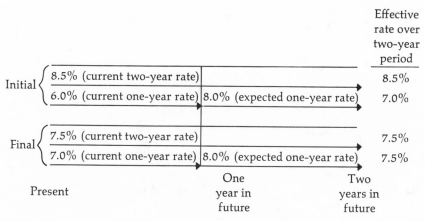

FIGURE 7–8 **EXAMPLE OF EXPECTATIONS HYPOTHESIS**

---

[6] This simplified method of calculating effective interest rates ignores compounding the interest earned on previous interest by assuming $(i_1 + i_E)/2 = i_2$

The expectations hypothesis can be applied to longer periods of any length. For any period, it says that the current, observed long-term rate equals the average of the current observed short-term rate and the expected future short-term rates through the maturity of the long-term security. The hypothesis says that borrowers and lenders do no better or worse via a long-term security than via a series of short-term securities.

This hypothesis can be applied to the relation between interest rates and maturities of securities over the business cycle. If interest rates are expected to remain stable in the future, the expectations hypothesis says that the *term structure of interest rate curve*, or yield curve, the curve that shows interest rates versus maturities, would be as shown in Figure 7–9. Interest rates at all maturities would be the same because future short-term rates are expected to be equal to current short-term rates, and so the current long-term rates which are the average of those short-term rates will equal the same constant level.

Assume that interest rates are expected to increase in the future because of inflation. Would the curve shown in Figure 7–9 still apply? If this curve initially described interest rates, and interest rates were expected to increase, lenders would purchase short-term securities to avoid capital losses they would experience if they held long-term securities. Borrrowers would issue long-term securities to assure that they could continue to pay the presently low coupons on their securities for a long period of time, rather than issuing short-term securities at a low coupon

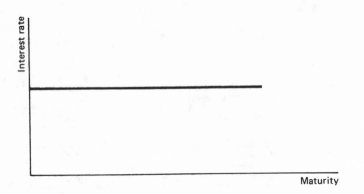

FIGURE 7–9 TERM STRUCTURE OF INTEREST RATES FOR EXPECTED CONSTANT INTEREST RATES

---

where i_1 and i_2 are the current one- and two-year rates, respectively, and (i_E) is the expected one-year rate one year in the future. The correct method is $(1 + i_1)(1 + i_E) = (1 + i_2)^2$.

The Domestic Financial System

and having to issue new securities at a higher coupon after the initial securities mature.

With lenders buying only short-term securities and borrowers issuing only long-term securities, there would be an excess supply of funds in the short-term market causing short-term interest rates to decrease, and an excess demand for funds in the long-term markets causing long-term interest rates to increase. The downward pressure on the short-term interest rates and the upward pressure on the long-term interest rates, shown in Figure 7–10, produce an upward sloping term structure of interest rate curve.

A question remains. From the initially assumed horizontal term structure curve, an excess supply of funds in the short-term market and an excess demand for funds in the long-term market make short-term rates decrease and long-term rates increase. But by how much? Certainly before the short-term rates become zero, lenders would cease buying short-term securities and borrowers start to issue them, thus preventing any further decrease in the short-term rate. And before the long-term reached 100 percent, lenders would start to buy long-term securities and borrowers would stop issuing them. What is the final relation among the rates? Or, how steep is the upward slope of the term structure curve? The expectations hypothesis provides the answer. The current long-term rate will equal the average of the current short-term rate and the expected short-term rates for future years. For example, if today's one-year rate is 7 percent, the one-year rate expected one year from today is 8 percent, and the one-year rate expected two years from today is 9 percent, the current three-year rate will be the average of these three one-year rates, or 8 percent. Consequently, the expectations hypothesis

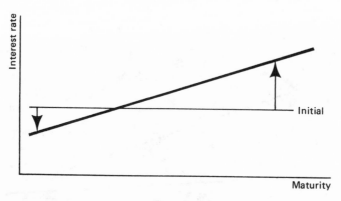

FIGURE 7–10 TERM STRUCTURE OF INTEREST RATES—INTEREST RATE EXPECTED TO INCREASE

says the current one-year rate will be 7 percent, and the current three-year rate will be 8 percent.

Assume, on the contrary, interest rates were as in the curve in Figure 7–11, but interest rates were expected to decrease in the future. Lenders would purchase only long-term securities to assure themselves of the presently high coupons for a long period of time and to capture the capital gains as the interest rates decreased. Borrowers would issue only short-term securities, thus paying the presently high coupons for only a short period of time, and waiting until interest rates decreased, as expected, to issue long-term securities. With lenders purchasing only long-term securities and borrowers issuing only short-term securities, there would be an excess supply of funds in the long-term market tending to cause long-term interest rates to decrease, and an excess demand for funds in the short-term market, tending to cause short-term interest rates to increase. The downward pressure on the long-term interest rate and the upward pressure on the short-term interest rate, shown in Figure 7–11, produce a downward sloping term structure of interest rate curve.

In sum, if interest rates are expected to increase, pressures in the financal markets tend to give the term structure curve an upward slope, as shown in Figure 7–10. If interest rates are expected to decrease, the pressures tend to give the term structure curve a downward slope, as shown in Figure 7–11. The relation between the short rate and the long rate is explained by the expectations hypothesis, which says that the long rate equals the average of the current short rate and the expected future short rates.

The pure expectations hypothesis concludes that if interest rates are expected to remain the same, the term structure curve will be horizontal; if rates are expected to increase, the curve will be upward slop-

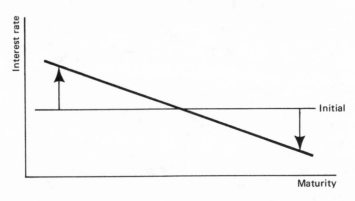

FIGURE 7–11 TERM STRUCTURE OF INTEREST RATES—INTEREST RATES EXPECTED TO DECREASE

ing; and if rates are expected to decrease, the curve will be downward sloping. But, in practice, the expectations hypothesis is always supplemented with the liquidity hypothesis. The liquidity hypothesis projects an upward slope, as shown in Figure 7–7. Adding the liquidity hypothesis to the expectations hypothesis gives the yield curves an upward bias as shown in Figure 7–12.

Observed term structure curves are normally upward sloping, as would be expected from a combination of the expectations and liquidity hypotheses. During recessions, interest rates are normally low and are expected to increase; the term structure curve usually has a steep upward slope. During times of tight credit and high interest rates, the term structure curve is downward sloping, reflecting expectations of decreasing interest rates after the crunch.

Figure 7–13 shows a downward sloping term structure curve during the high interest rate period of August, 1974, and a steep upward slope during 1976 when rates were even lower than during the recession year of 1976.

Segmentation Hypothesis. The expectations hypothesis is based on the assumption that lenders and borrowers shift between short-term maturities and long-term maturities in response to small interest rate differentials. The segmentation hypothesis, however, is based on the assumption that most borrowers and lenders do not readily switch among

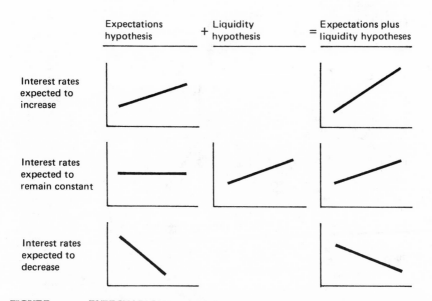

FIGURE 7–12 EXPECTATIONS HYPOTHESIS PLUS LIQUIDITY HYPOTHESIS

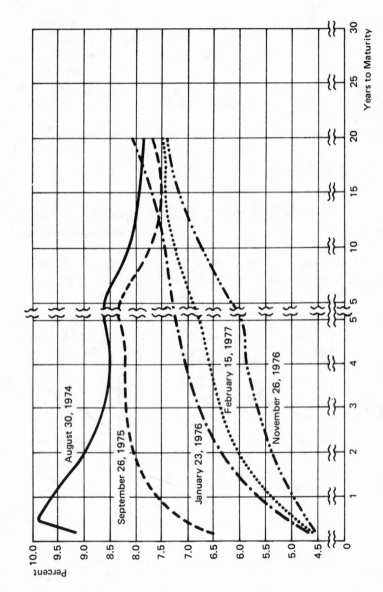

FIGURE 7-13 YIELDS ON U.S. GOVERNMENT SECURITIES

Source: U.S. Financial Data, February 23, 1977, Federal Reserve Bank of St. Louis.

securities of differing maturities. In other words, proponents of the segmentation hypothesis believe that long and short maturities are not considered to be substitutes by market participants.

It is asserted that sufficient institutional preferences and legal constraints exist that prevent most lenders and borrowers from switching between the long-term market and the short-term market in response to changes in the interest rate differential between these two markets. For example, life insurance companies purchase only small amounts of short-term corporate or Treasury securities; commercial banks do not purchase appreciable amounts of long-term corporates or Treasuries; house purchasers issue only long-term mortgages.

If most borrowers and lenders participate in only one maturity of the financial markets and do not shift among maturities when interest rate differentials change, the markets for securities of various maturities are *segmented*. The interest rate for a security of a particular maturity is determined by the supply and demand for funds in that market. And the supply and demand in one market are independent of the conditions in markets for other maturities. A change in the supply or demand for securities in a particular market will cause a change in the interest rate in that market but will not affect the interest rates in markets for securities of other maturities.

Resolution. The expectations hypothesis and the segmentation hypothesis are based on opposing assumptions and offer different explanations about how interest rates of various maturities are related. The liquidity hypothesis can be viewed as a supplement to either of the other two.

The expectations hypothesis is based on the assumption that there is substantial shifting by borrowers and lenders among securities of different maturities in response to changing interest rate differentials. The segmentation hypothesis is based on the assumption that there is little or no shifting by borrowers and lenders among securities of different maturities in response to interest rate differentials.

Which hypothesis—expectations or segmentation—is correct? Unfortunately, they are difficult to test. The expectations hypothesis is based on expected short-term interest rates which are not observable. The segmentations hypothesis does not definitively state what the relation among interest rates will be.

The real world probably contains elements of both hypotheses and does not completely satisfy either extreme. Undoubtedly, contrary to the segmentations hypothesis, some borrowers and lenders do shift among various maturities in response to changing interest rate differentials. Business borrowers, as is discussed in Chapter 11, change the maturity composition of their borrowing as interest rates change. And

The Interest Rate

the expectations hypothesis does not assert that all borrowers and lenders must shift among maturities but only enough to cause the described changes in the interest rates.

But some segmentation is present in the financial markets. Many borrowers and lenders cannot shift because of restrictions on their portfolios or do not wish to shift because of risk considerations.

The truth is probably somewhere between the pure expectations and the pure segmentation hypotheses. But the expectations hypothesis complemented by the liquidity hypothesis seems to have the stronger support.

It has been shown that there is a structure of interest rates for two elements of liquidity, credit risk and market risk (maturity). There is also a structure of interest rates for the other element of liquidity, marketability. Interest rates on securities increase as their marketability decreases.

forecasting interest rates

This section explains how the three previously discussed methods of determining interest rates are applied to forecasting interest rates.

LIQUIDITY PREFERENCE

The liquidity preference method of forecasting interest rates can be used in both simple and complex ways.

The simple way involves first forecasting the future level of nominal GNP and then determining or calculating the money supply necessary to support this level of GNP (from the equation discussed in Chapter 6, $M = 1/V \times GNP$, where V is the velocity of money). If the actual level of the money supply is expected to be less than this needed amount, interest rates will rise, and vice versa. Although this seems simple in principle, forecasting changes in nominal GNP, and particularly the money supply, is difficult.

The complex way provides a quantitative description of each step in the money supply and money demand processes. The money supply process starts with the provision of reserves by the Fed, the use of a portion of reserves to support demand deposits and time deposits, and the demand for bank loans as part of this process. The money demand process is based on the demands by individuals, corporations, and other sectors for cash (part of the high-powered money), demand deposits, time deposits, and other financial assets. This method is sufficiently complex that it is used only in the large econometric models of the U. S. economy.

There is also a third method of forecasting interest rates by considering the money supply; that is, by using liquidity preference effect. It involves forecasting short-term—weekly—changes in both short-term and long-term interest rates. The Fed announces each week, on Thursday afternoon, the changes in the money supply—both M1 and M2—for the previous week. These announcements are reported each Friday in the *Wall Street Journal* in a form shown in Table 7–3 for the Fed announcement on Thursday, July 28.

Interest rates are very sensitive to these announcements, through the liquidity preference effect. But, interestingly, the relationship between what is announced and subsequent changes in interest rates has reversed during the last five years. This reversal is due primarily to the change in the Fed's use of indicators of monetary policy, as discussed in Chapter 6.

During the 1960s and early 1970s, when the Fed was using interest rates as an indicator, when an announcement was made of an increase in the money supply, interest rates declined as would be expected for the liquidity preference hypothesis. When the money supply increased, there was more liquidity so interest rates decreased. This relationship which

TABLE 7–3   MONEY SUPPLY DATA FROM FED ANNOUNCEMENT

MONETARY AND RESERVE AGGREGATES
(daily average in billions)

	One week ended:	
	July 20	July 13
Money supply (M1) sa	329.0	324.0
Money supply (M2) sa	785.8	780.3
Money supply (M1) nsa	329.4	327.9
Money supply (M2) nsa	786.2	784.4
	Four weeks ended:	
	July 20	June 22
Money supply (M1) sa	325.3	321.4
Money supply (M2) sa	780.2	771.6
Adjusted bank deposits sa	555.3	551.4
Bank time deposits sa	518.5	513.6

sa–Seasonally adjusted. nsa–Not seasonally adjusted.

was typical during the 1960s and early 1970s is indicated in the following quote:

> A 9¾ per cent prime rate is likely to gain wide acceptance in the banking industry this week. The move to 9¾ per cent level was started Friday morning by First National City Bank, New York's largest, which lowered its base rate from the record 10 per cent in effect since mid-September. . . . The move resulted from a sharp decline in open-market rates on short-term debt instruments in recent weeks as the Federal Reserve System, the nation's money manager, relaxed somewhat its tight credit stance.[7]

Since the early 1970s the Fed has been using prespecified ranges for $M1$ and $M2$ as indicators for changes in monetary policy as discussed in Chapter 6 and shown in Figure 6–3. Now current announcements of money supply figures are interpreted in terms of what the Fed will have to do in the future to stay within its ranges. For example, an announcement of a large increase in the money supply is interpreted by investors as a sign that the Fed will have to tighten monetary policy in the near future so that the actual increase will not be higher than the upper limit of its range. Because of the expectation of future tightness, interest rates rise due to an announcement of a large increase in the money supply. This type of relationship is indicated in the following quotes:

> Interest rates in the short-term credit market jumped upward in late dealings after the Federal Reserve Board reported an unexpectedly large rise in the nation's money supply. The Fed reported the basic money supply, which is cash and checking accounts, climbed to a seasonally adjusted daily average of $330.4 billion in the week ended August 31, up $3 billion from the preceeding week. Money market analysts generally had anticipated a rise in the basic money supply, but most estimates were for a gain of $1.5 billion or less. The money supply figures are closely followed by market participants who interpret sharp gains as raising the possibility that Fed money managers will tighten credit conditions, boosting interest rates.

> Bond prices slipped a bit further as apprehension mounted prior to release of the weekly monetary figures in the late afternoon, dealers said. . . . Anxiety over the weekly data was well-founded, as increases in both money supply and bank loans were reported late yesterday. Previously, Aubrey G. Lanston & Co. had remarked that "recently bloated monetary levels represented a constant threat of further credit tightening by the Federal Reserve Board. The market is keenly aware that the Fed is committed to bringing the money supply under control in order to

---

[7] Reprinted with permission of the *Wall Street Journal*. © Dow Jones & Company, Inc. (1973). All rights reserved.

The Domestic Financial System

contain future inflation," the firm had said. Thus, market prices moved sharply lower after the figures were released.

Accelerated selling in the final hour drove the stock market sharply lower yesterday and halted its five-day rally on low volume. Analysts said the entire session was colored by expectations of another surge in the nation's money supply, conjuring up renewed worry over rising short-term interest rates. . . . With the "money supply cloud" hanging over the market, most "of the trading money stayed on the sidelines, waiting for clear directions of the market," said Charles Jensen, chief technical analyst at Merkin & Co. When sentiment grew stronger that the rise in the money supply would be large, selling intensified near the close, he said.[8]

Currently, not only money market interest rates but also bond prices (and rates) and stock prices respond to the Thursday announcement of money supply statistics in this way. The money supply data are closely watched by the entire investment community today.

During the 1960s, interest rates decreased due to the liquidity preference effect when the money supply increased. Today interest rates increase when the money supply increases. This is also due to the liquidity preference effect but is based on what investors expect future changes in the money supply to be in view of the announced change. Because of the Fed's money supply changes, future changes are usually expected to be the opposite of the recent change, particularly if the recent change was large.

Today's expectational type of liquidity preference effect causes changes in the same direction as the inflationary expectations effect. An announcement of a large increase in the supply of money not only causes interest rates to go up due to expectations of future tightening of the money supply, but also due to expectations of future inflation. Because both responses are in the same direction, interest rates have become even more sensitive to the money supply. Because of the strength of these relations between interest rates and the money supply, "Fed watching," or scrutinizing the Fed's moves, trying to anticipate what monetary policy they will implement, and investing on the basis of these anticipations, has become very popular among the financial community.

LOANABLE FUNDS

The loanable funds method is used to explain interest rates, as discusssed above, by comparing the supply and demand for loanable funds. An excess demand for funds causes interest rates to increase, and vice versa. Forecasting interest rates by this method requires a forecast of the total supply and the total demand for funds. This involves three

---

[8] Reprinted with permission of the *Wall Street Journal.* © Dow Jones & Company, Inc. (1977). All rights reserved.

steps. First, a structure of the individual components of the supply of funds must be developed; similarly for the demand for funds. Then a forecast for each component of supply and demand must be developed. Finally, the components of supply and demand must be added. If total supply is greater than total demand, an increase in interest rates would be forecast and vice versa.

The structure for the supply and demand for funds can be derived from the flow-of-funds structure of economy that was discussed in Chapter 2. One caution is necessary. As shown in Figure 7–14, funds are transmitted from savers to ultimate borrowers either directly along path P_1, or indirectly through financial intermediaries, along paths P_2 and P_3. Care must be taken not to double-count funds that flow through the financial intermediaries; that is, not to count either supplies or demands at both P_2 and P_3. To prevent double-counting, supplies and demands can be considered at either cut A or cut B in the figure.

The taxonomy developed in Table 7–4 uses cut A; the supply of funds considers loans from financial intermediaries but not supplies from the ultimate suppliers of funds to the financial intermediaries. The suppliers of funds are listed on the left, the demanders of funds on the right.

A number must be assigned to each of the categories in Table 7–4 for the period of the forecast. The numbers in each column are summed to give the total supply and the total demand. These totals can then be compared to determine whether interest rates are forecast to rise or decline. The magnitude of the difference between supply and demand will give an indication of how much interest rates will rise or decline. This assessment is judgmental, however.

Of course, after the forecast period has passed, total supply over the period will equal total demand because every dollar borrowed by one agent must also be lent by another. The supplies and demands that are forecast are the desired amounts. And desired borrowing and de-

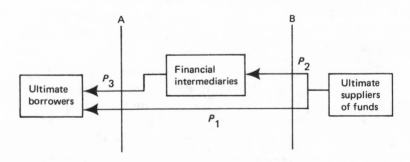

FIGURE 7–14 FLOW OF LOANABLE FUNDS

The Domestic Financial System

TABLE 7-4 TAXONOMY FOR LOANABLE FUNDS

Suppliers of funds (Lenders) (Sources of Funds)	Demanders of funds (Borrowers) (Uses of Funds)
Federal Reserve System	U.S. Government and agencies (Deficits are +; surpluses are —)
Commercial banks	State and local governments (Deficits are +; surpluses are —)
Non-bank financial intermediaries Savings and loan institutions Mutual savings banks Life insurance companies Other financial intermediaries	Nonfinancial business Short-term debt Long-term debt Equity
Direct supply by domestic nonfinancial sources Households Business Other	Households Mortgages Installment debt Other debt
Foreign supply	Foreign demand
TOTAL SUPPLY	TOTAL DEMAND

sired lending are not necessarily equal. If they are not equal, interest rates will change, the actual amounts of borrowing and lending will deviate from that desired amount, and at the new equilibrium rates of interest the actual amount of borrowing will equal the actual amount of lending. Forecasting all the specific supplies and demands for funds, as required by this method, requires a detailed familiarity with the financial markets.

One often unappreciated limitation of this method results from the interdependencies among the various supplies and demands for funds. For example, an increased federal budget deficit, while causing an increased demand for funds, may also lead to a strong economy. A stronger economy increases personal income and personal savings which increase the supply of funds. Business may also increase its demand for funds because of the stronger economy. So an increase in the demand for funds by the federal government may also generate an increase in the supply of funds by individuals and an increase in the demand for funds by business. The net effect on interest rates depends on the magnitudes of these changes. This point emphasizes that the various supplies and demands for funds cannot be forecast in isolation, but their interdependence must be considered.

Table 7-5 shows a taxonomy for forecasting interest rates by the loanable funds method; the table supplies actual data for 1970–1975 and predicted data for 1976 for each of the categories.

The Interest Rate   **131**

TABLE 7–5 SUMMARY OF SUPPLY AND DEMAND FOR CREDIT ($ BILLIONS)

	Annual Net Increase in Amounts Outstanding							Amounts Outstanding 12/31/76e
	1971	1972	1973	1974	1975	1976e	1977p	
Net Demand								
Privately held mortgages	44.3	68.8	68.7	42.8	38.5	61.3	69.5	760.1
Corporate bonds	24.7	18.9	13.5	27.5	32.7	27.6	24.1	334.3
Domestically held foreign bonds	0.9	1.0	1.0	2.2	6.3	9.3	10.4	34.2
Subtotal long-term private	69.9	88.7	83.2	72.5	77.5	98.2	104.0	1,128.6
Business loans	7.7	24.8	38.4	34.3	−14.5	−1.1	14.0	236.6
Consumer installment credit	9.3	15.6	19.7	9.0	6.9	16.0	21.0	178.2
All other bank loans	7.7	11.0	7.4	3.2	2.8	10.0	12.0	89.4
Open market paper	−0.1	1.6	8.3	16.6	−1.3	5.6	7.0	72.0
Subtotal short-term private	24.6	53.0	73.8	63.1	−6.1	30.5	54.0	576.2
Privately held Treasury debt	19.0	15.2	−2.0	10.2	75.8	61.8	49.5	406.7
Privately held federal agency debt	2.7	9.0	21.2	17.9	7.7	13.1	18.5	119.5
Subtotal federal	21.7	24.2	19.2	28.1	83.5	74.9	68.0	526.2
State and local tax-exempt bonds	16.4	14.1	13.3	11.9	16.9	17.8	19.0	228.6
State and local tax-exempt notes	5.3	−1.3	0.8	2.6	−1.2	−4.1	−2.0	13.8
Subtotal tax-exempt	21.7	12.8	14.1	14.5	15.7	13.7	17.0	242.4
Total net demand for credit	137.9	178.7	190.3	178.2	170.6	217.3	243.0	2,473.4
Net Supply [1]								
Mutual savings banks	9.0	8.8	5.3	3.1	10.4	11.9	11.9	121.1

e estimated
p projected

[1] Excludes funds for equities, cash, and miscellaneous demands not tabulated above.

Savings and loan associations	30.2	37.1	27.5	21.7	42.0	51.0	53.0	362.7
Credit unions	2.0	2.9	3.5	3.3	5.1	6.9	8.0	38.9
Life insurance companies	7.2	8.8	10.0	10.3	15.2	18.0	18.6	228.1
Fire and casualty companies	3.7	3.8	3.5	4.6	5.4	4.1	4.5	55.3
Private non-insured pension funds	−1.7	−0.7	2.0	5.8	7.9	7.4	7.6	59.0
State and local retirement funds	3.6	3.1	3.4	8.0	7.0	8.8	9.0	82.3
Personal and common bank trust funds	3.9	2.7	4.1	2.0	3.6	4.0	4.7	52.3
Foundations and endowments	1.7	−0.1	0.6	0.9	1.1	1.2	1.5	18.2
Closed-end corporate bond funds	0.2	1.2	1.1	0.2	0.0	0.0	0.0	2.8
Money market funds	0.0	0.0	0.0	1.0	0.6	0.3	0.4	1.8
Municipal bond funds	0.3	0.4	0.7	1.1	2.1	2.8	4.5	8.9
Open-end stock funds	0.0	0.0	−0.2	−0.4	0.7	0.4	−0.3	8.0
Real estate investment trusts	2.3	4.1	5.6	0.2	−4.6	−4.6	−2.2	6.2
Finance companies	4.2	7.5	8.8	2.4	0.5	8.1	10.1	84.4
Total non-bank institutions	66.6	79.6	75.9	64.2	97.0	120.3	131.3	1,130.0
Commercial banks[2]	50.9	73.3	77.6	59.8	31.0	44.5	58.0	785.9
Business corporations	2.4	0.9	3.4	8.0	10.6	7.1	8.1	74.2
State and local governments	−3.5	5.5	3.3	1.2	2.5	6.7	7.7	44.1
Foreigners	26.4	9.1	2.1	10.9	4.5	14.2	15.7	100.4
Subtotal	142.8	168.4	162.3	144.1	145.6	192.8	220.8	2,134.6
Residual: households direct	−4.9	10.3	28.0	34.1	25.0	24.5	22.2	338.8
Total net supply of credit	137.9	178.7	190.3	178.2	170.6	217.3	243.0	2,473.4

[2] Includes loans transferred to non-operating holding and other bank-related companies.

Source: *Prospects for the Credit Markets in 1977*, Salomon Brothers. In reference to this table, the similar 1976 document states, "The summary table on the opposite page, as well as the supporting tables on following pages, present our current estimates for credit flows in 1976. The 1976 estimates do not show all of the potential transaction flows, but rather those we believe will be realized. They are, therefore, directly comparable with the realized flows shown for 1975 and earlier years.

INFLATIONARY EXPECTATIONS

The inflationary expectations method bases its interest rate forecast on a forecast of the rate of inflation. This forecast rate of inflation is added to the normal real rate of interest (which is approximately 3 percent for a long-term bond, as shown in Figure 7–7) to give the forecast rate of interest. The basic real rate of interest may also be adjusted if economic conditions are not expected to be normal during the forecast period. In particular, the real rate should be adjusted downward if a recession is forecast. This would cause a downward adjustment in the nominal rate of interest.

In principle, this method is simple. In practice, however, forecasting the rate of inflation, which is necessary to forecast the rate of interest, may be as difficult as the initial goal of forecasting interest rates. Forecasting changes in the real rate of interest also complicates the use of this method.

SYNTHESIS OF THE THREE FORECASTING METHODS

Because each method of forecasting interest rates has limitations in practice, each is used for different purposes.

Forecasts of short-run changes in the short-term interest rates (Treasury bill rate, commercial paper rate, or federal funds rate) are usually based on the liquidity preference method. For this, data on the money supply are closely followed (money supply data are released weekly by the Fed). The financial markets use current money supply data to forecast future changes in the money supply and current short-term interest rates respond to these expectations as discussed.

For most participants in the financial markets, however, forecasting short-run changes in the short-term interest rates is not sufficient. For example, business borrowers need to know something about longer-term changes in long-term interest rates or the whole structure of interest rates. For these purposes, the loanable funds method of forecasting is often used. Forecasts of the quantities of supplies and demands for various types of funds are developed and compared. As discussed, this includes forecasting the posture of both monetary and fiscal policies.

The forecast of the direction of the movement in interest rates is thought to apply to the whole structure of interest rates, from short to long. To predict the magnitude of the changes of the interest rates of various maturities requires additional knowledge about whether expectations both now and at the time for which interest rates are being forecast would cause an upward sloping or a downward sloping term structure of interest curve.

Finally, the magnitude of the changes in interest rates forecast by the loanable funds method should be adjusted by the forecast change in inflation. This composite method of forecasting uses the inflationary expectations hypothesis in conjunction with the loanable funds hypothesis.

The loanable funds hypothesis gives the direction of change of the whole structure of interest rates and a general indication of the magnitudes of the change. To get a more precise forecast of the magnitude of the changes of various interest rates, additional information about present and future slopes of the term structure curve and the expected rate of inflation is necessary.

In the last decade, large economic models of the U.S. economy have been developed that forecast, in considerable detail, the state of the economy. The interest rate forecasts in these models are usually based on the liquidity preference hypothesis, the loanable funds hypothesis, and the inflationary expectations hypothesis. Businesses, governments, and government agencies have increasingly come to depend on these models for interest rate forecasts even though the users of these models do not always understand the technical methods used by the models in generating forecasts.

interrelations among interest rates

The various interest rates in the financial system, despite their differences, are integrally related. The expectations hypothesis of the term structure of interest rates stresses the fundamental reason for this relationship: borrowers shift among various sources of funds to get the lowest cost funds; and, lenders shift among assets to get the highest return on their investments. These shifts cause various interest rates to be related.

The general principle describing these shifts is called *arbitrage*. Pure arbitrage refers to a situation in which two identical securities are selling at different prices in two different locations. Investors, then, would buy the security at its low-priced location, and sell it at its high-priced location, thus making a net profit on the combination buy-sell transaction equal to the price differential between the securities (less transaction costs, of course). But buying the low-priced security would tend to increase its price and selling the high-priced security would tend to decrease its price, both changes tending to bring the security's prices into equality. When the prices in the two locations become equal, there would be no further gain from the combination buy-sell transactions. Consequently, the combination buy-sell transactions of identical securities, called arbitrage, is a response to price differentials and the arbitrage tends to eliminate the initial price differential.

Pure arbitrage refers to buy-sell transactions in response to price differentials between identical securities. An immediate profit results from pure arbitrage. In general, however, arbitrage refers to buy-sell transactions between similar, but not identical, securities on the basis of the perceptions that the prices or interest rates on the securities are "out of line." This combined transaction is done in expectation of future profit as the rates are brought into line. But the profit is not immediate as in pure arbitrage, and may not even result. The shifting by borrowers and lenders between long-term and short-term securities, as described in the section on the expectations hypothesis, is an arbitrage between long-term and short-term securities.

Figure 7–15 shows the similarity in the movements of the interest rates on Treasury bills and commercial paper. This similarity is not an

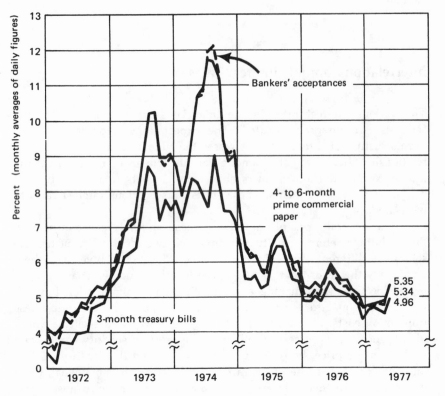

FIGURE 7–15 MONEY MARKET RATES
Source: Monetary Trends, Federal Reserve Bank of St. Louis.

The Domestic Financial System

accident. It is primarily due to arbitrage by investors between Treasury bills and commercial paper. Consider the following example. Assume that initially the commercial paper rate is 50 basis points above the Treasury bill rate. Assume, then, that a sudden large increase in the corporate issues of commercial paper causes an increase in the commercial paper interest rate by 10 basis points. Assume that there is no increase in the level of issues of Treasury bills and no increase in the Treasury bill rate. Investors, quickly perceiving that commercial paper is now paying 60 basis points more than Treasury bills rather than the normal 50 basis points, begin to buy the higher yielding commercial paper and sell the lower yielding Treasury bills. But these actions would drive the commercial paper rate down and the Treasury bill rate up, tending to reduce the spread. These transactions continue until the commercial paper rate returns to its 50 basis point premium over Treasury bills. Both rates might be higher than initially, because of the increase in the level of borrowing, but the interest rate differential returns to 50 basis points because of the arbitrage. And in the United States financial system such arbitrage occurs very rapidly.

Of course, arbitrage could be accomplished not due to shifts by investors as described here, but due to shifts among borrowers. However, there is much more segmentation of markets by borrowers than by lenders. For example, corporations cannot issue Treasury bills and the Treasury cannot issue commercial paper. Most arbitrage in the U.S. financial system is accomplished by shifts among investors or lenders.

Figure 7–16 shows how arbitrage among the various long-term debt issues keeps the movements in their interest rates similar. Arbitrage between stocks and bonds is discussed in Chapter 9.

The *spreads,* or differences between the interest rates on different securities, do change. That is, arbitrage does not keep all spreads constant. If the perceived degree of credit risk of one of the securities changes, the spread will change. Or if there is a large volume of issues of one of the securities, the segmentation hypothesis predicts the spread will change and spreads do change for this reason. The spreads between the interest rates on various securities are constantly changing for these and other reasons. And investors in the securities closely watch the spreads as part of their investment strategies. Despite the changes in these spreads, arbitrage does moderate the changes in the spreads and permits these changes to occur only in response to changes in fundamental factors such as changes in credit risk and supplies of specific securities.

This completes the discussion of concepts related to the interest rate and its role in the financial system. The next two chapters discuss the roles of the financial markets and financial institutions in the financial system.

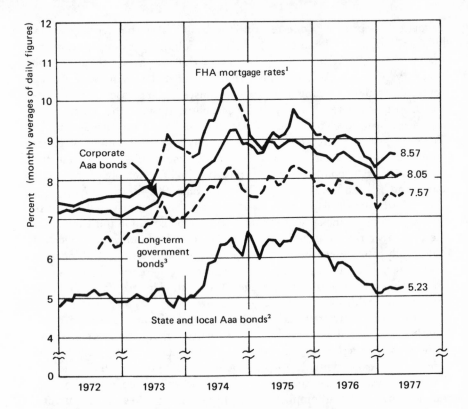

1 FHA 30-year mortgages. Dashed lines indicate data not available.

2 Monthly averages of Thursday figures.

3 Average of yields on coupon issues due or callable in ten years or more, excluding issues with federal estate tax privileges. Yields are computed by this bank.

FIGURE 7–16 LONG-TERM INTEREST RATES

Source: Monetary Trends, Federal Reserve Bank of St. Louis.

questions

1. Assume that in 1977 the nominal rate of interest is 9 percent and the rate of inflation is 6 percent. (The rate of inflation in 1976 was 6 percent also.) Assume also that in subsequent years the expected rate of inflation always equals the actual rate of inflation during the past year, and that the nominal rate of interest always changes by the change in inflationary expectations. Assume that the following rates of inflation actually occur:

1978	5 percent
1979	5 percent
1980	6 percent
1981	6 percent

The Domestic Financial System

What will be the nominal and real rates of interest during 1978–81? How would you use this information in your investment strategy? In your borrowing strategy? Evaluate the observation, "During periods of inflation borrow and pay back later in cheap dollars."

2. Assume that today's one-year interest rate is 5.0 percent, the two-year rate is 5.5 percent and the three-year rate is 6.0 percent. On the basis of the expectations hypothesis, what would the one-year rate be one year from today? Two years from today? If the Treasury issued a large volume of three-year securities, what would the expectations hypothesis and segmentations hypothesis say should happen to the yield curve (up to three years out)?

3. Discuss in detail the assumptions on which the expectations hypothesis and the segmentation hypothesis are based.

4. What does the expectations hypothesis conclude from the following yield curve and what behavior causes the yield curve to have this curvature?

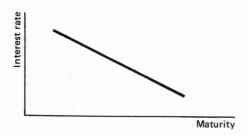

5. For 1978 you make the following estimates (billion $)
Federal budget deficit = $50
State and local budget deficit = $5
Household purchases of marketable securities = $30
Mortgage borrowing = $20
Business long-term borrowing = $20
Commercial bank lending = $50
Business short-term borrowing = $10
Non-bank financial institution lending = $25
On the basis of these estimates, what will be the total demand and the total supply of funds in 1978 and in which direction will interest rates move?

6. What is arbitrage? Apply the concept of arbitrage to the markets for commercial paper and Treasury bills. How does arbitrage relate to yield spreads among various securities? How can these spreads be used to formulate investment strategies?

7. If, starting today, the money supply began to increase at the rate of 15 percent per year, how would bond prices change over the next month? Over the next year?

the financial institutions

8

The two major components of the financial system, the financial institutions and the financial markets, are introduced in Chapter 2. This chapter examines the major individual financial institutions in more detail. Chapter 9 elaborates on the individual financial markets.

Financial institutions (FIs), often referred to as financial intermediaries, borrow funds from units with excess funds and relend these funds to other borrowing units. The funds the FIs borrow are their sources of funds, or in terms of a balance sheet, their liabilities. The funds the FIs lend are their uses of funds or in balance sheet terminology, their assets. The various sectors in the financial system differ from each other because they tend to specialize. Specialization in the financial system means that the funds supplied to the financial sector take a specific form and thus appeal to a certain type of supplier of funds; and the funds supplied by the financial sector take a specific form and thus appeal to a certain type of borrower. The nature of the individual FIs and the form of their specialization can thus be investigated by considering their balance sheets. Their liabilities show the form of their sources of funds and their assets the form of their uses of funds or their lending. The financial balance sheets of the major FIs are examined in this chapter to show their nature.

FIs are profit-making organizations.[1] Their major source of rev-

---

[1] These profits may accrue to the stockholders as they do for any corporation. Some financial institutions, however, have no stockholders and are instead owned by their depositors or other suppliers of funds. These are called *mutual* financial institutions. Mutual savings banks are owned by their depositors; mutual life insurance companies are owned by their policy-holders.

enues is the return on the funds they supply, such as the interest charges on loans made and the coupon and dividend returns on bonds and stocks purchased, respectively. A major cost of the institutions is the return they must pay on funds they raise; for example, the interest they pay on their deposits and the coupons and dividends they must pay on bonds and stocks issued, respectively. Of course, financial institutions also incur labor costs and capital costs because of their buildings and equipment. Their profits are the differences between these revenues and costs. The differential between the return they earn on the funds they supply and the return they pay on funds they raise is a critical determinant of these profits.

The nature of the various FIs and the ways in which they specialize are shown in the following sections.

commercial banks (CBs)

Several aspects of CBs are discussed in Chapter 3. As indicated, the unique aspect of CBs is their ability to issue demand deposits or checking accounts.[2] The rest of the major sources and uses of funds of the commercial banking sector, as of the end of 1975, are shown in Table 8–1.

THE COMMERCIAL BANK BALANCE SHEET

Several other aspects of the bank balance sheet, although not unique to banks, do distinguish CBs from other FIs. The largest source of funds to CBs is their time deposits. Time deposits are different from demand deposits in two important respects. Demand deposits can be used as a means of payment to settle accounts, which is why they are included in the definition of the money supply. Time deposits cannot be used as a means of payment. Also, CBs are prevented from paying any interest on demand deposits by the Fed's Regulation Q while they can pay interest on time deposits, although there is also a Regulation Q ceiling on the interest rates. There are several types of time deposits, and the level of the interest rate on them depends on the nature of the time deposit.

---

[2] This uniqueness has been disappearing recently, however. In some states mutual savings banks can also issue demand deposits. And recently some states have allowed these institutions to issue something very similar to checking accounts (called negotiable orders of withdrawal, or NOW accounts). And the development of techniques to transfer funds electronically from deposits to settle accounts is substantially reducing the distinction between checking accounts and other types of deposits.

TABLE 8–1 COMMERCIAL BANKING SECTOR (BALANCE SHEET, SELECTED PARTS, END OF YEAR, 1975) (BILLION DOLLARS)

Uses of Funds (Financial Assets)	
Vault cash and other reserves	$ 38.3
U.S. government securities	119.0
State and local government obligations	102.0
Corporate bonds	8.1
Mortgages	134.8
Consumer credit	90.3
Business loans[1]	257.3
Open market paper	10.2
Security credit	14.3
Total financial assets[2]	822.3
Sources of Funds (Liabilities)	
Demand deposits	236.8
Time deposits	453.1
Large negotiable CDs	82.9
Other	370.2
Corporate bonds	4.5
Total liabilities	775.1

[1] Some other minor categories are included in business loans.
[2] The categories shown do not add up to the total because some categories are not included.

Source: Flow of Funds Data, Board of Governors of the Federal Reserve System.

A large and important category of time deposits is the large nego-tiable certificate of deposit (CDs) discussed in Chapter 2. These nego-tiable CDs are large ($100,000 or more) with fixed short-term maturities (less than one year) and have no Regulation Q interest rate ceilings. There is also a secondary market for CDs on which they can be sold prior to maturity. CDs are purchased mainly by businesses who wish to earn an interest on a safe, short-term asset. Since CDs are short-term liabilities of mainly large CBs, and commercial paper is a short-term liability of large nonbank corporations, the interest rates on CDs and commercial paper are almost equal.

No other CB time deposits are either negotiable or immune from Regulation Q interest rate ceilings. A traditionally important form of time deposit for CBs is the passbook savings account. Passbook savings accounts have a lower interest rate ceiling than other time deposits, 5 percent at present, but the depositors can withdraw their funds at any time. Households, rather than businesses, are the largest holders of pass-book savings accounts. Not until November 10, 1975, were businesses allowed to maintain savings accounts in commercial banks.

The other forms of time deposits are essentially passbook savings accounts with fixed maturities and in some cases with minimum deposits. But the interest rate ceilings are higher on these deposits than on passbook savings accounts, ranging from 5.5 percent for a three-month minimum maturity and a $500 minimum deposit to 7.5 percent for minimum deposits of $1,000 held for six years or more. If the funds are withdrawn before maturity, however, an interest rate penalty equal to 90-days interest is imposed (and the rate is reduced to the passbook rate if the remaining deposit is below the minimum denomination).

Demand deposits and time deposits are the largest source of bank funds. The actual source of usable funds for each deposit, however, is less than the amount of the deposit because there are reserve requirements on each. Of course, banks, like any other corporation, also raise funds by issuing bonds and equities. These are important but, in magnitude, very small sources of funds for commercial banks.

CBs, however, are not allowed to issue commercial paper as a source of funds like other corporations. But in recent years commercial banks have devised a device, called the *bank holding company*, that permits the bank to issue commercial paper indirectly. A bank holding company is a corporation that holds all the stock of a CB. A bank can transform itself into a bank holding company by transferring its stock to another corporate entity called the bank holding company. The bank holding company is permitted to engage in activities not allowed banks. One of these activities is the issuance of commercial paper to raise funds. An advantage of commercial paper issues is that there are no reserve requirements on them.

Another source of funds that has at times been important for CBs is related to the Eurodollar. In the last decade a market has developed for bank deposits and loans in Europe which are denominated in dollars. These dollar-denominated European deposits are called Eurodollars. Many of the European banks engaged in the Eurodollar market are actually European branches of U.S. banks. During the periods of very tight credit in 1966 and 1969, the U.S. parent banks found it profitable to transfer their dollar deposits from their European branches to the parent for subsequent lending in the U.S. The advantage was that during these times there was no reserve requirement on these transfers from foreign banks. The Fed, which was trying to implement tight monetary policy during these periods, was being frustrated by the transfer of foreign deposits to the U.S. to finance bank lending. Consequently the Fed used its power under Regulation M to impose a reserve requirement on foreign branch deposits as of October 16, 1969. Since then banks have continued to derive some funds from these transfers but the level has been much lower and more stable.

CBs thus raise their funds from many sources. Households, businesses, and governments hold demand deposits. Businesses purchase CDs. Households are the primary holders of passbook savings accounts and other time deposits. Many investors purchase bank commercial paper, bonds, and stocks. European depositors are the source of Eurodollar transfers to banks.

Banks use these sources of funds in many ways. They keep some as reserves in the form of vault cash and reserves at the Federal Reserve Banks so they can honor withdrawals and meet reserve requirements. They invest a large amount in U.S. government securities, mainly short-term Treasury bills. Investments in Treasury bills are called *secondary reserves* because they can easily be converted into cash and there is little potential for a capital loss because of their short-term nature. Investments in longer-term Treasury bonds experience capital losses if interest rates rise.

Banks also invest in state and local government securities. The advantage of these securities is that their coupon payments are not subject to the federal income tax. New bank investments in these securities have slowed markedly since 1971, however, as shown in Table 8–2. Two principal reasons cause this reduction. First, banks have increasingly used other means of tax avoidance, such as depreciation expenses associated with their increasing leasing activity and the recent increased level of bad loans. Second, the market for state and local securities is rather thin; there are not many buyers. Consequently, during tight credit times when many banks attempt to sell some of these securities to generate funds to make business loans, the absence of buyers has caused sharp decreases in the prices of these securities and large capital losses for the banks. Banks became increasingly aware of this phenomenon during the tight credit periods of 1969, 1973, and 1974 and responded by adding fewer of these securities to their portfolios. The data in Table 8–2 also show that even prior to the decline in bank investment in

TABLE 8–2   ACQUISITIONS OF STATE AND LOCAL SECURITIES BY COMMERCIAL BANKS (BILLION DOLLARS)

Year	Acquisitions
1968	$ 8.6
1969	0.6
1970	10.5
1971	12.8
1972	7.1
1973	5.6
1974	5.2
1975	1.6
1976	2.6

Source: Flow of Funds Data, Board of Governors of the Federal Reserve System.

The Domestic Financial System

state and local securities, banks tended to add little during times of tight credit, such as 1969, when they were using their funds for business loans and added substantially to their portfolios during recessions, such as 1970–1971, when the demand for business loans was weak.

Holdings of U.S. Treasury, state and local securities are called bank *investments* because there are secondary markets for these assets. The holdings of the next three bank assets listed in Table 8–1—mortgages, consumer credit, and business loans—are called bank *loans* because there are essentially no secondary markets for these assets (there is actually a rudimentary secondary market for mortgages). Banks make mortgage loans to households and businesses. The nature of mortgages is discussed in more detail in the next section on savings and loan institutions.

The largest and the most important use of bank funds is the business loan. Banks make loans to credit-worthy businesses of all sizes. Of course, for a variety of reasons, large banks tend to lend to large businesses and small banks to small businesses. The basic bank loan interest rate is called the *prime rate* of interest. It is the rate the biggest banks charge their prime customers. Less credit-worthy businesses pay an increment over the prime rate. For example, a "prime plus 2 percent" company pays 2 percent over the prevailing prime rate for a loan. Banks, particularly during times of tight credit, require businesses to keep a *compensating balance* on their loans. This means that the business must keep a stated percentage of its loan in its checking account while the loan is outstanding. For example, a 20 percent compensating balance means that the business must keep a minimum balance in its checking account at the lending bank equal to 20 percent of the loan. Compensating balances reduce the usable part of the loan and thus increase the effective interest charge on the loan. Compensating balances also tend to increase the level of bank demand deposits and increase their sources of funds.

Bank loans to businesses are called *commercial and industrial loans*. Most bank business loans are short-term, with a maturity of less than one year, and self-liquidating; that is, the business uses the loan to finance an asset that will be converted into cash within one year and can be used to repay the loan. For example, business loans used to finance seasonal increases in accounts receivables or inventories are self-liquidating. However, increasingly in recent years banks have granted long-term business loans (maturities from one to seven years) called *term loans*. Business uses term loans to purchase longer-term assets such as equipment and often the asset purchased is used as collateral for the loan. Typically, term loans require higher interest rates and are repaid on an installment basis (that is, the loan is repaid by annual payments rather than by a lump sum at the maturity of the loan). On May

25, 1977, large commercial banks had $117.6 billion of commercial and industrial loans outstanding and of these $46.1 billion were term loans.[3]

The interest rate on the term loan is usually "tied" to the prime rate, so that when the prime rate increases, the rate on the outstanding term loans also increases. However, a variation of the term loan, called the *cap loan*, was developed in 1971 when loan demand was weak. The cap loan puts a ceiling or cap on the interest charged over the life of the loan, no matter how high the prime rate rises.

Consumer credit is an important bank asset because the interest charges on it are higher than on any other bank asset. Security credit is lending to those who purchase corporate stock on margin (that is, borrow part of the purchase price of the stock). Banks normally keep the purchased stock as collateral on these loans.

Over the business cycle, banks change the composition of their funds used to purchase their three major assets: U.S. government securities, business loans, and consumer credit. Such variation is shown in the flow of funds data in Table 8–3.

During years of strong economic growth and tight credit the demand for business loans and consumer credit is strong. And since the return on these uses of bank funds is greater than the return on U.S. government securities, banks typically sell some of their government securities to finance large increases in their business and consumer loans. During 1969 and 1973, for example, large bank increases in business and consumer loans were partially financed by selling U.S. government se-

TABLE 8–3   BANK PURCHASES OF SELECTED ASSETS (BILLION DOLLARS)

Year	U.S. Government Securities	Business Loans	Consumer Credit
1968	$ 3.3	$14.4	$ 5.5
1969	−10.1	11.5	4.7
1970	10.9	4.7	2.9
1971	7.2	11.7	7.4
1972	6.0	26.9	10.8
1973	−1.3	46.2	11.6
1974	1.2	32.6	3.6
1975	30.3	−12.7	2.9
1976	19.3	11.8	7.4

Source: Flow of Funds Data, Board of Governors of the Federal Reserve System.

---

[3] Federal Reserve Bulletin, June, 1977, p. A24, Board of Governors of the Federal Reserve System.

curities. During recessions the demand for both business and consumer loans is usually weak and since banks cannot use their funds for these preferred uses, they instead increase their investments in U.S. governments. During the recession years of 1970 and 1975, bank investments in U.S. governments increased substantially because of the anemic growth in business and consumer loans (business loans actually decreased during 1975). So the ratio of bank loans to investments increases during times of strong economic growth and tight credit and decreases during recessions.

This phenomenon is shown clearly in Figure 8–1. During the growth periods of 1973 and early 1974, loans increased greatly and investments very slowly. With the onset of the recession during 1974, however, loans leveled off and investments began to increase quickly.

LIABILITY MANAGEMENT

During the 1950s and early 1960s, commercial banks had adequate funds from their normal depository sources to meet their lending needs. They encountered more difficulty in making loans than in getting deposits. During the mid-sixties, however, this balance changed. At most times since then, there has been a greater demand for bank loans than banks could finance from their normal depository sources. And raising funds has become more difficult than making loans. *Liability management,* or managing their sources of funds, has, because of this shift, become a much more important concern for banks.

One aspect of liability management is that banks have devoted more resources to soliciting demand and time deposits by advertising, establishing many convenient branches, and other means. Despite this, the ratio of bank loans to bank deposits has increased considerably in the last decade. Data on the major types of bank liabilities and bank loans outstanding over the 1967–1975 period are shown in Table 8–4. The ratio of bank loans to bank deposits is calculated from these data and shown in Table 8–5. This ratio increased from 50.2 percent in 1967 to 63.6 percent in 1974. Note also that the ratio tends to increase during years of tight credit (1973 and 1974) and decrease during years of recession (1970 and 1975).

Finally, banks have become more dependent on new sources of funds on which interest rates are high and on which the level of supplies of these types of funds to banks is very sensitive to the level of interest paid, mainly CDs and commercial paper issued by bank holding companies. Relative to the traditional sources of funds—the demand deposit and the nonnegotiable time deposit—CDs and commercial paper have the disadvantages to banks that during times of tight credit the interest rates are much higher and the suppliers of these types of funds

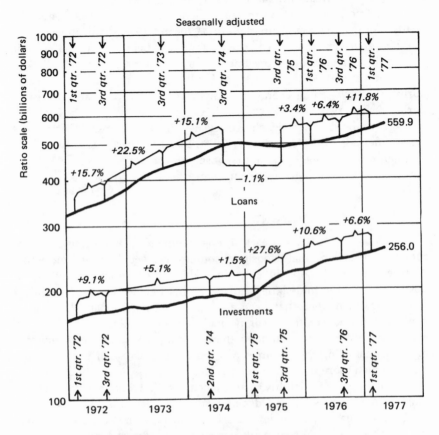

1 Averages of seasonally adjusted data for current and preceding last
Wednesday of each month.
Percentages are annual rates of change for periods indicated.

FIGURE 8–1 BANK LOANS AND INVESTMENTS[1]
Source: *Monetary Trends*, Federal Reserve Bank of St. Louis.

are very interest sensitive. But their advantages are that banks have
more flexibility in bidding for these funds since the rates they can pay
are not constrained by Regulation Q and that the pool of available
money is very large. Because of these advantages, banks, particularly
large banks, have become much more dependent on these new sources
of funds. As shown in Table 8–6, the ratio of certificates of deposit and
commercial paper to demand deposits and nonnegotiable time deposits

TABLE 8-4 END OF YEAR LEVELS OF SELECTED BANK LIABILITIES AND ASSETS (BILLION DOLLARS)

	Demand Deposits	Total Time Deposits[2]	Certificates of Deposit	Commercial Paper Issues[3]	Loans (Consumer Credit plus Business Loans)
1967	$160.57	$183.10	$20.33	$0	$162.19
1968	172.73	203.67	23.47 (3.14)[1]	0	182.12
1969	177.37	194.09	10.92 (−12.55)	4.29 (4.29)	198.81
1970	182.50	231.68	26.07 (15.15)	2.35 (−1.94)	206.31
1971	195.47	272.79	34.76 (8.69)	1.97 (−0.38)	225.42
1972	219.58	315.59	44.52 (9.76)	2.64 (0.67)	263.18
1973	232.49	365.92	64.53 (20.01)	4.88 (2.24)	320.96
1974	231.37	423.50	93.05 (28.52)	8.33 (3.45)	357.42
1975	236.83	453.09	82.90 (−10.15)	8.65 (0.32)	347.90

[1] The numbers in parentheses are changes in the levels during the year.
[2] This category includes certificates of deposit.
[3] This category is a liability of domestic affiliates of commercial banks, mainly holding-company parents of banks.

Source: Flow of Funds Data, Board of Governors of the Federal Reserve System.

TABLE 8-5 BANK LOANS AS A PERCENTAGE OF BANK DEPOSITS (EXCLUDING LARGE CDs)

Year	Percentage
1967	50.2%
1968	51.6
1969	55.2
1970	53.2
1971	52.0
1972	53.6
1973	60.1
1974	63.6
1975	57.3

Based on data of Table 8-3.

has increased from 6.3 percent during 1967 to 18.0 percent during 1974. Note also the numbers in parentheses in Table 8-4, which show that these sources of funds are particularly important to banks during times of tight credit. During the tight credit years of 1973 and 1974, CDs and commercial paper increased substantially and during the next recession year of 1975, they, taken together, decreased.

TABLE 8-6 PERCENTAGE OF CDs AND COMMERCIAL PAPER RELATIVE TO DEMAND DEPOSITS AND NONNEGOTIABLE TIME DEPOSITS

Year	Percentage
1967	6.3%
1968	6.7
1969	4.2
1970	7.3
1971	8.5
1972	9.6
1973	13.0
1974	18.0
1975	15.1

Calculated from the data in Table 8-3.

BANK REGULATION

The issue of who regulates banks and how they are regulated is quite complex; only a few highlights are given here. Banks may be either federally chartered, in which case they are regulated by the federal government, or chartered by the state in which they operate. Federally chartered banks are supervised by the Comptroller of the Currency. Federally chartered banks must also be members of the Federal Reserve System, which allows them to borrow from the Fed and use the Fed's check-clearing facilities. The Fed also regulates and supervises its members. State-chartered banks are regulated by their state's regulatory body. They may also choose to join the Federal Reserve System to avail themselves of the Fed's services but they then also become subject to the Fed's supervision and regulation.

The Federal Deposit Insurance Corporation (FDIC) insures bank deposits, currently up to $40,000. All federally chartered banks must be members of the FDIC. Most state-chartered banks have voluntarily joined the FDIC and are insured.

BANK INNOVATION

Banks have been quite innovative, particularly in devising new ways to raise funds. The CD was devised in 1961 when a large bank agreed to issue them and another financial institution agreed to make a secondary market in them; that is, buy and sell them before their maturity. Eurodollars were also used as a way of compensating for tight domestic credit conditions. But the bank holding company has perhaps been the most important innovation. There are many incentives for holding companies to acquire banks and for banks to transform themselves into holding companies. These incentives, and the legal limitations on

        The Domestic Financial System

bank holding companies, are too complex to be discussed here in detail. But among the major incentives were the ability to issue commercial paper to raise funds and the ability to engage in types of businesses and in geographical areas not allowed to commercial banks. Some of these types of businesses are insurance, some types of leasing, real estate investment trusts, and consumer and business finance companies. And for these reasons the number of banks in bank holding companies, particularly large banks, has increased greatly in recent years.

BANK BEHAVIOR OVER THE BUSINESS CYCLE

As shown in Tables 8–4 and 8–5, during times of tight credit banks increase their loans in response to strong loan demand. As a result, their loan to deposit ratio increases and they finance an increased portion of their loans from high interest rate–interest rate sensitive sources of funds. Both of these factors put banks in a more precarious situation during periods of tight credit.

During recessions, the loan to deposit ratio and the degree of dependence on CDs and commercial paper both decrease. However, during recessions, banks typically experience losses due to business and consumer loans that have gone bad because of the recession. Traditionally, these have included many types of business loans. During the recession of 1974–1975, however, banks were particularly affected by bad real estate loans. The banks themselves had made many loans for office buildings, condominiums, apartment houses, and shopping centers which, because of overbuilding and the recession, could not be repaid. And many real estate investment trusts (REITs) that were part of bank holding companies experienced the same problems. And in some cases the banks in holding companies either lent to the REITs or purchased some of the REITs' questionable loans, thus exacerbating the banks' problems.

savings and loan associations (SLAs)

As shown in Table 8–7, SLAs are very specialized in that about 82 percent of their financial assets are mortgages and 90 percent of their liabilities are savings shares. The SLA sector is the second largest financial sector, somewhat less than half as large as the commercial banking sector as measured by financial assets. SLAs exist in all 50 states, although six states (California, Illinois, Ohio, New York, Florida, and Pennsylvania) account for over 50 percent of the assets of all SLAs.

SLAs supply funds mainly to the mortgage market and they are given a tax advantage for being primarily mortgage lenders. Mortgages

TABLE 8-7 SAVINGS AND LOAN INSTITUTIONS SECTOR (BALANCE SHEET, SELECTED PARTS, END OF YEAR, 1975) (BILLION DOLLARS)

Uses of Funds (Financial Assets)	
Mortgages	$278.70
Consumer credit	2.80
Currency, demand deposits, time deposits	8.08
U.S. Treasury and government agency securities	22.58
Total financial assets[1]	338.40
Sources of Funds (Financial Liabilities)	
Savings shares	286.04
Federal home loan bond advances	17.85
Total liabilities[1]	318.62

[1] The categories do not add up to the totals because some categories are not included.

Source: Flow of Funds Data, Board of Governors of the Federal Reserve System.

are long-term loans with original maturities of between twenty-five and thirty years. However, mainly because of early payment, on the average mortgages stay with SLAs for only about seven years. Even so, this is a much longer loan than the average commercial bank loan.

Savings and loan associations get most of their funds from the savings account. They are, consequently, in direct competition with the time deposits of commercial banks for these depository funds. There are many types of savings and loan savings accounts, similar to the variety of commercial bank time deposits. The basic account is the passbook savings account that has no minimum account and can be withdrawn at any time with no interest penalty. SLAs are permitted by law to pay 0.25 percent more on passbook accounts than commercial banks, partly to compensate for the natural advantage commercial banks have due to their ability to offer checking accounts. At present commercial banks can pay up to 5 percent on their passbook accounts and SLAs up to 5.25 percent.

SLAs also offer other accounts that require minimum deposits or that can be withdrawn only after a fixed period. For example, they offer 90-day maturity accounts that now pay a maximum of 5.75 percent through six-year, $1,000 minimum accounts that pay a maximum of 7.75 percent. Banks can pay 0.25 percent less on these accounts also. On fixed maturity deposits there is an interest rate penalty on early withdrawals similar to that on commercial bank deposits. The importance of passbook accounts as a source of funds to SLAs has declined considerably in recent years. During 1966, 88.3 percent of all savings and loan accounts were of the passbook type; at the end of 1975, this ratio was only 42.7 percent.[4] This change has raised the interest costs of SLAs but has also made their deposits somewhat more stable during times of high interest rates than they otherwise would have been. Despite this, the average life of a savings account was only slightly more than two years at the end of 1975.[5]

SLAs can be organized under either federal or state charters. All federally chartered SLAs are mutual organizations; they are owned by their depositors and have no stockholders. State-chartered SLAs can be either mutual or stock (that is, owned by their stockholders) organizations. All federally chartered SLAs must belong to the Federal Home Loan Bank System (FHLBS), which regulates and provides credit to its members in a way similar to that in which the Federal Reserve System does for commercial banks. Many state-chartered SLAs voluntarily join the FHLBS (at the end of 1975 there were 2,048 federally-chartered SLAs in the FHLBS and 2,029 state-chartered members).[6] In addition to regulating its members, the System extends credit in the form of advances to its members to preserve their liquidity and support the mortgage markets. The System also supervises the Federal Savings and Loan Insurance Corporation (FSLIC), to which all federally chartered SLAs must belong, and which insures the deposits of its members up to $40,000. At the end of 1975, SLAs accounting for 97.6 percent of all SLA assets were insured by the FSLIC.

A fundamental problem that affects the mortgage and housing markets results from the fact that SLAs hold long maturity assets and much shorter maturity liabilities. During times of rising interest rates, the average return on the SLAs' mortgage portfolio increases only slowly because the average mortgage turns over only once every seven years and the SLAs earn the new, higher interest only on the new mortgages extended. However, to keep their deposit rates competitive with other rates, the SLAs would have to increase the interest rates on their entire stock of deposits (or at least those deposits without a long maturity). SLAs are limited by legal Regulation Q–type interest rate ceilings in the extent to which they can raise their rates on deposits. But even in the absence of these ceilings they would be limited in the extent to which they can raise their rates by the average return on their assets, or else they would operate at a loss. Consequently, during times when market interest rates are increasing, the rates on SLA deposits increase less and there is an inducement for SLA depositors to withdraw their funds and invest them elsewhere. As shown in Table 8–8, during the tight credit periods (or "credit crunches") of 1966, 1969,

---

[4] *Savings and Loan Fact Book, 1976*, p. 58.

[5] Ibid., p. 61.

[6] Ibid., p. 96.

TABLE 8–8 CHANGES IN SAVINGS AND LOAN ASSOCIATIONS—SAVINGS SHARES, FHLB ADVANCES, AND MORTGAGES (BILLION DOLLARS)

	Average Annual Yield on Savings Deposits in SLAs[1]	Three-month Treasury Bill Rate[2]	Change in Savings Shares[3]	Change in FHLBS Advances[3]	Change in Mortgages[3]
1965	$4.23	$3.95	$ 8.5	$0.7	$ 9.0
1966	4.45	4.88	3.6	0.9	3.7
1967	4.67	4.32	10.6	−2.5	7.3
1968	4.68	5.34	7.4	0.9	8.9
1969	4.80	6.68	3.9	4.0	9.5
1970	5.06	6.46	10.9	1.3	9.8
1971	5.33	4.35	27.8	−2.7	23.6
1972	5.39	4.07	32.6	0.0	31.8
1973	5.55	7.04	20.2	7.2	26.5
1974	5.98	7.89	16.0	6.7	17.6
1975	6.24	5.84	43.1	−4.0	29.7
1976	6.31	5.00	50.3	−2.0	44.4

[1] Source: *Savings and Loan Fact Book, 1976*, p. 15.
[2] Source: Economic Report of the President.
[3] Source: Flow of Funds Data, Board of Governors of the Federal Reserve System.

1973, and 1974, the rate on three-month Treasury bills exceeded that on SLA deposits; the increase in savings shares declined substantially as potential depositors instead invested in Treasury bills, commercial papers, and other marketable securities. As shown in Figure 8–2, there were absolute decreases in SLA deposits during periods of 1973 and 1974. The phenomenon of savers withdrawing funds from financial intermediaries in general, and SLAs in particular, and investing in marketable securities is called *disintermediation*.

Of course, with smaller increases in deposits, the SLAs' ability to finance new mortgages is reduced. Table 8–8 shows the reduced mortgage financing by SLAs during the credit-crunch years. For these reasons, typically during years of strong economic activity and high interest rates, the mortgage market becomes weaker.

The plight of the SLAs is exacerbated by the tendency of mortgage borrowers to refinance their mortgages financed during high interest rate periods at lower rates once interest rates have declined. The trend away from passbook savings accounts toward fixed maturity deposits, however, tends to "lock in" the SLAs' depositors and make the SLAs less susceptible to disintermediation.

Loans to SLAs from the FHLBS have to some extent reduced the variation in the sources of funds to SLAs. As shown in Table 8–8, in

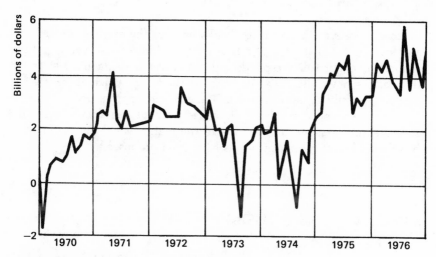

FIGURE 8–2 SAVINGS GAINS AT INSURED ASSOCIATIONS (SEASONALLY ADJUSTED)

Source: *Savings and Loan Fact Book*, 1976, p. 64.

1969, 1973, and 1974 advances to SLAs by the FHLBS increased substantially, thus supporting the SLAs' ability to extend mortgages. After interest rates decline and SLA deposits increase, SLAs repay these advances, as shown in the table.

Commercial banks, due to their time deposits, also experience disintermediation, as shown in Table 8–9. But rising interest rates have

TABLE 8–9 CHANGES IN COMMERCIAL BANK TIME DEPOSITS (OTHER THAN LARGE, NEGOTIABLE CERTIFICATES OF DEPOSITS) (BILLION DOLLARS)

Year	Changes in Time Deposits
1965	$16.4
1966	13.8
1967	19.1
1968	17.4
1969	2.9
1970	22.4
1971	32.4
1972	33.0
1973	30.3
1974	28.3
1975	39.7
1976	58.7

Source: Flow of Funds Data, Board of Governors of the Federal Reserve System.

The Financial Institutions

caused a less severe problem for banks because the average maturity of their loans is much shorter than SLA loans and hence the average return on their loan portfolio responds more quickly to rising interest rates. Also, banks have alternative sources of funds on which there are no interest rate ceilings, such as the CD and commercial paper.

There has been much public concern about the volatility in the mortgage and housing markets due to the maturity imbalances in SLA portfolios. Several types of reforms have been proposed.

mutual savings banks (MSBs)

The financial balance sheet for the MSB sector in Table 8–10 shows that MSBs are similar to SLAs in two important aspects. First, savings deposits are responsible for almost all the funds raised by each sector. Second, the mortgage is the largest asset of each sector. However, MSBs do hold more corporate bonds and stocks than do SLAs. MSBs also hold a large quantity of Treasury and agency securities for liquidity and a small amount of consumer credit.

MSBs are all mutual organizations, are all state chartered, and exist in only seventeen states, mostly in the northeast. Their limited geographical coverage is the main reason that the total assets of the MSB sector are only about 35 percent those of the SLA sector. MSBs are very impor-

TABLE 8–10 MUTUAL SAVINGS BANK SECTOR (FINANCIAL BALANCE SHEET, SELECTED PARTS, END OF YEAR, 1975) (BILLION DOLLARS)

Uses of Funds (Financial Assets)	
Currency, demand deposits, and time deposits	$ 2.32
Corporate equities	4.40
U.S. Treasury and government agency securities	10.87
Corporate bonds	17.54
Mortgages	77.25
Consumer credit	1.81
Total financial assets[1]	121.14
Sources of Funds (Liabilities)	
Savings deposits	109.87
Total liabilities	112.63

[1] The categories do not add up to the total because some categories are not included.

Source: Flow of Funds Data, Board of Governors of the Federal Reserve System.

TABLE 8–11 CHANGES IN MUTUAL SAVINGS BANK SAVING SHARES
AND MORTGAGES (BILLION DOLLARS)

	Savings Shares	Mortgages	U.S. Treasury and Government Agency Securities
1965	$ 3.6	$4.0	$ −0.3
1966	2.6	2.7	−0.5
1967	5.1	3.2	−0.2
1968	4.2	2.8	−0.1
1969	2.6	2.7	−0.4
1970	4.4	1.8	0.3
1971	9.9	3.9	0.9
1972	10.2	5.5	1.3
1973	4.7	5.7	−0.4
1974	3.1	2.2	−0.2
1975	11.2	2.3	3.9
1976	13.0	4.4	4.0

Source: Flow of Funds Data, Board of Governors of the Federal Reserve System.

tant in some states, however. In New York, Massachusetts, New Hampshire, Connecticut, Rhode Island, and Maine, mutual savings banks hold more savings deposits than do the SLAs and commercial banks combined.

Many MSBs have joined the Federal Deposit Insurance Corporation so that their deposits have the same protection commercial bank depositors have ($40,000), and many have joined the Federal Reserve System so they can borrow from the Federal Reserve Banks.

The similarity of MSBs to SLAs extends to the susceptibility of MSBs to disintermediation during times of high interest rates. The acquisition of new deposits and extension of new mortgages by the MSB sector is shown in Table 8–11. The growth in savings shares declined substantially during the tight credit years of 1966, 1969, 1973, and 1974. However, the reductions in mortgages extended by MSBs were smaller than in savings shares because MSBs tended to liquidate U.S. Treasury and government agency securities during these times to counteract the reduced growth in savings shares.

credit unions (CUs)

Like SLAs and MSBs, credit unions raise most of their funds from savings deposits, called credit union shares, as shown in Table 8–12. However, CUs differ from SLAs and MSBs in several ways. The prin-

TABLE 8–12 CREDIT UNION SECTOR (FINANCIAL BALANCE SHEET, SELECTED PARTS, END OF YEAR, 1975) (BILLION DOLLARS)

Uses of Funds (Financial Assets)	
Currency and demand deposits	$ 1.65
Savings and loan shares	3.40
U.S. government securities	5.04
Home mortgages	1.60
Consumer credit	25.35
Total financial assets[1]	37.04
Sources of Funds (Liabilities)	
Credit union shares	33.05

[1] The categories do not add up to the total because some categories are not included.

Source: Flow of Funds Data, Board of Governors of the Federal Reserve System.

cipal asset of the CU is consumer credit, rather than the mortgage. Much of this credit is for consumer durables such as automobiles and furniture. The rest is for a wide variety of purposes such as debt consolidation and education. Since the maturity of consumer credit is much shorter than the maturity of a mortgage, the average returns on the CUs' portfolios respond more quickly to increases in interest rates than do those of SLAs and MSBs. CUs also hold demand deposits, currency, savings and loan shares, and U.S. government securities for liquidity and a small amount of mortgages.

A distinguishing feature of the CU is the "common bond" of its members. To qualify as a CU, its members must have a common bond such as being employed by the same firm or being members of the same profession. These two types of bonds account for more than 95 percent of all credit unions. Most individual credit unions are small and the CU sector is less than one-third the size of the MSB sector. Often the costs of CUs' operations are low because some of the work is provided by volunteers and office space is provided by the employer of its members. In addition, CUs are exempt from federal taxation. For these reasons, CUs are usually able to pay higher rates on the deposits of their members and charge lower rates on the loans to their members. And for these reasons, CUs are often regarded as a fringe benefit to their members.

CUs are nonprofit cooperative associations—its members are its owners. They may be either federally or state chartered. Deposits of federally chartered and some state-chartered CUs are insured by the National Credit Union Administration to a maximum of $40,000, the same as commercial banks, SLAs, and MSBs.

Commercial banks, SLAs, MSBs, and CUs are all *deposit-type financial institutions;* their liabilities are in the form of deposits. Other financial institutions are of a *contractual type;* their liabilities are commitments for future payment under conditions specified in the contract. Insurance companies and pension funds are the major contractual-type financial institutions. Mutual funds and trust funds are *investment-type financial institutions* whose liabilities are shares of a common interest in a portfolio of securities. *Finance companies* are institutions whose liabilities consist mainly of debt and equity securities they have issued. The deposit-type financial institutions are discussed above. Some of the contractual, investment, and finance types of financial institutions are discussed below.

life insurance companies (LICs)

The contractual-type financial institutions—LICs and pension funds—are characterized by regular inflows of funds, under a long-term contract, in the form of insurance premiums or pension fund contributions. Because of the regular inflow of funds and the ability of life insurance companies and pension funds accurately to predict their payments, liquidity is not an important problem for these institutions. And for these reasons, also, these institutions purchase mainly long-term financial assets to get the normally higher returns.

There are two major categories of life insurance. The first is *term insurance.* Term life insurance provides protection only over a specific period, or term, such as one year or ten years. If the insured dies within the period, the face value of the policy is paid to the beneficiary. Normally, at the expiration of the period, the policy has no cash value and while a new term policy can be purchased, the current, probably higher, rates will be applicable. The second category of insurance, including whole life, limited life, and endowment policies, is unlike the term policy in that these types provide insurance over the entire life of the insured and have a fixed premium over the payment period (which is the insured's entire life for whole life, and for a fixed number of years—for example, until age 65—for limited-life). The most important distinction is that the second category of insurance has a cash value against which the insured can borrow, which can be withdrawn, or which can be used to purchase a smaller amount of completely paid insurance with no further premiums.

Term life insurance is similar to other types of insurance such as most automobile, home owners, and health insurance in that it is strictly a purchase of insurance with no cash value or savings component. In the second type of insurance, the insured pays premiums greater than would be necessary just to buy insurance; this excess is savings and is reflected in the cash value of the policy. It is this savings component that makes life insurance companies truly financial intermediaries. Their term insurance business makes them like other insurance companies but does not make them financial intermediaries.

The 1975 financial balance sheet of the LIC sector is shown in Table 8–13. Their main liability is their reserves, which represent the funds necessary to meet the LICs' future obligations to policy-holders and their beneficiaries.[7] As indicated above, LICs have a small need for liquidity. Consequently, they have small levels of currency, demand deposits, and U.S. government securities. Since their liabilities are long-term, they hold mainly long-term corporate bonds and mortgages as assets. Because the guaranteed return on the savings component of their policy-holders' policies is relatively low, the return on these assets is adequate to cover the guaranteed return and other LIC expenses.

Insurance companies acquire many of their corporate bonds by *direct placement* (also called *private placement*). In direct placement, the LIC deals directly with the borrowing company (perhaps with the assistance of an investment banker) for the purchase of a large block of bonds at an interest rate and with other terms that are negotiated by the two parties. In direct placement, borrowers save the costs of registration with the Security and Exchange Commission (S.E.C.) and some under-

TABLE 8–13 LIFE INSURANCE COMPANY SECTOR (FINANCIAL BALANCE SHEET, SELECTED PARTS, END OF YEAR, 1975) (BILLION DOLLARS)

Uses of Funds (Financial Assets)	
Currency and demand deposits	$ 1.93
Corporate equities	28.06
U.S. government securities	6.16
State and local obligations	4.51
Corporate bonds	105.54
Mortgages	89.36
Policy loans	24.47
Total financial assets[1]	279.87
Liabilities	
Reserves	228.77
Total liabilities[1]	267.05

[1] The categories do not add up to the total because some categories are not included.

Source: Flow of Funds Data, Board of Governors of the Federal Reserve System.

---

[7] These reserves, while a liability of LICs, are not a source of funds to LICs in the way that the liabilities of commercial banks, SLAs, MSBs, and CUs are sources of funds to them. The sources of funds to LICs are the premiums paid and their returns on their investments, which provide the basis for the reserves.

The Domestic Financial System

writing costs but normally pay a slightly higher interest rate than if they sold marketable bonds on the open market. Companies whose bonds are not rated highly enough to be able to sell them on the open markets are often able to place their bonds directly.

Policy loans are a small but important asset of LICs. They represent loans by LICs to policy-holders based on the holders' cash values of their policies. Most policies have a provision for loans based on the cash value at a fixed interest rate stated in the policy. When market interest rates become high, policy-holders can borrow on their policy cash value at a lower rate than elsewhere. An increase in policy loans during times of high interest rates is a form of disintermediation for LICs. Table 8–14 shows that policy loans have increased during the credit crunch years of 1966, 1969, 1973, and 1974.

In total assets, the LIC sector is approximately four-fifths the size of the SLA sector and over double the size of the MSB sector. LICs may be either mutual or stock organizations.

During recent years, LICs have grown less quickly than have most other financial institutions. And in their overall growth, the growth in term life insurance has been more rapid than the growth in the cash value type of insurance. A possible explanation is that because the guaranteed rate of return on the savings component is low, and the policy value is fixed, people may be purchasing pure term insurance and investing the excess of the premiums that must be paid on cash value over the term policy premiums in other financial assets at a higher rate of return. LICs have begun to respond to this by offering "variable an-

TABLE 8–14 INCREASE IN LIFE INSURANCE COMPANY POLICY LOANS
(BILLION DOLLARS)

Year	Increase in Policy Loans
1965	$0.54
1966	1.44
1967	0.94
1968	1.25
1969	2.52
1970	2.24
1971	1.00
1972	0.93
1973	2.20
1974	2.66
1975	1.61
1976	1.40

Source: Flow of Funds Data, Board of Governors of the Federal Reserve System.

The Financial Institutions

nuity" policies in which the policy value and the annuity payments are tied to the stock market value or a cost of living index.

PENSION FUNDS

A pension fund is essentially a retirement fund. Typically, it is a program established by an employer to which both the employer and the employee contribute (although sometimes contributions are made only by the employee) while the employee is working for the employer and from which the employee receives a stream of benefit payments after a certain period of time, usually beginning at retirement. Usually, employee participation in a pension fund is mandatory and the employee has no access to the funds until retirement.

Payments into a pension fund are invested in a portfolio of financial assets, the return on which provides the funds for the benefit payments. Pension funds can be sponsored by either government units, federal, state, and local, or private units, mainly corporations. The federal Old Age, Survivors, and Disability Insurance Program (OASDI), usually called social security, invests its funds in governmental securities. The portfolios of state and local government pension funds are invested in corporate stocks and bonds as well as in U.S. government securities and state and local government securities (even though pension fund income is exempt from taxation). The portfolios of corporate pension funds may be administered by trust departments of banks, the corporations themselves, or life insurance companies. Some corporations invest their pension funds primarily in their own stocks and bonds. The financial balance sheets for private pension funds and state and local pension funds are shown in Table 8–15.

TABLE 8–15 PRIVATE PENSION FUNDS AND STATE AND LOCAL GOVERNMENT RETIREMENT FUNDS (FINANCIAL BALANCE SHEETS, SELECTED PARTS, END OF YEAR, 1975) (BILLION DOLLARS)

	Private Pension Funds	State and Local Funds
Uses of Funds (Financial Assets)		
Currency, demand deposits, and time deposits	$ 3.86	$ 1.70
U. S. government securities	10.76	6.81
State and local obligations	0	2.50
Corporate equities	88.56	25.80
Corporate bonds	37.81	60.89
Mortgages	2.38	8.25
Total financial assets[1]	148.88	105.95

[1] The categories do not add up to the total because some categories are not included.
Source: Flow of Funds Data, Board of Governors of the Federal Reserve System.

investment-type financial institutions

The principal investment-type financial institution is the mutual fund. When investors buy shares of a mutual fund they essentially buy shares of a portfolio of securities that the mutual fund purchases with the funds so received. The potential advantages to small investors of buying a share in a mutual fund instead of buying, say, a single stock, are that the investors get a more diversified portfolio of securities, get more expert management of their portfolios, and save on transactions costs because of the large quantities in which mutual funds trade. A mutual fund is also called an *open-end* investment company because mutual funds sell as many shares as they can. The value of a mutual fund's outstanding shares is the current value of assets in the fund's portfolios. Mutual fund shareholders can also redeem their shares with the mutual fund at the asset value of the share.

Mutual funds specialize in various ways. Some are *growth funds*—they emphasize capital gains and purchase mostly common stock, often speculative stocks. Others emphasize income and have mostly conservative stocks with high dividends and bonds. These are called *income funds*. Some funds offer a combination of growth and income.

Recent studies have indicated that mutual funds have performed no better or worse than stock market averages. Many analysts now claim that the transactions costs due to frequent purchases and sales of stock and the research and management costs of mutual funds do not benefit their shareholder. The response has been the development of low stock turnover mutual funds.

Table 8–16 shows the financial balance sheet of the mutual fund sector (open-end investment company sector). It is invested preponderantly in corporate equities and corporate bonds.

TABLE 8–16 MUTUAL FUNDS (OPEN-END INVESTMENT COMPANIES) (FINANCIAL BALANCE SHEET, SELECTED PARTS, END OF YEAR, 1975) (BILLION DOLLARS)

Uses of Funds (Financial Assets)	
Demand deposits and currency	$ 1.17
U.S. government securities	1.07
Open-market paper	1.51
Corporate bonds	4.77
Corporate equities	33.66
Total financial assets[1]	42.18

[1] The categories do not add up to the total because some categories are not included.

Source: Flow of Funds Data, Board of Governors of the Federal Reserve System.

The closed-end investment company is similar to a mutual fund (open-end investment company) in many ways but it differs because it issues a fixed number of shares which are not redeemable by the company. This sector is much smaller than the mutual fund sector.

The high interest periods of 1973 and 1974 served as a stimulus for a new type of mutual fund, one that holds money market securities, commercial paper, certificates of deposit, and U.S. Treasury bills in its portfolio. Because during times of high interest rates, short-term interest rates are higher than long-term interest rates (the term structure of interest rate curve is downward sloping) money market securities are attractive at these times. But because money market securities come in large denominations ($100,000 for CDs, $5,000 for commercial paper, and usually $10,000 for Treasury bills) and generally trade in much larger amounts, small investors find them out of their range. Consequently, money market funds were devised to permit small investors to invest indirectly in money market securities. Table 8–17 shows the financial balance sheet of money market funds. But during times of low or normal levels of the interest rate, short-term interest rates are lower than long-term interest rates and at times lower than deposit rates at commercial banks, SLAs, and MSBs. At these times, money market securities are not very attractive. Table 8–18 shows that the net share issues of money market funds have decreased and become negative as the high interest rate period passed and the recession began.

Trust companies and trust departments of banks, both of which manage portfolios of financial assets primarily for wealthy individuals, can also be considered investment-type financial intermediaries. Safety is the primary goal in the management of these portfolios. Common stocks dominate the portfolios but they also consist of corporate bonds, U.S. government bonds, state and local bonds, and mortgages.

The final investment-type financial intermediary is the real estate

TABLE 8–17 MONEY MARKET FUNDS (FINANCIAL BALANCE SHEET, SELECTED PARTS, END OF YEAR, 1975) (BILLION DOLLARS)

Uses of Funds (Financial Assets)	
Currency and demand deposits	$0.03
Time deposits (including CDs)	2.13
U.S. government securities	0.93
Open market paper	0.52
Total financial assets[1]	3.65
Shares outstanding	3.65

[1] The categories do not add up to the total because some categories are not included.

Source: Flow of Funds Data, Board of Governors of the Federal Reserve System.

TABLE 8–18 NET NEW SHARE ISSUES OF MONEY MARKET FUNDS (BILLION DOLLARS)

Year	Quarter	Net New Share Issues
1974	I	$ 1.1
	II	1.2
	III	3.3
	IV	4.0
1975	I	5.0
	II	0.2
	III	0.2
	IV	−0.2
1976	I	−0.1
	II	−1.3
	III	−0.2
	IV	0.6
1977	I	0.3

Source: Flow of Funds Data, Board of Governors of the Federal Reserve System.

TABLE 8–19 REAL ESTATE INVESTMENT TRUSTS (BALANCE SHEET, SELECTED PARTS, END OF YEAR, 1975) (BILLION DOLLARS)

Uses of Funds (Assets)	
Physical assets—Total	$ 7.30
Multifamily structures	2.41
Nonresidential structures	4.89
Financial assets—Total	11.64
Home mortgages	1.37
Multifamily mortgages	4.79
Commercial mortgages	7.02
Sources of Funds (Liabilities)	
Open market paper	0.83
Bank loans	10.52
Corporate bonds	2.10
Mortgages	2.02
Multifamily residential	0.67
Commercial	1.35
Total liabilities	15.46

Source: Flow of Funds Data, Board of Governors of the Federal Reserve System.

The Financial Institutions

investment trust (REIT) and is not a pure financial intermediary because many of its assets are not financial but real. The REIT industry began in 1960 with the passage of legislation that exempted REITs from federal corporate income taxes if 75 percent of their assets was in real estate, cash, or government securities and 90 percent of their income was paid in dividends. The balance sheet for REITs in Table 8–19 shows that in addition to purchasing mortgages, REITs purchase property directly, much of which is in turn mortgaged. In addition to raising money from equity issues, REITs borrow from banks, issue commercial paper, and use mortgages to finance property purchases.

During 1974–1975 several REITs became insolvent because they overbuilt apartment houses, office buildings, condominiums, and shopping centers. Since REITs borrow heavily from banks and several are owned by bank holding companies, commercial banks were severely affected by financial problems in the REIT industry.

finance companies

Finance companies make loans to consumers and businesses. There are three types of finance companies: sales, consumer, and business. Sales finance companies purchase installment credit contracts from the retail dealers who issue the credit. The sales finance company may be a part of the same parent company to which the retailer belongs. For example, General Motors Acceptance Corporation finances the purchase of cars sold by General Motors dealers. Or the sales finance company can be independent of the retailer.

Consumer finance companies make general loans to individuals, often with real estate or furniture as collateral. The interest rates on the consumer credit of these companies is higher than on the consumer credit of commercial banks or credit unions.

Business finance companies make loans to businesses, usually to businesses that cannot qualify for commercial bank loans. Typically, these loans are secured by inventories, accounts receivables, or other assets. The interest rates on business finance company loans is higher than that on commercial bank business loans.

The balance sheet of the finance company sector, which includes all three types, is shown in Table 8–20. Finance companies borrow both short-term via commercial paper and bank loans, and long-term via corporate bonds. Not shown in the table, however, is that they have a large amount of equity capital.

Many consumer and business finance companies are owned by bank holding companies.

TABLE 8–20 FINANCE COMPANIES (FINANCIAL BALANCE SHEET, SELECTED PARTS, END OF YEAR, 1975) (BILLION DOLLARS)

Uses of Funds (Financial Assets)	
Demand deposits and currency	$ 3.90
Consumer credit	46.11
Home mortgages	9.33
Business loans	39.03
Total financial assets	98.37
Sources of Funds (Liabilities)	
Open market paper	28.03
Bank loans	16.25
Corporate bonds	30.73
Total liabilities	94.28

Source: Flow of Funds Data, Board of Governors of the Federal Reserve System.

relevance of the institutions to nonfinancial business

The various financial institutions are not equally relevant to the business sector. SLAs, MSBs, and CUs neither lend to business nor accept the funds of business to any significant degree. Commercial banks are very important to the business sector because they make a large volume of direct loans to businesses of all sizes. In addition, the CDs of commercial banks are an important means of short-term business investment.

Life insurance companies are important to business finance because they make direct loans to business via the private placement market and also buy corporate stocks and bonds on the secondary markets. Pension funds, mutual funds, money market funds, and trust funds all purchase business securities on the secondary markets. Finally, business finance companies make loans to businesses that often have no other source of funds.

questions

1. What are the major responses of commercial banks to the business cycle? How have bank innovations contributed to this behavior?

2. Explain why the mortgage market exhibits such large variations

over the business cycle. What are the potential ways to reduce this volatibility?

3. Discuss the importance of life insurance companies as business sources of funds.

4. How would you expect the assets of money market mutual funds to vary over the business cycle?

5. Discuss the nature of the competition between commercial banks and savings and loan associations.

the financial
markets

9

This chapter expands on the discussion of financial markets that began in Chapter 2. As indicated, financial markets are the markets on which marketable securities are traded. Supply and demand determines the price at which these securities are traded and consequently the prices of marketable securities are variable, not fixed. Marketable securities are divided into capital and money market securities on the basis of their maturity. *Money market* securities have maturities of less than one year and the markets on which these securities trade are the money markets. *Capital market* securities have maturities greater than one year and the markets that trade them are the capital markets. After a brief introduction, this chapter discusses the general nature of the financial markets and then the individual capital and money markets and securities.

introduction

As discussed in Chapter 2, there is an important distinction between the initial sale of a security at its time of issue and subsequent sales or exchanges of the security. At the initial sale, the ultimate borrower receives funds from an agent with excess funds. This exchange provides the ultimate borrower with the funds needed to engage in real invest-

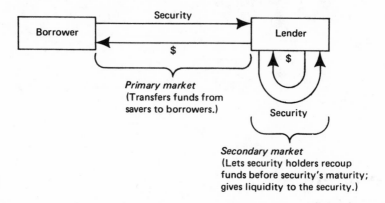

FIGURE 9–1   PRIMARY AND SECONDARY MARKETS

ment. The security at the time of initial sale is called a *primary security* and the market that facilitates this sale is called a *primary market*.

Initial purchasers of the security cannot recoup their funds from the initial borrower until the maturity of the security (and common and preferred stock never mature so purchasers can never recoup their funds from the issuer). But the holders of the security can recoup their funds by selling the security to a third party before its maturity. Securities exchanged subsequent to their initial sale are called *secondary securities* and the markets that facilitate these exchanges are called *secondary markets*. Secondary markets make a security more liquid since they enable the security's holders to recoup their funds before the security's maturity. But the maturity value of a security, if any, is fixed while its sale price if sold before maturity is variable and determined by the secondary markets.

The primary and secondary markets and their functions are shown in Figure 9–1.

the primary and secondary markets

The modes of exchange in the primary and secondary markets are quite different. And for each market, the modes of exchange differ among various securities. This section discusses the major types of primary and secondary markets in a way that is mainly unrelated to the specific securities. The following sections relate these general types of markets to specific securities.

SECONDARY MARKETS

The two different types of secondary markets are *organized exchanges* and *over-the-counter markets*. Organized exchanges are physical locations at which representatives of the buyers and sellers of the securities meet and exchange securities. The transaction prices are determined by a continuous auction for the securities and they change frequently as the supply and demand conditions for the securities change. The New York Stock Exchange, and the various regional stock exchanges are examples of organized exchanges.

There are two major types of participants in organized exchanges. One type, called the *specialist*, actually conducts the auction in one or more securities (they specialize in that they conduct auctions for only one or a small number of securities). In addition to conducting the auction for buyers and sellers, specialists also at times buy and sell the securities for their own accounts. Only firms that are members of an exchange (member firms) can buy or sell securities on an exchange. To become a member, a firm must purchase a "seat" on the exchange. These member firms and their employees are called *brokers* in the securities sold on the exchange.[1] An individual, or a nonmember firm, who wishes to sell a security on the exchange must contact an employee of a member firm who then arranges for the transaction on the "exchange floor" where the auction is held.[2] The broker never owns the security but only arranges for the exchange of the security. For arranging this exchange, the broker charges a *commission*, the broker's profit.

While stock brokers are related to the organized exchanges in stock, *brokers*, in general, are agents who arrange for exchanges of any assets between buyers and sellers and get a fee for this service but never take ownership of the assets. And not all brokers are associated with organized exchanges. For example real estate brokers arrange for real estate transactions without being associated with an organized exchange.

Over-the-counter markets are not physical locations like organized exchanges, but are essentially telephone connections among agents willing to purchase or sell specific securities for their customers. Specific firms or departments within firms make it known that they will "make a market" in a specific security. They do this by making available to the public their "bid-ask quotations," or prices they will pay to buy the security (bid price) and prices they will charge to sell the security (ask price). These *dealers* (the name for the market makers) buy and sell for their own accounts or portfolios; that is, they actually take possession of the securities. The difference between the bid price and the ask price, the *spread*, represents their profit. Of course, since they actually take owner-

---

[1] Actually the specialists also own seats on the exchange.
[2] There are exceptions to this, as discussed below.

ship of the securities, they can experience a capital loss if the prices of the securities they own go down.

The bid-ask quotations of different dealers in a security tend to be very similar at any time. Someone wishing to buy or sell a security will typically contact several dealers to get their quotes and sell to the dealer with the highest bid quote or buy from the dealer with the lowest ask quote. A dealer with a low bid quote or high ask quote would get few orders.

Dealers specialize in the types of securities in which they trade. For example, some trade only in stocks, others only in government securities. And the dealers may be members of a firm that only deals in specific securities or of other types of financial institutions such as commercial banks or investment banks.

Several characteristics of financial markets indicate how well they are performing their function. Three characteristics of secondary markets indicate the market's potential for capital gain or loss, its degree of market risk: depth, breadth, and resiliency. The *depth* of a market refers to how closely bunched the buy and sell orders for a security are around its last sales price. For example, if the last security sold at 60½ and there are buy orders of large quantites at 60⅜, 60¼, and 60⅛, and large sell orders at 60⅝, 60¾, and 60⅞, the market is said to be deep. Given these buy orders, the price of the security will not decline much before a buy order prevents it from falling further. And given the sell orders, the price of the security will not rise much before a sell order prevents it from rising further. If, however, there were buy orders only at 58, 55, and 52, and sell orders at 62, 65, and 69, the price of the security would have to either decline or rise substantially before there were buy or sell orders, respectively. The deeper the market—the more closely the buy and sell orders are bunched around the last transaction price—the less likely it is that the price will substantially increase or decrease. Of course, even closely bunched buy and sell orders can be withdrawn by their offerers if conditions change, thereby making substantial price changes possible.

The *breadth* of a market refers to the number of different types of investors supplying buy and sell orders. For example, if small individual investors, mutual funds, and trust funds are all placing buy and sell orders for a stock, the market is considered broad, whereas if only mutual funds are placing orders, the market does not exhibit breadth. It is thought that buy and sell orders from a broad market are less likely to be withdrawn at the same time than are buy and sell orders from a narrow market, because different types of investors have different motivations for investing. Consequently, a broad market should exhibit less price volatility; that is, it should have less market risk.

Resiliency refers to the tendency for a market to rebound after price changes in either direction, because of the placement of new orders which reverse the direction of the past price change. For example, in a resilient market if the price of a security declined sharply, new buy orders would be placed above the current price tending to reverse the decline. Resiliency refers to the depth and breadth of *potential* investors, investors currently "on the sidelines" but willing to enter the market under advantageous conditions, rather than to the depth and breadth of investors who have actually placed orders.

The *efficiency* of a primary or secondary market refers to how well the market is fulfilling its function of channeling funds from surplus sectors to deficit sectors. The *operational efficiency* of a market refers to the cost of supporting the market, how cheaply the market is performing its function. The cost of an over-the-counter market can be measured by the difference between the bid and ask quotes of the dealers, the spread. The cost of an organized exchange can be measured by the commission charged by the brokers (expressed as a percentage of the sales price of the security). These costs reflect both the costs incurred by the brokers and dealers in supporting the markets (they will not remain in the business unless they cover their costs) and the profit margin of the brokers and dealers, which in turn depends on the degree of competition in the markets. Improved technologies for placing and transacting orders and for record-keeping would reduce operating costs. An increase in the number of brokers and dealers and the removal of any restraints on price competition would reduce profit margins. In general, the U.S. financial markets are thought to be operationally very efficient.

The *allocational efficiency* of a market refers to its ability to channel funds to borrowers with the greatest need, as measured by their ability to pay the highest interest rates, and to charge interest rate differentials among borrowers that reflect their risk differentials. Allocational efficiency is difficult to measure. But some observers claim that the financial markets discriminate against small and less credit-worthy borrowers, because even though these borrowers are willing to pay higher interest rates which reflect their higher risks, at times no credit is available to them. If so, this reflects a high degree of risk averseness among market participants. Allocational efficiency applies to both the primary and the secondary markets. If there is no demand for a security on the secondary markets, it will be difficult to issue the security on the primary markets.

PRIMARY MARKETS

The mode used to issue new securities depends, to some extent, on the type of security. The *investment bank*, a type of financial institution not discussed in Chapter 9, is instrumental in most issues of corporate equities, corporate bonds, state and local bonds, and some issues of commercial paper. Investment banks also provide many other services to their business customers. Investment banks are so important to so many of the primary markets, they are discussed in some detail in the following section.

Investment Banks (IBs). Investment banks typically assist businesses in their issues of stocks and bonds in three steps: 1) the IB assists the business in designing stocks or bonds that can be easily sold to the public at a minimum cost to the issuer; 2) the IB then buys the stocks or bonds from the business; and, 3) the IB sells the stocks or bonds to the public.

The first step is called *origination*. The IB provides consultation to the business on the timing, the price, and other characteristics of the issue. Bonds are usually designed to sell at approximately their maturity value, $1,000, so the coupon of the bond must be set accordingly on the basis of the current yields of bonds of a similar type. Other characteristics of the bonds, as discussed below, are also determined. Since new issues of corporate stock will be paid the same dividends as previous issues, the price of the new stock must be set at least equal to the current market value.

In the second step, *underwriting*, the IB buys the issue from the business. By underwriting or buying the issue, the IB bears the risk of selling the issue and essentially provides insurance to the business that the business will get the agreed quantity of funds from the issue. Of course, the IB purchases the issue at a price less than it intends to sell them for on the market; this difference between the IB's purchase price and the anticipated market price, the spread, is the return to the IB for bearing the risk. For example, if a bond issue is designed to sell for $1,000 and the IB buys the bonds from the business for $990, the IB's spread is $10 or 1 percent. If the market price of the issue declines between when the IB purchases and sells the issue, the spread will be less than intended and perhaps negative, which means that the IB loses money on the issue. For example, if, as in the above example, the IB purchases the issue for $990 and can sell it for only $995 rather than $1,000, the actual spread would be $5 or about 0.5 percent; if it can sell the issue for $985 the spread would be −$5 or about −0.5 percent. Of course, if the market price rises during this period, the IB's profits would be greater than had been anticipated. For a large issue, one investment bank may not wish to bear the risk of the entire issue, so a *syndicate* of IBs each underwrites a portion of the issue. The lead IB in the syndicate, the IB that forms the syndicate, is called its manager.

A business can choose the IB, or syndicate of IBs, that underwrites its issue in either of two ways. In the *negotiated* method of selecting an

IB, the IB that provides the consultation to the company in designing the issue also manages the syndicate. The price the company receives for the issue is negotiated between the issuing company and the lead IB. By the *competitive method* of placing an issue, after designing the issue, perhaps with the consultation of an IB, the business auctions the issue. The IB or syndicate that offers the highest price to the business for the specific issue will be its underwriter. Most public utilities are required to select their underwriters by competitive bids.

In the third step the members of the IB sell or distribute the issue to the public. In practice, members of the syndicate sell some of their underwritten shares themselves and also solicit the assistance of other firms which specialize in distribution to sell some of the issue. The latter firms do not bear any risk but receive a fee for their sales effort. Often these firms are brokers or dealers in the security being sold.

To prevent declines in the price of underwritten securities during the distribution phase (and to protect against a reduction or elimination of the underwriting profits), the syndicate manager often attempts to *stabilize* the price of the security during distribution. It does so by placing buy orders for the security with the dealers or brokers in the security at a price equal to or slightly below the offering price. Such stabilization efforts may prevent temporary declines in the price of the security but cannot protect the underwriters against general declines in the security market prices. Consequently, underwriters attempt to sell their securities very quickly after they actually purchase or underwrite them. Many issues are 100 percent sold on the first day after the actual purchase by the underwriters. If the securities remain "on the shelf" of the underwriters because they cannot sell them at their planned offering price, three bad effects occur. First, the underwriter may have to take a loss to sell them. Second, in the interim the underwriters may not be able to participate in subsequent underwritings because their funds are tied up in the securities on their shelves. Finally, if there is a general "overhang" of underwritten securities with several investment banks, new issuers of securities will not receive as much interest from investment banks to underwrite their new issues and may, therefore, have to accept a lower price for their securities and a higher cost of issue.

In negotiated underwritings, IBs often begin soliciting orders for the securities before the actual underwriting to assure rapid distribution. In competitive underwritings, the orders are not solicited until the winning IB or syndicate is announced. Negotiated underwritings, then, provide more safety for the IBs and cause less consternation in the securities markets.

The total profits from a primary security placement are divided up among the manager or managers of the syndicate, the IBs that underwrite the securities, and the firms that distribute them. During recent years, on average, about 20 percent of the profits have gone to the manager or managers of the syndicate, about 30 percent to the underwriters, and about 50 percent to the firms that distribute the securities. Of course, the same IB may both underwrite and distribute the securities, and perhaps manage the syndicate. The total profits as a fraction of the dollar size of the issue, the *spread* for the issue, depends on the type of security issued. The size of these spreads for various securities are discussed in the sections below on the individual securities.

Table 9–1 lists the twelve largest IBs in the United States during 1974, by issues managed or comanaged.

Not all issues by businesses in which IBs participate are underwritten; in some issues only consultation and marketing support are provided. For small or new companies, IBs may not be willing to accept the risk of purchasing the issue outright and will provide only *best effort* assistance; that is, the IB will not purchase the issue but will make its best effort to sell the issue for the company for a fee based on the amount sold. (Securities issued in this way are also said to be sold on an *agency basis*.) Very large, credit-worthy companies may not wish to pay for the underwriting service and may, therefore, solicit only best effort service.

At times, new issues of common stock are issued, not through IBs, but directly to existing stockholders through "rights offerings," which are discussed below. In this case, the issuing company may also commission an IB to underwrite any shares that are not purchased by the existing stockholders. This is called a *stand-by agreement*.

TABLE 9–1   THE TWELVE LARGEST UNDERWRITERS IN 1974

Firms	Volume of Underwritings Managed or Comanaged (000 Omitted)
Merrill Lynch, Pierce, Fenner & Smith, Inc.	$9,614,559
First Boston Corp.	7,835,975
Goldman, Sachs & Co.	7,527,048
Salomon Brothers	7,287,167
Morgan Stanley & Co., Inc.	6,914,449
Blyth Eastman Dillon & Co., Inc.	5,674,451
White, Weld & Co., Inc.	4,493,706
Lehman Brothers, Inc.	4,416,542
Kidder, Peabody & Co., Inc.	4,410,946
Halsey Stuart & Co., Inc.	4,050,196
Dean Witter & Co., Inc.	3,725,849
Smith Barney & Co., Inc.	3,027,452

Source: *Investment Banking Arrangements*, The Conference Board, Inc., New York, 1976, p. 1.

State and local governments use IBs to issue their bonds in the same way businesses do. Under the Glass-Steagall Act of 1933, commercial banks are not permitted to participate in the issues of business securities; that is, commercial banks cannot also be investment banks for business. Commercial banks are, however, allowed to participate in the issues of state, local, federal government, and government agency securities.

Other ways of issuing securities include auctioning the securities and selling the issues directly to the investing public at a fixed price. These and other methods are discussed in the context of the specific securities that use them.

The primary markets can be evaluated according to their allocational and operational efficiencies, as discussed for the secondary markets. The spread for investment banks is a measure of their operational efficiency.

The next two sections discuss the individual capital and money market securities and their markets in detail. Each section examines the nature of the security, including the type of issuer; the primary and secondary markets for the security; the principal buyers of the security; and, the level of the interest rate of the security.

capital market securities

There are six types of capital market securities: 1) federal government securities; 2) federal government agency securities; 3) state and local government securities; 4) corporate bonds; 5) corporate equities; and, 6) mortgages. Each is discussed individually in this section.

TREASURY SECURITIES
(FEDERAL GOVERNMENT SECURITIES)

Nature of Treasury Securities. When the U.S. government runs a budget deficit, it must borrow funds to finance the deficit. The government borrows funds by selling securities issued by the U.S. Treasury. The Treasury issues several types of securities, some marketable and others nonmarketable. The major types of marketable Treasury securities are Treasury bills, notes, and bonds. Treasury bills have a maturity ranging from three months to one year.[3] Recently, the minimum de-

---

[3] Even though Treasury bills are a money market instrument, certain aspects of bills are discussed in this section on Treasury capital market securities.

nomination of Treasury bills has been $10,000 (and in multiples of $5,000 above $10,000).[4] Treasury bills pay no explicit interest but are sold on a *discount basis*. For example, if a one-year $10,000 bill is initially issued or sold for $9,400, the $600 appreciation during the year represents a 6.38 percent return.

Treasury notes have maturities ranging from one to seven years. Treasury bonds have maturities over seven years. Both notes and bonds have minimum denominations of $1,000. And both initially sell at (or approximately at) their maturity value rather than at a discount, and pay a fixed coupon every six months (they are called *coupon instruments* for this reason).

Treasury bills, notes, and bonds are, for the most part, in *bearer form*. This means that they are not registered by the issuer in the owner's name and because of this the bearer of the security can sell the security, and title changes with delivery without endorsement and without notice to the issuer. Bearer-type securities are essentially negotiable. Coupons are attached to bearer securities and must be presented to the issuer when interest is due.

Other securities, called *registered* securities, are registered by the issuer in the owner's name. Interest payments are mailed to the owner of record without notice and only the owner of record can sell the security. Treasury bonds and most issues of notes are also available in registered form.

The major types of nonmarketable Treasury securities are United States Savings Bonds, which can be of either the Series E or Series H types. Series E bonds are sold at a discount and appreciate over their five-year maturity. For example, a $25 savings bond is initially sold for $18.75 and is redeemed for $25 after five years, representing an average annual return of about 6 percent. Series H bonds are sold at par in denominations of $500, $1,000, and $5,000, and interest is paid semi-annually by check. Both Series E and H bonds are registered.

U.S. Retirement Plan Bonds and U.S. Individual Retirement Bonds are other types of nonmarketable Treasury securities individuals may purchase under certain circumstances for retirement purposes. Treasury bond investments and foreign series securities are large nonmarketable securities which are sold to large institutional investors and foreign governments, respectively. Of all these types of Treasury securities, only Treasury bonds and notes are properly capital market securities.

---

[4] At times, Treasury bills have had minimum denominations of $1,000. But because during times of high interest rates, many savers were withdrawing funds from banks, savings and loan associations, and mutual savings banks to purchase Treasury bills, the minimum denomination was raised to $10,000 to reduce this disintermediation.

Table 9–2 shows the composition of the public debt, by type of issue, at the end of fiscal year 1976.

This debt was issued to finance the budget deficits of the Treasury. Recent deficits are shown in Table 6–1. However, not all this debt affects the private financial system and the level of the interest rates. Some of the Treasury's debt is purchased by the Federal Reserve System in its implementation of monetary policy (the Fed must purchase Treasury securities to increase the money supply). A large part of this debt is also purchased by government trust funds, such as Social Security, and other government accounts. The remainder is purchased by financial institutions, nonfinancial corporations, individuals, and other investors, and it is this portion that affects the level of private credit and the interest rates. Table 9–3 shows the composition of the ownership of public debt securities.

Markets for Treasury Securities. The primary market for marketable Treasury bills, notes, and bonds is conducted by the regional Federal Reserve Banks and their branches. Treasury bills are sold on an auction basis. Treasury bills with maturities of thirteen and twenty-six weeks are auctioned every week (on Monday); bills with maturities of fifty-two weeks are auctioned on an irregular basis approximately every month. Tenders or bids are submitted by investors to the Federal Reserve Banks. The bids are expressed on the basis of 100; for example, a bid of 98.21 for a $10,000 bill represents a bid of $9,821. (Recall that a higher price represents a lower yield for the purchaser.) To choose the bidders to whom the Treasury actually sells, the Treasury starts with the highest bid and continues down the bid list until they have issued the desired quantity of bills. The Treasury also sells bills on a *noncompetitive basis,* usually to smaller private investors. Noncompetitive bidders state the face value of the bills they wish to purchase but do not submit

TABLE 9–2   INTEREST-BEARING PUBLIC DEBT, BY TYPE OF OBLIGATION, END OF FISCAL YEAR, 1976 (BILLION DOLLARS)

Total Interest-bearing Debt	$619.3
Marketable	392.6
Bills	161.2
Notes	191.8
Bonds	39.6
Nonmarketable	226.7
U.S. savings bonds	69.7
Other	157.0

Source: Economic Report of the President, 1977.

TABLE 9–3 ESTIMATED OWNERSHIP OF PUBLIC DEBT SECURITIES, END OF FISCAL YEAR, 1976 (BILLION DOLLARS)

Total	$620.4
Held by government accounts	149.6
Held by Federal Reserve Banks	94.4
Held by private investors	376.4
Commercial banks	91.8
Mutual savings banks and insurance companies	15.6
Corporations	25.0
State and local governments	39.5
Individuals	96.4
Miscellaneous investors	108.0

Source: Economic Report of the President, 1977.

a bid price. Rather they agree to pay the average price of the competitive bids accepted by the Treasury. Table 9–4 shows an excerpt from the *Wall Street Journal* describing the results of a recent Treasury bill auction.

If P_a is the price paid for the Treasury bill and P_m its maturity value the capital gain by holding the bill to maturity is $(P_m - P_a)/P_a$. This is the amount earned over the maturity of the bill. To express this return on an annual basis—that is, to annualize the return—this gain must be

TABLE 9–4 DESCRIPTION OF TREASURY BILL AUCTION ON MARCH 21, 1977

Yields are determined by the difference between the purchase price and face value. Thus, higher bidding narrows the investor's margin of return, while lower bidding widens the yield. The percentage rates are based on the discount from par and are calculated on a 360-day year rather than the 365-day year on which yields of bonds and other coupon securities are figured.

	13-Week	26-Week
Applications	$4,350,350,000	$5,611,335,000
Accepted bids	$2,101,290,000	$3,100,190,000
Accepted at low price	52%	80%
Accepted noncompetitively	$271,925,000	$139,545,000
Average price (Rate)	98.849(4.553%)	97.560(4.826%)
High price (Rate)	98.855(4.530%)	97.568(4.811%)
Low price (Rate)	98.847(4.561%)	97.556(4.834%)
Coupon equivalent	4.67%	5.02%

Both issues are dated March 24. The 13-week bills mature June 23 and the 26-week bills mature September 22.

Source: Reprinted with permission of the *Wall Street Journal*. © Dow Jones & Company, Inc. (1977). All rights reserved.

multiplied by a factor correcting for the number of times a bill of this maturity could be purchased and held to maturity during a year. This correction factor is $365/M$ where M is the maturity of the bill and $365/M$ the number of periods of duration M in a 365-day year. Thus, the annual return on a bill of maturity M purchased at issue for P_a is $(365/M) \times (P_m - P_a)/P_a$. This is the true annual return on bills and is called the *coupon equivalent yield* because this is the method used to calculate the return on coupon-bearing securities such as Treasury bonds and notes. However, the method used to calculate the quoted return on Treasury bills deviates from this "true" method in two ways. First, the return on Treasury bills is calculated on the basis of a 360-day year. Second, the total gain is calculated on the basis of the maturity value rather than the purchase price (this is called the discount method). The quoted return on Treasury bills is, therefore, calculated by $(360/M) \times (P_m - P_a)/P_m$, and is called the *discount rate*. It is the coupon equivalent yield that should be compared to other interest rates rather than the discount rate. The discount rate can be converted to the coupon equivalent yield by [5]:

$$\text{Coupon Equivalent Yield} = \frac{365}{360} \times \frac{P_m}{P_a} \times \text{Discount Rate}$$

Treasury note and bond issues are conducted irregularly after public announcements by the Treasury. Notes and bonds can be sold on an auction basis, in a manner similar to bills, and also by cash offerings, or subscriptions, and exchanges. In *cash offerings* the Treasury sets the terms of the issue including the issue date, maturity date, coupon rate, and the price at which the securities will be sold. Subscriptions may then be submitted to the Federal Reserve Banks and branches for this issue. They are accepted on a first come–first served basis subject only to the intended allotment by the Treasury.

At times, the Treasury also issues new securities in exchange for specific outstanding Treasury securities mentioned in the exchange announcement. Once the terms of the exchange are set by the Treasury, the exchange is at the option of the security holder. The Treasury can offer new securities in exchange for securities, either just before their maturity or for those whose maturity is not imminent. In the former case, called *exchange refunding*, the Treasury offers a new security instead of cash for a maturing security. To make the exchange attractive and to keep the amount of attrition (the securities turned in for cash) small, the Treasury usually offers a security with an attractive return. *Advance re-*

---

[5] The rates in Table 9–4 can be calculated as follows:
Discount Rate = (360/91) (100–98.849)/100 = 4.553
Coupon Equivalent Yield = (365/91) (100–98.849)/98.849 = 4.67
Coupon Equivalent Yield = (365/360) (100/98.849) × Discount Rate

funding, the Treasury offering of a new security for an outstanding maturity that will mature some time in the future, is used to lengthen the maturity of Treasury debt and to take advantage of current credit conditions without increasing total indebtedness.

The Treasury has used both the auction and subscription bases for its issues of new securities as well as refunding of outstanding issues in recent years. Obviously, a refunding has less effect on the financial markets than does an issue for new cash, because the former is just a rolling over of existing securities and does not take any new cash from the financial markets.

The secondary market for Treasury securities is an over-the-counter market. The market is made by a small group (about two dozen) of Treasury security dealers, some of which are departments of commercial banks and investment banking houses. The transactions in this extremely well-organized and efficient market are conducted by telephone and teletype. These dealers purchase and sell Treasury securities for their own accounts, making markets for customers by quoting firm prices or spreads at which they will buy and sell. Table 9–5 shows the quotes for the outstanding Treasury bills, notes, and bonds on March 21, 1977.

At the center of the dealer market is the group of dealers with whom the Federal Reserve Bank of New York deals in implementing the open market operations decided upon by the Federal Open Market Committee. These dealers, in addition to getting the added business from the Fed, get a current view of the Fed's actual trading.

Treasury security dealers, besides making the secondary market for these securities, also contribute to the primary market by making large purchases of new issues for resale to their customers.

The levels of securities held in the portfolio of the Treasury security dealers (their positions) and their purchases and sales (transactions) decline for longer maturity securities as shown in Table 9–6. The turnover of these securities is very high. As shown, these dealers sold more than their average holding of each maturity with the exception of "others within one year" during the week ending April 20, 1977.

Purchasers of Treasury Securities. Treasury securities are held by investors because of their low credit risk (their market risk depends, of course, on their maturity). Because of their lower credit risk, the return on Treasury securities is less than the return on other securities of equivalent maturity. Table 9–7 shows that commercial banks, nonbank financial institutions, and state and local governments hold the largest quantities of Treasury securities. Commercial banks and nonbank financial institutions hold Treasury bills as a form of secondary reserves. Households also hold large amounts of Treasury bills because of their low credit and market risks.

TABLE 9–5 QUOTES ON TREASURY SECURITIES

Monday, March 21, 1977

Over-the-Counter Quotations: Source on request.

Decimals in bid-and-asked and bid changes represent 32nds. 101.1 means 101 1-32. a–Plus 1-64. b–Yield to call date. d–Minus 1-64.

U.S. TREASURY BONDS

Rate	Mat.	Date	Bid	Asked	Bid Chg.	Yld.
6½s,	1977	Mar n..............	100	100.2	....	3.54
7⅜s,	1977	Apr n..............	100.7	100.9	− .1	4.55
6⅞s,	1977	May n..............	100.9	100.11	....	4.55
9s,	1977	May n..............	100.19	100.21	− .1	4.55
6¾s,	1977	May n..............	100.11	100.13	....	4.50
6½s,	1977	Jun n..............	100.13	100.19	....	4.47
7½s,	1977	Jul n..............	100.28	101	− .1	4.62
7¾s,	1977	Aug n..............	101.3	101.7	....	4.62
8¼s,	1977	Aug n..............	101.11	101.15	− .1	4.80
8⅜s,	1977	Sep n..............	101.21	101.25	....	4.88
7½s,	1977	Oct n..............	101.11	101.15	....	5.01
7¾s,	1977	Nov n..............	101.17	101.21	....	5.12
6⅝s,	1977	Nov n..............	100.27	100.31	....	5.18
7¼s,	1977	Dec n..............	101.12	101.16	....	5.25
6⅜s,	1978	Jan n..............	100.23	100.27	....	5.36
6¼s,	1978	Feb n..............	100.21	100.25	+ .1	5.35
8s,	1978	Feb n..............	102.9	102.13	+ .1	5.34
6¾s,	1978	Mar n..............	101.6	101.10	....	5.42
6½s,	1978	Apr n..............	100.29	101.1	....	5.53
7⅛s,	1978	May n..............	101.19	101.23	....	5.56
7⅞s,	1978	May n..............	102.13	103.17	....	5.57
7⅛s,	1978	May n..............	101.20	101.24	....	5.59
6⅞s,	1978	Jun n..............	101.12	101.16	....	5.65
6⅞s,	1978	Jul n..............	101.13	101.17	+ .1	5.69
7⅝s,	1978	Aug n..............	102.13	102.17	....	5.69
8¾s,	1978	Aug n..............	103.28	104	+ .1	5.74
6⅝s,	1978	Aug n..............	101.3	101.7	+ .1	5.73
6¼s,	1978	Sep n..............	100.18	100.22	+ .1	5.77
5⅞s,	1978	Oct n..............	99.31	100.3	+ .1	5.81
6s,	1978	Nov n..............	100.3	100.7	+ .1	5.86
5¾s,	1978	Nov n..............	99.22	99.26	+ .1	5.87
5¼s,	1978	Dec n..............	98.24	98.28	+ .1	5.93
8⅛s,	1978	Dec n..............	103.16	103.20	....	5.94
5⅞s,	1979	Jan n..............	99.24	99.28	+ .1	5.95
7s,	1979	Feb n..............	101.23	101.27	+ .1	5.96
5⅞s,	1979	Feb n..............	99.23	99.25	+ .1	6.00
7⅞s,	1979	May n..............	103.17	103.21	+ .1	6.03
7¾s,	1979	Jun n..............	103.11	103.15	+ .1	6.09
6¼s,	1979	Aug n..............	100.4	100.8	+ .2	6.14
6⅞s,	1979	Aug n..............	101.16	101.20	+ .3	6.14

TABLE 9-5—Continued

Rate	Mat.	Date	Bid	Asked	Chg.	Yld.
8½s,	1979	Sep n................	105.5	105.9	+ .1	6.21
6¼s,	1979	Nov n................	99.30	100.2	+ .2	6.22
6⅝s,	1979	Nov n................	100.24	100.28	+ .3	6.26
7s,	1979	Nov n................	101.21	101.25	+ .2	6.26
7½s,	1979	Dec n................	102.31	103.3	+ .2	6.27
4s,	1980	Feb	93.30	94.14	....	6.12
6½s,	1980	Feb n................	100.10	100.14	+ .2	6.33
7½s,	1980	Mar n................	102.30	104.6	+ .2	6.32
6⅞s,	1980	May n................	101.5	101.13	+ .2	6.38
7⅝s,	1980	Jun n................	103.5	103.13	+ .3	6.46
9s,	1980	Aug n................	107.5	107.13	+ .3	6.54
6⅞s,	1980	Sep n................	100.27	101.3	+ .4	6.52
3½s,	1980	Nov	90.28	91.12	....	6.18
5⅞s,	1980	Dec n................	97.18	97.22	+ .6	6.58
7s,	1981	Feb n................	101	101.8	+ .2	6.63
7⅜s,	1981	Feb n................	102.6	102.14	+ .4	6.65
6⅞s,	1981	Mar n................	100.20	100.22	+ .5	6.68
7⅜s,	1981	May n................	102.5	102.13	+ .2	6.70
7s,	1981	Aug................	101.6	102.6	+ .4	6.42
7⅝s,	1981	Aug n................	103	103.4	+ .3	6.79
7s,	1981	Nov n................	100.19	100.27	+ .4	6.79
7¾s,	1981	Nov n................	103.14	103.22	+ .1	6.81
6⅛s,	1982	Feb n................	97	97.8	+ .4	6.83
6⅜s,	1982	Feb................	98.10	98.26	....	6.67
8s,	1982	May n................	104.19	104.27	+ .5	6.86
8⅛s,	1982	Aug n................	105.2	105.10	+ .4	6.93
7⅞s,	1982	Nov n................	104	104.8	+ .4	6.96
8s,	1983	Feb n................	104.19	104.27	+ .3	6.99
3¼s,	1978-83	Jun................	82.10	83.10	+ .4	6.55
7s,	1983	Nov n................	99.21	99.25	+ .3	7.04
7¼s,	1984	Feb n................	100.19	100.23	+ .4	7.12
6⅜s,	1984	Aug................	96.6	97.6	....	6.87
3¼s,	1985	May................	77.12	78.12	+ .2	6.74
4¼s,	1975-85	May................	83	84	+ .4	6.84
7⅞s,	1986	May n................	103.6	103.14	+ .5	7.35
8s,	1986	Aug n................	104.2	104.6	+ .4	7.37
6⅛s,	1986	Nov................	95.4	96.4	....	6.68
3½s,	1990	Feb................	72.6	73.6	+ .2	6.62
8¼s,	1990	May................	106	106.16	+ .4	7.46
4¼s,	1987-92	Aug................	74.6	75.6	+ .2	6.89
4s,	1988-93	Feb................	72.30	73.30	....	6.69
6¾s,	1993	Feb................	95.22	96.22	+ .2	7.10
7½s,	1988-93	Aug................	99.26	100.26	....	7.42
4⅛s,	1989-94	May................	72.22	73.22	+ .2	6.74
3s,	1995	Feb................	71.16	72.16	+ .2	5.42

The Domestic Financial System

TABLE 9–5—Continued

Rate	Mat.	Date	Bid	Asked	Chg.	Yld.
7s,	1993–98	May..............	97.16	98.16	+ .8	7.14
3½s,	1998	Nov.................	71.14	72.14	+ .6	5.74
8½s,	1994–99	May..............	107	107.16	+ .6	7.70
7⅞s,	1995–00	Feb..............	101.20	101.28	+ .5	7.68
8⅜s,	1995–00	Aug..............	106.2	106.18	+ .6	7.70
8s,	1996–01	Aug..............	102.20	103.4	+ .5	7.69
8¼s,	2000–05	May..............	105.4	105.20	+ .6	7.73
7⅝s,	2002–07	Feb..............	98.22	98.30	+ .6	7.72

U.S. Treas. Bills

Mat.	Bid Discount	Ask	Mat.	Bid Discount	Ask
3–24	4.59	4.31	7–14	4.70	4.63
3–31	4.58	4.34	7–21	4.72	4.64
4– 5	4.54	4.34	7–26	4.74	4.64
4– 7	4.53	4.35	7–28	4.73	4.65
4–14	4.52	4.32	8– 4	4.76	4.68
4–21	4.54	4.36	8–11	4.78	4.70
4–28	4.54	4.36	8–18	4.79	4.73
5– 3	4.56	4.44	8–23	4.81	4.75
5– 5	4.57	4.47	8–25	4.81	4.75
5–12	4.57	4.45	9– 1	4.81	4.75
5–19	4.57	4.45	9– 8	4.83	4.77
5–26	4.57	4.47	9–15	4.82	4.80
5–31	4.57	4.45	9–20	4.88	4.80
6– 2	4.57	4.47	10–18	4.92	4.84
6– 9	4.57	4.47	11–15	5.00	4.92
6–16	4.56	4.52	12–13	5.05	4.97
6–23	4.60	4.52	1–10	5.09	5.03
6–28	4.64	4.56	2– 7	5.15	5.07
6–30	4.63	4.55	3– 7	5.14	5.10
7– 7	4.67	4.59			

n = Treasury notes

FEDERAL AGENCY SECURITIES (AGENCIES)

Nature of Agencies. As indicated, the U.S. Treasury is a substantial borrower. In addition, the federal government has also authorized several federal government-related agencies to borrow funds for certain specific uses. Some of these agencies are owned by the federal government and hence their debt issues have federal government guarantees. Among these are the Government National Mortgage Association

TABLE 9–6 U.S. GOVERNMENT SECURITIES DEALERS' POSITIONS AND TRANSACTIONS FOR WEEK ENDING APRIL 20, 1977 (MILLION DOLLARS)

	Positions	Transactions (Purchases and Sales)
U.S. government securities	$7,667	$15,260
Bills	6,566	9,502
Others within one year	278	163
1–5 years	403	3,366
5–10 years	216	1,905
Over 10 years	203	325

Source: Federal Reserve Bulletin, June, 1977, Board of Governors of the Federal Reserve System.

TABLE 9–7 HOLDINGS OF MARKETABLE TREASURY SECURITIES, BY SECTOR, END OF YEAR, 1975 (BILLION DOLLARS)

	Bills	Notes and Bonds*
Total outstanding	$219.0	$150.9
Total holdings, by sector		
Government-sponsored credit agencies	2.9	0.0
Federal Reserve System	52.4	35.5
Foreign	35.3	31.2
Private domestic sectors		
Households (Hold savings bonds of 62.9)	30.2	16.8
Corporate business	11.8	2.5
State and local governments	21.6	9.0
Commercial banking	48.5	36.8
Private nonbank finance	16.2	19.1

* This category includes a small amount of nonmarketable issues.

Source: Flow of Funds Data, Board of Governors of the Federal Reserve System.

(GNMA or Ginnie Mae), the Export-Import Bank, and the Farmers' Home Administration. The expenditures of some of these agencies are counted as part of the federal budget: they are "on-budget" agencies. Other of these agencies are "off-budget": their expenditures do not count as part of the federal budget.

Other federally related agencies are not presently owned by the federal government, although they were initially authorized by the government and some were owned by the government at one time. They are called government-sponsored agencies, and are presently owned by: investors in general, such as the Federal National Mortgage Association

(FNMA or Fannie Mae), whose shares are traded on the New York Stock Exchange; the institutions the agency serves, such as the Federal Home Loan Banks, whose shares are owned by savings and loan associations; or, by another agency, such as the Federal Home Loan Mortgage Corporation (FHLMC or Freddy Mae), whose shares are owned by the Federal Home Loan Banks.

Despite not having government guarantees, the debt securities of these government-sponsored agencies appear to be as acceptable to the investing public as those of government-owned agencies. In general, the yield on government agencies is somewhat greater than that of Treasury securities, but less than that of AAA corporate issues. Agency securities, thus, are deemed to have more credit risk than Treasuries but less than corporates.

Most of the government-related agencies are essentially financial intermediaries, borrowing funds from the investing public, the Treasury, or another agency and relending to those who qualify according to the agencies' objectives. Two principal objectives of these agencies are to provide agricultural credit (as do the Federal Land Banks, the Farmers' Home Administration, the Bank for Cooperatives, and the Federal Intermediate Credit Banks) and mortgage credit (as do GNMA, FNMA, FHLMC, and the Federal Home Loan Banks).

Table 9–8 lists the outstanding debt of the federally sponsored credit agencies at the end of 1976.

The public debt issues of government-owned agencies have decreased substantially since the creation of the Federal Financing Bank (FFB) by Congress in December, 1973. The FFB's purpose is to coordinate more efficiently the borrowing of the other agencies with that of the Treasury and to reduce the interest rates paid by the agencies on their borrowing. To achieve these goals, the FFB is authorized to raise its own

TABLE 9–8   OUTSTANDING DEBT OF FEDERALLY SPONSORED CREDIT AGENCIES, END OF YEAR, 1976 (MILLION DOLLARS)

Agency	Outstanding Debt
Federal Home Loan Banks	$16,811
Federal Home Loan Mortgage Corporation	1,150
Federal National Mortgage Association	30,565
Federal Land Banks	17,127
Federal Intermediate Credit Banks	10,494
Banks for Cooperatives	4,330
Student Loan Marketing Association	410

Source: Federal Reserve Bulletin, May, 1977, Board of Governors of the Federal Reserve System.

funds in the capital markets or borrow from the Treasury, and relend to the eligible agencies. Only agencies whose securities have government guarantees, however, are eligible to borrow from the FFB. The government-sponsored agencies, therefore, are not eligible. Most eligible agencies have eliminated their public borrowing and now borrow only from the FFB. And recently the FFB has been borrowing all its funds from the Treasury rather than by issuing securities to the public. Effectively, then, government-owned agency borrowing has been replaced by Treasury borrowing.

Markets for Agencies. The primary market for agency securities is conducted by government security dealers, investment banks, and commerical banks (commercial banks are allowed to underwrite agency securities). This process is similar to that described above for corporate securities.

The secondary market for government agency securities is an over-the-counter market and is conducted mainly by the same dealers who make the secondary market in Treasury securities. Quotes appear daily in the *Wall Street Journal* for the following agency securities: 1) Federal Home Loan Bank; 2) Bank for Cooperatives; 3) GNMA Issues; 4) Postal Service; 5) FNMA Issues; 6) Federal Land Bank; and 7) Federal Intermediate Credit Bank Debentures.

Purchasers of Agencies. The principal buyers of agency securities are commercial banks, savings and loan associations, mutual savings banks, and state and local governments. The Federal Reserve System also occasionally buys agency securities in the secondary market as part of its open market operations. These securities provide a slightly higher return than do Treasuries at only a slightly higher credit risk.

STATE AND LOCAL GOVERNMENT BONDS (MUNICIPALS)

Nature of Municipals. Bonds are issued by states, counties, towns, cities, and districts mainly to finance their expenditures. Such issues are called municipal securities; those with long-term maturities are called municipal bonds. The most important aspect of municipal bonds is that their coupon is exempt from the federal income tax. The coupons are also generally exempt from the state and local income taxes in the jurisdiction that issues the security.

There are two types of municipals. The first is called a *general obligation* (GO) or "full faith and credit" bond, which is secured by the general taxing authority of the issuing government. The second type is the *revenue bond*, which is secured only by the revenues generated from the project for which the funds were borrowed. Revenue bonds are issued by agencies responsible for providing water, highways, bridges, and other similar services, and are secured by the revenues generated from these specific services.

Municipal bonds are rated according to credit risk by the same agencies that rate corporate bonds. These ratings are based on the financial, economic, and demographic characteristics of the issuing jurisdiction. Traditionally, general obligation bonds have had higher ratings than have revenue bonds but the recent financial problems of New York City and other large cities have lessened their perceived advantage.

Many municipal issues are *serial bonds,* a single issue composed of a series of securities of varying maturities, from very short to very long. Typically, the longer maturities have a higher yield. Purchasers, then, can select the maturity and yield they prefer in the issue.

Purchasers of Municipals. During the last decade, municipal indebtedness has grown much more quickly than has federal indebtedness. Purchasers of this large volume of municipal securities tend to be in high tax brackets and purchase the securities because of their tax exemption. As shown in Table 9–9, commercial banks are the largest holders of municipal securities. Recently, however, commercial banks have been purchasing a smaller fraction of new municipal issues. One reason is that banks have developed alternative means of tax avoidance through such means as leasing, which permits use of the investment tax credit and the depreciation of the leased assets. Another reason for the reduction in the bank demand for municipals is mentioned below. There has been considerable concern that this reduced bank demand for municipals will cause higher yields on these securities and a thinner market.

TABLE 9–9 HOLDINGS OF MUNICIPAL SECURITIES BY SECTOR, END OF YEAR, 1975 (BILLION DOLLARS)

Sector	Holdings
Households	$ 74.2
Corporate business	4.5
State and local government general funds	4.4
Commercial banks	102.8
Mutual savings banks	1.5
Life insurance companies	4.5
State and local government retirement funds	2.5
Other insurance companies	34.3
Brokers and dealers	0.6

Source: Flow of Funds Data, Board of Governors of the Federal Reserve System.

Individuals in high income tax brackets and property and liability insurance companies are also large purchasers of municipal securities. Other types of life insurance companies have low or no income taxes and hold small volumes of municipal securities.

Markets for Municipals. The primary market for municipals is conducted by large, national investment banks, some small regional and local investment banks, and commercial banks, which are allowed to underwrite municipal issues. In most states, general obligation bonds must be sold to the underwriters by competitive bidding. The underwriting spread for municipals (the difference between the price paid by the underwriter to the municipality and the offering price by the underwriter) averages about 0.875 percent for general obligation bonds and about 1.125 percent for revenue bonds but varies with the quality of the issuer and the size of the issue.

The firms that make the secondary market for municipal issues tend to be the same firms that underwrite them. Dealers in the underwriting firms make an over-the-counter market in the issues. The *turnover* of municipals (that is, the trading on the secondary market relative to the amount outstanding) is much lower than that of Treasuries. Investors in municipals tend to hold them until maturity.

The yields on municipal securities, because of their tax exemption, tend to be lower than even the yields on Treasury securities as shown in Figure 7–19 in Chapter 7. However, the yields on municipals tend to fluctuate more over the business cycle than do the yields on Treasuries and corporates. A major reason is that most municipals are held by commercial banks, and commercial banks as a group tend to want to liquidate municipals during times of tight credit so they can finance business loans. At these times there are few buyers of municipals and municipal yields rise substantially. The thinness of this market causes the higher fluctuation in yields. For this reason also commercial banks have reduced their purchases of municipal securities in recent years. Essentially, banks have been keeping a smaller portion of the issues they underwrite. The serial nature of municipal securities also means that there is a smaller volume of securities at each maturity which reduces their marketability.

MORTGAGES

Nature of Mortgages. A greater volume of debt exists in the mortgage market than in any other sector of the capital markets. A mortgage is a security in which real property is used as collateral or backing to secure the loan. If the borrower defaults on the loan, the lender has claim to the property. Mortgages can be classified into four types according to the type of property used as collateral: 1) farm; 2) one- to four-family residences; 3) multi-family (apartments); and, 4) commercial property. Their volumes are shown in Table 9–10. Mortgage loans are long-term, running up to forty years in maturity.

The mortgage market is quite complex and only a few of its highlights are given here. One reason for its complexity is the degree of government involvement in it. The government became involved in the mortgage and housing markets because of the perceived social value of housing and because of the intrinsic problems of the mortgage markets, as discussed below.

The earliest form of government involvement was the government insurance of mortgages. With government insurance, the lender bears no risk even if the borrower defaults. Federal Housing Administration (FHA) insurance was initiated in the 1930s and is now being applied mainly to low- and middle-income housing. The Veterans Administration has guaranteed the mortgage loans of veterans since 1944. Lower down-payments are typically required of borrowers under each of these programs (that is, the loan-to-assessed value of the property is higher). Interest rate ceilings have also often been imposed by the FHA

TABLE 9–10 HOLDERS OF MORTGAGES, AMOUNTS OUTSTANDING END OF YEAR, 1975 (BILLION DOLLARS)

Holder of Mortgage	Home Mortgages	Multi-Family Residential Mortgages	Commercial Mortgages	Farm Mortgages
Households	$ 38.3	$ 5.8	$ 10.5	$18.1
U.S. government	6.9	5.9	0.2	0.5
U.S. government-sponsored credit agencies	31.0	6.4	—	16.0
Commercial banks	77.2	5.9	46.9	6.4
Savings and loan associations	224.7	25.4	28.6	—
Mutual savings banks	50.0	13.8	13.4	0.6
Credit unions	1.6	—	—	—
Life insurance companies	17.6	19.7	45.3	6.8
Real estate investment trusts	1.4	4.8	7.0	—
TOTAL*:	492.6	100.4	158.7	51.6

* The totals do not add up to the categories shown because some categories have been omitted.

Source: Flow of Funds Data, Board of Governors of the Federal Reserve System.

and VA for qualifying loans. Mortgage loans that are not FHA-insured or VA-guaranteed are called *conventional loans*.

Purchasers of Mortgages. As shown in Table 9–10, savings and loan associations, mutual savings banks, commercial banks, life insurance companies, and U.S. government-sponsored credit agencies are the primary holders of mortgages.

Markets for Mortgages. Several important aspects of the primary market for mortgages can be examined. One important distinction is between financing new construction and financing the change of ownership of old construction. For new construction, the financing during the actual construction is distinct from the financing after the construction is completed and the structure is sold to its initial owner. The construction financing is of a short-term nature and is usually supplied by commercial banks. However, before construction financing is provided, commercial banks often require the commitment of mortgage financing by another institution when the structure is completed and ready for sale.

The primary market for mortgages refers to the origination of mortgages, the finding of mortgage borrowers by the lenders. Some lenders originate their own mortgages. Savings and loan associations essentially originate all their own mortgages, make the mortgage loans, and often keep the mortgages until maturity. Other lenders, such as insurance companies, do not originate the loans they make. *Mortgage companies* (also called *mortgage bankers*) originate and often service mortgage loans (that is, collect the interest and principal payments) for institutional lenders such as insurance companies which do not have the resources or geographical distribution to originate loans. The mortgage companies identify the potential mortgage borrowers, perhaps arrange for interim commercial bank financing until the lending institution can make the mortgage loan, resell the mortgage to the lending institution, and often continue to service the loan. The mortgage company gets a fee for the origination and the servicing. Mortgage banks originate residential, commercial, and industrial loans.

The secondary mortgage market remains the least well developed of the secondary capital markets even though its development has improved substantially since the late 1960s. This lack of development can be attributed to the small size, great variety in quality, and local nature of the mortgage security. And the improvement in the secondary mortgage market since the late sixties has been primarily because of three government-related agencies: the Federal National Mortgage Association (FNMA), the Government National Mortgage Association (GNMA), and the Federal Home Loan Mortgage Company (FHLMC).

The FNMA, now privately owned, supports a secondary mortgage market by making advance commitments to buy mortgages, mainly from mortgage companies, on an auction basis. Although the FNMA originally purchased only FHA and VA mortgages, it now purchases conventional mortgages as well.

The GNMA, within the Department of Housing and Urban Development, was established in 1968 with one of its functions being to make real estate mortgage investment attractive to a broad range of investors. It has done this by guaranteeing securities issued by mortgage banks, savings and loan associations, and commercial banks which represent shares in a pool of FHA and/or VA mortgages. Purchasers of these "Ginnie Mae pass-through" securities get a share of the interest and principal from the pool of mortgages and the GNMA guarantee of the security assures prompt monthly payments.

The FHLMC, which is owned by the Federal Home Loan Banks, issues securities and uses the proceeds to purchase FHA, VA, and conventional mortgages, mainly from savings and loan associations. Savings and loan associations can use the receipts from the sales of these mortgages to originate new mortgages. The Federal Home Loan Banks also support savings and loan association mortgage lending by making loans to savings and loan associations, as indicated in Chapter 8.

The yields on conventional mortgages tend to be higher than those on corporate AAA bonds, as shown in Figure 7–19 in Chapter 7. But mortgage yields are less volatile and their movements tend to lag corporate yields. Mortgage yields also have lower volatility and longer lags than short-term interest rates and this is a major reason for the disintermediation and severe cycles in the housing market discussed above.

CORPORATE BONDS

Nature of Bonds. Corporate bonds represent the long-term indebtedness of corporations. Chapter 11 examines factors that affect whether corporations raise long-term or short-term funds, and if long-term whether it is in the form of debt or equity. This section discusses the nature of the corporate long-term debt issues.

Corporate bonds have fixed maturities, usually ranging from about ten to forty years. They have a fixed coupon set at the time of issue which is paid semi-annually. Most corporate bonds are in bearer form so they are easily transferable. Some, however, are in registered form. The most common denomination for corporate bonds is $1,000.

The legal conditions pertaining to a bond are specified in the bond indenture at the time of its issue. The indenture specifies the nature of the bond, including any possible restrictions on corporate behavior while the bond is outstanding, such as on dividend payments, working capital requirements, and debt-equity ratios. A *trustee*, usually an official of a financial institution, is one who assures that the corporation abides by the indenture. Unsecured bonds (that is, bonds having no specific assets as collateral) are called debentures. Bonds may also be secured by various types of assets. Bonds secured by mortgages are called *mortgage bonds;* those secured by marketable securities are called *collateral trust bonds;* and those secured by rolling stock such as railroad cars and airplanes are called *equipment trust certificates.*

Some bond indentures have *sinking fund provisions;* that is, they require that the corporation set aside a certain amount each year which is invested by the trustee and used to retire the bonds at maturity. Bonds issued as *convertible bonds* can be converted into the common stock of the company under certain specified conditions at the option of the bondholder, as discussed in the next section.

Another characteristic of some bonds refers to the right of the issuing corporation to repay and retire the bond prior to its maturity. This is referred to as *calling* the bond. One reason a corporation may choose to call a bond is because interest rates have declined since the issue and it could now re-issue bonds at a lower rate—this is called *refunding.* Corporations can also call bonds before maturity without issuing new ones, because, for instance, they have excess cash. Bond indentures usually specify a certain date before which the corporation cannot either refund the bond or call the bond for other reasons. This date is referred to as the *call date.* If a corporation retires a bond before its maturity, the price it has to pay to retire it is called the *call price.* The call price is usually at a premium over the maturity value. For example, if the maturity value of a 25-year bond is $1,000, a corporation retiring it after the tenth year may have to pay $1,030 for each bond. These call (or refunding) dates and prices are specified in the indenture.

Examples of bond description are shown below [6]:

Date Issued	Rating	Amount (million)	Issue	Coupon	Maturity Date	Call Date and Price
3/15/77	A	$250	Standard Oil Co (Ohio)	8⅜	2007	NR 87 – 104.52
3/ 9/77	Aaa	$210	South Central Bell Tel.	8¼	2017	NC 82 – 106.57

The South Central Bell issue cannot be called for any reason until 1982 (NC 82) and can be called in 1982 at a call price of $1,065.70 for a $1,000 maturity value bond. The Standard Oil issue cannot be called for purposes of refunding (NR) before 1987. However, it can be called for

---

[6] Bond Market Roundup, Week Ending March 25, 1977, Salomon Brothers, New York.

The Domestic Financial System

other reasons prior to that. Noncallability provides stronger protection to the bondholder than nonrefundability.

Obviously, the bond issuer would like to be able to recall the bond at any time. Bond buyers, however, do not want to have their bonds retired at the issuer's option, particularly if they bought them at a time when interest rates were high. Consequently, bonds with an early call date usually require higher interest rates to induce investors to purchase them.

Purchasers of Bonds. Financial institutions are the largest holders of corporate bonds. Of these, life insurance companies hold the largest amount, as shown in Table 9–11. The institutions tend to purchase bonds as new issues and hold them to maturity. This is typical because liquidity is not an important issue for insurance companies, pension funds, and retirement funds.

Markets for Bonds. Corporate bonds are issued on the primary markets in two different ways, *public issue* and *direct placement* (direct placement is also called *private placement*). Public issues are through investment banks, which use the mechanisms described above. Most corporate bond issues are underwritten by the investment banks. Competitive bidding for choosing the underwriter is usually required for public utility or railroad issues; other corporate issues are usually awarded to an investment bank by negotiation. Best effort arrangements and standby underwriting or convertible bonds are used less frequently. Public issues of bonds must be registered with the Securities and Exchange Commission and a prospectus for the issue must be made public; these requirements cause both a cost and a time delay.

TABLE 9–11 HOLDINGS OF CORPORATE (AND FOREIGN) BONDS BY SECTOR, END OF YEAR OUTSTANDING, 1975 (BILLION DOLLARS)

Households	$ 65.9
Commercial banks	8.6
Mutual savings banks	17.5
Life insurance companies	105.5
Private pension funds	37.8
State and local government retirement funds	60.9
Other insurance companies	12.2
Open-end investment companies	4.8
Brokers and dealers	1.4
TOTAL	317.2

Source: Flow of Funds Data, Board of Governors of the Federal Reserve System.

Direct placement is when new issues of corporate bonds are entirely sold directly to a financial institution, rather than to the public. Most direct placements are purchased by life insurance companies, although commercial banks and pension funds also buy direct placements. Often an investment bank serves as an intermediary between the issuer and the purchaser, for which the investment bank receives a commission.

The interest rate on direct placements is usually higher than that on public issues. However, with direct placements, the time delays are shorter and the corporation saves on the cost of underwriting (although if an investment bank finds the purchaser of the issue, the corporation pays a commission).

Often, corporations whose bond ratings are low cannot publicly issue their bonds because there is no market for them. But they can privately place their bonds directly with life insurance companies. Of course, the interest rates on these privately placed bonds would be high due to the high credit risk of the issues and due to the fact that rates on private placements are higher independent of credit risk. In addition, often other restrictions may be placed on the corporation by the life insurance company, such as on working capital, debt-equity ratio, and dividend payments which can constrain future activities of the corporation.

The underwriting spread averages about 0.875 percent for publicly issued corporate bonds and about 0.375 percent for bond issues privately placed by investment banks, but both spreads vary considerably by issue. Table 9–12 shows the volume of corporate bonds publicly offered and directly placed (privately placed) in recent years.

Direct placements of corporate bonds are at times competitive with commercial bank term loans, discussed in Chapter 8. Normally, commercial bank term loans extend only up to about seven years in maturity,

TABLE 9–12 VOLUME OF CORPORATE BONDS BY TYPE OF ISSUE (BILLION DOLLARS)

	Publicly Offered	Directly Placed
1969	$ 9.31	$ 4.43
1970	22.18	4.29
1971	19.78	6.58
1972	14.94	8.50
1973	12.40	7.73
1974	24.89	6.13
1975	30.16	10.17

Source: Statistical Bulletin, Securities and Exchange Commission, February, 1977, p. 31.

The Domestic Financial System

and directly placed corporate bonds down to about ten years. However, at times when both commercial banks and life insurance companies have excess funds, as during early 1977, the maturities of these two corporate sources of funds tend to overlap and they become competitive.

The secondary market for corporate bonds consists of both organized exchanges and over-the-counter markets. Virtually all of the bond trading on organized exchanges occurs on the New York Stock Exchange, and much of this is for convertible bonds. Most corporate bond trading, however, occurs on the over-the-counter markets. And, since most corporate bonds are purchased by financial institutions when issued and held to maturity, the trading on the secondary markets is small relative to the volume of bonds outstanding; that is, their turnover is low. Again, much of the trading is in convertible bonds. The secondary market for nonconvertible corporate bonds is, therefore, fairly thin. Despite this thinness, the bid-ask spread is narrow, partly because the volume of each trade is large.

Due to credit risk, the yields on corporate bonds are higher than those of Treasury securities of the same maturity, as shown in Figure 7–19 in Chapter 7. And, again due to credit risk, the yields on corporate bonds increase as the credit rating decreases.

CORPORATE STOCK (EQUITIES)

Nature of Equities. The first five types of capital market securities discussed have several similarities. Treasury, agency, municipal and corporate bonds, and mortgages have specific maturities, fixed coupon or interest payments, and in each the supplier of funds becomes a creditor of the security's issuer. Corporate stock (equities) never matures. This factor increases the importance of the secondary markets for equities in providing liquidity to equity holders. Corporate stock also pays no fixed return because the holder of corporate stock is an owner, not a creditor, of the corporation. And as an owner, the stockholder shares in the profits of the corporation, getting a high return if profits are high and a low or no return if profits are low. And in the event of the liquidation of the corporation, the stockholder, as an owner, gets no payments until the creditors are fully reimbursed.

There are two components of the total return on common stock. The first is the dividend payment, usually paid quarterly. The annual dividend divided by the current price of stock is called the *dividend yield.* It is analogous to the current yield for bonds. The second component is the capital gain or loss on the stock. The current market price of the stock reflects the future profits and dividends of the firm since stock has no maturity or maturity value. The *total yield* on common stock is the sum of its dividend yield and its annual percentage capital gain over some period. The capital gain for a stock is known only for the past and can only be estimated for the future.

Corporations also issue another type of stock called *preferred stock* which has some characteristics of bonds as well as of common stock. Preferred stock has no maturity date, like common stock, but has a fixed dividend or coupon payment, like bonds. However, although nonpayment of bond coupons is considered default, nonpayment of preferred dividends is not. But dividends cannot be paid on common stock until the past and current dividend payments on preferred stock are made. In the event of liquidation, preferred stockholders are paid after all creditors but before common stockholders.

Another corporate security that has some characteristics of both common stock and bonds is the *convertible bond*. Convertible bonds are essentially bonds that can be converted into the common stock of the issuing company at the option of the security holder under specified conditions. For example, if the convertible bond has a *conversion price* of $40, its holder may use the $1,000 maturity value of the bond to purchase common stock of the corporation at a price of $40 per share. The bondholder may therefore convert the bond into twenty-five shares of stock (this number is called the *conversion ratio*). If the current market value of the corporation's stock is $35, the convertibility feature is not of current value; if the market value is currently $45, however, the convertability feature is of value and the market price of convertible bonds will be higher than those of otherwise similar non-convertible bonds. Convertible bonds are bonds that can become stocks.

Purchasers of Equities. As shown in Table 9–13, the household sector has the largest holding of corporate equities. The "household" category in the flow of funds structure, however, includes bank-

TABLE 9–13 TOTAL HOLDINGS OF CORPORATE EQUITIES BY SECTOR, END OF YEAR, 1975 (BILLION DOLLARS)

Households	$630.5
Foreign	26.7
Commercial banks	0.9
Mutual savings banks	4.4
Life insurance companies	28.1
Private pension funds	88.6
State and local government retirement funds	25.8
Other insurance companies	14.3
Open-end investment companies (mutual funds)	33.7
Brokers and dealers	1.7

Source: Flow of Funds Data, Board of Governors of the Federal Reserve System.

administered trust funds and nonprofit institutions, so a portion of the amount shown is really institutional holding of equities. Other institutions, such as life insurance companies, private pension funds, retirement funds, and mutual funds are the other major holders of corporate equities. A shift in stock ownership between households and institutions has occurred during recent years, as Table 9–14 indicates. Households have been net sellers and the institutions buyers of equities. The decline in the direct holdings of households is even greater than that shown in Table 9–14 because commercial bank trust departments, included in the household category, have been purchasers of equities.

This increase in the institutional holdings of corporate equities at the expense of the household's share has caused two concerns for the equities markets. First, the buying and selling behavior of the institutions tends to coincide, thus causing larger swings in stock prices than if the households, whose behavior does not conform to that of the institutions, were larger traders. Second, these institutions tend to purchase stocks of select, highly rated corporations, leaving little demand for the stocks of smaller, less highly rated corporations. Rules defining prudent investments for institutional investors (often restricting investments to stocks of companies rated BBB or A and above) add to this selectivity.

Markets for Equities. Corporate equities can be issued on the primary markets in two different ways. The most common way is through investment banks, which sell the securities to the public. Investment banks underwrite most issues but for some issues best effort or agency arrangements are used.

New issues of corporate stock may also be sold directly by the is-

TABLE 9–14   NET ACQUISITIONS OF CORPORATE EQUITIES BY SECTOR (BILLION DOLLARS)

	1970	1971	1972	1973	1974	1975	1976
Households	$−0.8	$−3.7	$−4.5	$−6.9	$−1.2	$−1.8	$−2.1
Foreign	0.7	0.8	2.4	2.8	0.5	4.7	2.7
Commercial banks	0.1	0.0	0.1	0.2	0.1	0.0	0.0
Mutual savings banks	0.3	0.5	0.6	0.4	0.2	0.2	0.1
Life insurance companies	2.0	3.6	3.5	3.6	2.3	1.9	3.0
Private pension funds	4.6	8.9	7.3	5.3	2.3	5.8	7.1
State and local government retirement funds	2.1	3.2	3.7	3.4	2.6	2.4	2.6
Other insurance companies	0.2	1.1	1.8	2.4	−0.5	−0.7	0.7
Open-end investment companies (mutual funds)	1.2	0.4	−1.8	−2.3	−0.5	−1.1	−2.4
Brokers and dealers	0.1	0.1	0.2	0.4	−0.9	0.0	0.9

Source: Flow of Funds Data, Board of Governors of the Federal Reserve System.

suing company in three ways. The issuing company itself may sell the issue to the general investing public without using an investment bank. This method is often used by new, small, and financially weak corporations. Corporate stock is also often sold directly to employees as part of savings or stock purchase programs or to managers as part of an incentive program.

The most common type of direct sale of a new issue, however, is by a *rights offering*. In a rights offering, current stockholders receive a number of rights in proportion to their current stock holdings which enable them to purchase new issues of stock at a price below the current market price. Current stockholders are thus able to maintain their share of the ownership of the corporation if they desire. Some states require that new common stock be issued by rights offering. In some rights offerings, the corporation retains an investment banker to sell any shares not purchased by current stockholders (who do not "exercise their rights") with a standby agreement. Table 9–15 shows the values of corporate stock, preferred stock, and bonds issues which were underwritten, sold on a best effort basis through investment banks, and placed directly, in 1975. Table 9–16 shows the proceeds from new issues of common stock, preferred stock, convertible bonds, and nonconvertible bonds, by industry, in 1975. Note the importance of public utilities (electric, gas, and water) in common and preferred stock issues.

The underwriting spread for corporate stock issues averages about 4.5 percent, substantially higher than the spread for corporate bond issues because of the greater risk of underwriting corporate stock.

Secondary trading of corporate stock occurs on both organized exchanges and over-the-counter markets. There are two national organized exchanges, the New York Stock Exchange (NYSE) and the American Stock Exchange (AMEX) and eleven regional organized exchanges, the

TABLE 9–15 PRIVATE CORPORATE REGISTRATIONS, BY METHODS OF DISTRIBUTION TO THE PUBLIC—CALENDAR YEAR, 1975 (MILLION DOLLARS)

	Total Underwritten	Total on Best Effort Basis	Total Issued Directly
Common stock	$ 5,763	$ 856	$ 677
Preferred stock	3,073	0	15
Bonds, notes, debentures	29,907	345	776
TOTAL	38,771	1,200	1,491

Source: Statistical Bulletin, Securities and Exchange Commission, February, 1977, p. 38.

TABLE 9-16 ESTIMATED GROSS PROCEEDS FROM PRIMARY OFFERINGS BY INDUSTRY, 1975 (CASH SALES IN MILLIONS OF DOLLARS)

	Nonconvertible Bonds	Convertible Bonds	Preferred Stock	Common Stock
Total Offering	$40,328	$1,338	$3,458	$7,413
Publicly offered	30,162	1,331	3,088	7,178
Privately placed	10,166	7	370	236
Manufacturing	16,242	776	537	1,134
Extractive	648	30	75	875
Electric, gas, and water	9,654	4	2,521	3,714
Transportation	2,610	25	0	1
Communication	3,462	0	112	889
Sales and consumer finance	1,010	0	0	1
Financial and real estate	4,884	458	126	361
Commercial and other	1,818	85	87	440

Source: Statistical Bulletin, Securities and Exchange Commission, February, 1977, pp. 30–34.

main ones being the Midwest, Pacific, and Philadelphia-Baltimore-Washington exchanges. To be traded on any of these exchanges the corporation's stock must be "listed" on the exchange and the corporation must be registered with the exchange. Listing and registration requirements pertain to publishing adequate financial data, disclosing trading in the corporation's stock by its managers and officers, and minimum standards for the distribution of ownership and volume of trading.

The listing requirements are strictest for the NYSE and for this reason more large, credit-worthy corporations tend to be listed on it than on other organized exchanges. The AMEX has somewhat less restrictive listing requirements and tends to list smaller, often younger companies.

The regional organized exchanges specialize in trading stocks of small corporations that have a regional but not a national interest. But, the regional exchanges also trade in the stocks of some corporations that are also traded on a national exchange (called dual or multiple listing). In fact, most of the trading on the regional exchanges is in stocks that are listed elsewhere. Table 9–17 shows the relative sizes of the organized exchanges both in number of shares listed and in market value of their listings.

Many stocks are not listed on any organized exchanges but are

TABLE 9–17 SECURITIES LISTED ON EXCHANGES (DECEMBER 31, 1974)

Exchange	Common Stock		Preferred Stock		Bonds	
	Number	Market Value (Millions)	Number	Market Value (Millions)	Number	Market Value (Millions)
New York	1,543	$493,293	537	$17,762	2,380	$255,449
American	1,222	22,011	83	1,303	202	2,250
Boston	62	159	3	1	1	1
Cincinnati	6	11	4	52	7	67
Detroit	5	13	1	0	0	0
Midwest	28	208	8	79	1	13
National	102	145	0	0	3	2
Pacific Coast	62	1,089	8	31	22	373
Philadelphia-Baltimore-Washington	28	87	100	644	5	28
Intermountain	34	20	0	0	0	0
Spokane	27	7	0	0	0	0
Honolulu	19	353	7	7	5	6

Source: Securities and Exchange Commission, Annual Report, 1975, p. 196.

traded exclusively on the over-the-counter (or unlisted) markets. Dealers buy and sell these unlisted stocks for their own accounts by making public bid-ask quotes for the stocks in which they make a market. Over-the-counter dealers in stocks must be members of the National Association of Security Dealers (NASD), an organization which self-regulates the over-the-counter markets in corporate securities. There are about 3,700 firms in the NASD. In 1971 the NASD established a quotation system (the National Association of Security Dealers Automated Quotation or NASDAQ) for over-the-counter stocks, which is an automated system for providing stock sales prices and volumes. One effect of the NASDAQ has been to narrow the bid-ask spreads in over-the-counter trading.

At the end of 1974, there were 2,593 stock issues in the NASDAQ system, approximately the same number listed on the organized exchanges (see Table 9–17). Many other stocks traded on over-the-counter markets, however, do not have sufficient trading volume to be included in the NASDAQ system: about 4,500 additional over-the-counter stocks are listed in the National Quotations Board pink sheets. However, the share volume traded on the organized exchanges was much greater. During 1974, 1.2 billion shares were traded over-the-counter while 4.9 billion were traded on the organized exchanges.[7] In dollar value of ex-

---

[7] Securities and Exchange Commission, Annual Report, 1974, pp. 158–59.

The Domestic Financial System

change, the difference was even greater because the average stock price on the organized exchanges is greater than on the over-the-counter markets. This is the opposite of the corporate bond market, in which most of the volume and value of bond trading is on the over-the-counter markets. The stocks of some large corporations, however, particularly commercial banks and life insurance companies, continue to be sold mostly on over-the-counter markets.

Not all listed stocks are traded only on organized exchanges. The so-called *third market* in stock transactions refers to dealers who have an inventory of stocks that are listed on exchanges and make an over-the-counter market in these stocks. Much of the third market trading is in large blocks (10,000 shares or more) of stock. During 1975, the value of stocks listed on the NYSE but traded over the counter was 6.0 percent of the value of trading on the NYSE (this ratio was 4.6 percent in terms of number of shares traded).[8]

The *fourth market* in stock trading refers to direct stock trades between institutions without the services of brokers or dealers. This market remains small.

As indicated in the last section, most bonds are purchased at issue and held to maturity and so the turnover of bonds is low. For comparison, the turnover of stocks and bonds listed on the NYSE is shown in Table 9–18. During 1974, 22.9 percent of the value of stocks but only 2.5 percent of the bonds listed on the NYSE were exchanged.

Table 9–16 shows that there is a much greater volume of new issues of bonds than of stock. Table 9–18 shows the volume of secondary trading of stocks is much greater than that of bonds. Consequently, the primary market dominates the market for bonds while the secondary market dominates the market for stocks. A casual reading of any financial periodical, such as the *Wall Street Journal*, confirms this. Most attention is devoted to the secondary market for stocks and the primary market for bonds.

TABLE 9–18 TURNOVER OF STOCKS AND BONDS, 1974

	Stocks	Bonds
Dollar value exchanged (million dollars)	$118,252	$ 6,457
Dollar value of securities listed (million dollars)	517,396	258,189
Turnover	.229	.025

Source: Securities and Exchange Commission, Annual Report, 1975, pp. 192 and 196.

---

[8] Statistical Bulletin, Securities and Exchange Commission, December 1976, p. 602.

Yield on Equities. The return to common stocks can be measured either by the dividend yield or by the total yield as discussed earlier. The dividend yield is analogous to the current yield on bonds; the total yield is analogous to the yield to maturity on bonds. Common stocks and bonds are comparable in the sense that both pay a periodic payment to their holders (quarterly dividend on common stocks and semi-annual coupon on bonds). The major differences, however, in this context are that common stocks have no maturity and maturity value, and so no yield to maturity can be determined, and also that the coupon payment on bonds is fixed but the dividend payment on common stock is variable and depends on the profits of the firm. Despite these differences, the same forces should tend to affect both stock and bond prices, since they are alternative assets in an investment portfolio. When interest rates increase, bond prices decrease. Stock prices should also decrease for the same reason, unless the dividend payments have increased significantly.

Before the mid-1960s, stock and bond prices moved fairly independently. And the total return on stocks, including capital gains, was considerably greater than the return on bonds (on average, about 4 to 5 percent higher). Since about 1965, however, two changes have developed in the relationship between stock and bond yields. Bond yields have increased substantially and stock yields, both dividend yields and the total yields, have declined so that the bond yield is now greater than the stock yield. In addition, movements in stock and bond prices tend to be much more similar.

Figure 9–2 shows the similarity in the recent movements in the yield to maturity on bonds and the dividend yield on stocks. Only shifts between stocks and bonds by investors, a general form of arbitrage, could cause these yield movements to be so similar. The price movements of these two securities move inversely to the yield movements. (This is always the case for bonds; it is also true in the short-run for stocks because dividend payments change slowly.) Of course, the total yield on stocks is the dividend yield shown plus the capital gain. But the net change in stock prices over the period covered in Figure 9–2 has been very small and so the total yield on stocks is approximately equal to the dividend yield.[9]

Stock and bond yields have not always been related in these ways. As Figure 9–3 indicates, before about 1960 the dividend yield on common stock was above the corporate AAA bond yield. And since about 1965 the spread in favor of bonds has widened substantially. The shift

---

[9] If bonds are not held until maturity, there can also be a capital loss on bonds even though their yield to maturity increases. When interest rates increase, the yield to maturity increases but the current bond price decreases, producing a capital loss if sold.

Dividend yields on the 30 stocks in the Dow Jones industrial average during
May averaged 4.69%, compared with a 7.79% average yield on Barron's best-
grade corporate bonds.

FIGURE 9–2 STOCK AND BOND YIELDS

Source: Reprinted with permission of the *Wall Street Journal*. © Dow Jones & Company, Inc. (1977). All rights reserved.

in the difference between the returns on the two securities is even more
pronounced when it is recalled that the percentage annual capital gains
on common stock were much larger before 1965 than after, as shown in
Figure 9–4. In addition, Figure 9–3 reveals that these two yields did not
change as similarly before 1965 as they have since.

Why has the relationship between stock and bond yields changed?
Although this question is still being debated, some aspects of the answer
seem clear. Interest rates have risen significantly since 1965, mainly because of inflation. The rise in interest rates has made the yield to maturity on bonds more attractive relative to stock returns.

Whereas many institutions and individuals did not hold significant
amounts of bonds in their portfolios before the mid-1960s because of

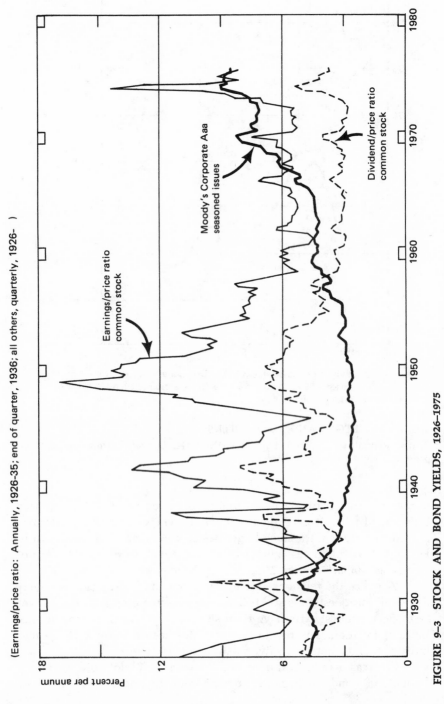

(Earnings/price ratio: Annually, 1926–35; end of quarter, 1936; all others, quarterly, 1926–)

Percent per annum

Earnings/price ratio common stock

Moody's Corporate Aaa seasoned issues

Dividend/price ratio common stock

FIGURE 9–3 STOCK AND BOND YIELDS, 1926–1975

Source: Historical Chart Book, Board of Governors of the Federal Reserve System.

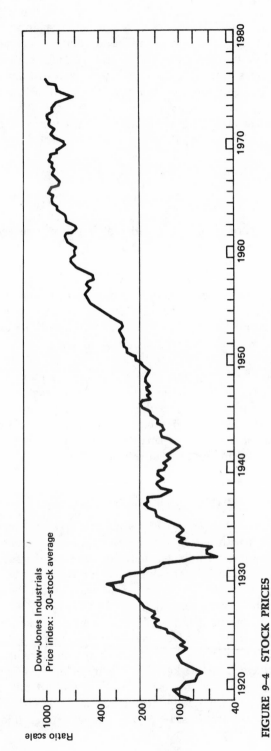

FIGURE 9-4 STOCK PRICES

Source: Historical Chart Book, Board of Governors of the Federal Reserve System.

the low return on bonds, they now hold substantial quantities of bonds and readily shift between stocks and bonds due to changes in their relative yields. Life insurance companies and individuals have both exhibited such changes in their portfolio behavior. And with investors now frequently shifting between stocks and bonds, their prices and yields tend to move together. When bonds and stocks were not portfolio substitutes, their prices and yields were independent of each other.

money market securities

Money market securities have maturities of less than one year. Therefore, short-term interest rates are determined in the money markets.

Capital and money market securities can also be distinguished in other ways than maturity. First, the money market securities are in general of much larger denominations. For this and other reasons the money markets tend to be more specialized and attract fewer but larger investors. As a result the money markets remain mostly unregulated by the government, whereas the capital markets operate under many government regulations.

No organized exchanges exist in the secondary money markets—all secondary trading is done on over-the-counter markets. The primary markets differ considerably among the various money market securities. Because of the expertise of its participants, the money markets are very competitive and the spreads are small. The various money market securities are discussed individually in this section.

TREASURY SECURITIES

Treasury money market securities include Treasury bills—that is, Treasury securities with less than one year maturity at time of issue—and Treasury securities with longer maturities at time of issue that have matured until they have less than one year until maturity. Most aspects of Treasury money market securities are discussed above in the section on Treasury capital market securities.

The most important aspect of Treasury money market securities is that they are essentially risk-free, certainly the most risk-free of any marketable security. They have no credit risk and, because of their short maturity, they have little market risk. Their yields vary considerably over time. At times of low interest rates, the Treasury bill rate is less than the Regulation Q ceiling rates on commercial bank passbook savings accounts, as was the case in early 1977. At times of high interest rates, the Treasury bill rate is higher than the Treasury bond rate, as it was in 1974. (The behavior of short-term interest rates is discussed in Chapter 7.)

Low risk is the major inducement to purchase Treasury money market securities. Commercial banks and other depository financial institutions use them as a form of secondary reserves. Households and state and local governments also hold substantial amounts as shown in Table 9–7.

Treasury bills are sold on an auction basis. The lowest accepted bid price is called the *stop-out price*. The principal buyers of bills on the auction are commercial banks, securities dealers, and the government trust accounts; noncompetitive bids by smaller, less experienced investors account for about 20 percent of the purchases.

SHORT-TERM AGENCY SECURITIES

Several government-related agencies that issue capital market securities are discussed above. The securities of these same agencies have also become important money market securities in recent years. Some agencies, such as the Federal Intermediate Credit Banks and the Banks for Corporations, issue securities with an initial maturity of one year or less. In addition, all securities with longer initial maturities eventually mature until they have less than one year until maturity and are then traded on the money markets. The yields on these securities are slightly greater than the yields on Treasury money market securities, because of higher credit risk and lower marketability.

SHORT-TERM MUNICIPAL SECURITIES

Traditionally, most state and local government debt issues have been long term. In recent years, however, governments have been issuing substantial amounts of short-term debt. For some governments, this has been interpreted as a sign of financial weakness, particularly in the case of New York City. One particular type of short-term issue is called the *tax anticipation bill* (TAB; the TAN or tax anticipation note is the intermediate term equivalent), which is an issue that will be retired with tax collections that are anticipated to occur at the time of maturity of the bill. The return on these issues is exempt from federal taxation.

Both initial short-term issues and longer-term municipal issues that have matured sufficiently that they have less than one year until maturity are traded on the money markets. The secondary market for municipal money market securities is the same as for the municipal capital market securities and is, as is that of the capital market securities, relatively thin.

COMMERCIAL PAPER

Commercial paper is important because it is the only money market instrument by which nonbank corporations can raise funds. Only the United States and Canada have marketable short-term business liabilities.

Commercial paper is unsecured; that is, it has no collateral. But at times the issuing corporation has an open line of credit at a commercial bank equal to the amount of the issue that assures it will be able to repay the lender at maturity. Commercial paper is short term, ranging from three days to 270 days. Any corporate security with a maturity of 270 days or less is exempt from Securities and Exchange Commission registration and prospectus requirements; therefore, the maturity of commercial paper never exceeds 270 days. Most commercial paper is issued in denominations of $100,000 and higher, although some is available in smaller denominations.

Only the largest and most highly rated corporations have a market for their commercial paper. Consequently, only a few hundred industrial corporations, public utilities, finance companies, and bank holding companies can sell commercial paper. Both Standard and Poor's and Moody's rate commercial paper issues. The grades usually acceptable to commercial paper investors are Standard and Poor's A–1, A–2, and A–3 and Moody's Prime–1, Prime–2, and Prime–3. Because of the high quality of the issuing corporations, commercial paper has usually been regarded as a very safe investment. However, the default of the Penn-Central Transportation Company on its commercial paper in the spring of 1970 raised concern about commercial paper's credit risk.

Commercial paper is usually sold on a discount basis; that is, it is sold at less than its maturity value, with no explicit interest or coupon payments.

Commercial paper can be initially placed (on the primary market) in either of two ways. Some corporations that regularly issue large amounts of commercial paper use their own staffs to sell the issues. This method is called *direct placement* and is used mostly by finance companies involved in financing personal loans, inventories, accounts receivables, and so on.

Most corporations do not issue sufficiently large volumes of commercial paper on a regular basis to be able effectively to employ their own staffs. They use dealers who sell commercial paper for many corporations to sell their commercial paper—this is called *dealer placed* paper. Even though many more corporations use dealers than use direct placement, about two-thirds of the total value of commercial paper placed is by direct placement. The dealer placed share has been increasing, however. Data on the nature of the issuers and the type of placement are shown in Table 9–19.

TABLE 9–19 COMMERCIAL PAPER OUTSTANDING, BY METHOD OF ISSUE AND TYPE OF ISSUER, END OF YEAR, 1974 (BILLION DOLLARS)

Directly placed paper	$31.6
Bank affiliates	6.1
Finance companies	25.3
Real estate investment trusts	0.2
Dealer placed paper	16.5
Corporate business	11.2
Bank affiliates	1.2
Finance companies	3.4
Real estate investment trusts	0.8
Total	48.1

Source: Flow of Funds Data, Board of Governors of the Federal Reserve System.

The main purchasers of commercial paper are nonfinancial corporate businesses, households, commercial banks, life insurance companies, investment companies, and foreigners, as shown in Table 9–20 (the data in Table 9–20 also include bankers' acceptances, a similar security discussed next).

At time of issue, the maturity of commercial paper is often tailored to the purchaser's needs, particularly in the case of direct placement. For example, if a lender has funds available for thirty-eight days, commercial paper with this maturity will be sold to the lender. Because commercial paper is often tailored to the maturity needs of the lender and be-

TABLE 9–20 HOLDINGS OF COMMERCIAL PAPER AND BANKERS' ACCEPTANCES BY SECTOR, END OF YEAR OUTSTANDING, 1975 (BILLION DOLLARS)

Total Holdings	$66.4
Households	6.8
Corporate business	27.9
Monetary authorities	1.1
Commercial banking	10.3
Savings and loan associations	2.7
Mutual savings banks	1.1
Life insurance companies	4.8
Investment companies	1.5
Money market mutual funds	0.5
Foreign	8.4

Source: Flow of Funds Data, Board of Governors of the Federal Reserve System.

The Financial Markets

cause of its short maturity, there is little secondary trading in commercial paper. However, usually the dealer who places the paper for other corporations or the corporation that places it directly will supply bid-ask quotes on the paper they place. Consequently, there is a fair secondary market for commercial paper, particularly dealer placed paper.

Because of credit risk, the commercial paper rate is higher than the Treasury bill rate. But these rates tend to move synchronously as shown in Figure 7–18 in Chapter 7.

BANKERS' ACCEPTANCES

The next three money market instruments discussed—bankers' acceptances, certificates of deposit, and federal funds—are all liabilities of commercial banks. Bankers' acceptances and certificates of deposit trade on secondary markets in which any investors can participate; only commercial banks (and some other financial institutions) can participate in the federal funds market.

Bankers' acceptances are generated mainly in international trade. Consider the following example. A U.S. firm is importing coffee from a Brazilian firm. The Brazilian exporter would like to receive its funds at time of shipment or delivery. The U.S. importer may not be able to pay for the coffee until ninety days after receipt of the coffee, the time it takes to process and sell the coffee. The bankers' acceptance is a device that allows the exporter to receive its funds at time of delivery without requiring the importing firm to supply the funds until ninety days later. A third party provides the interim financing.

The exporter, through its Brazilian bank, draws a draft on the U.S. importer, which when signed by the importer, obligates the importer to pay the agreed amount at a certain time, say ninety days after receipt of the coffee. The U.S. importer then presents this draft to its U.S. bank which "accepts" the draft, which means that the bank agrees to pay the exporter the stated amount in ninety days if the importer does not pay. Once this draft is accepted by a U.S. bank, the draft has sufficient credit standing that it can be sold to an investor, or marketed. This accepted draft is the bankers' acceptance. The exporter then immediately sells the bankers' acceptance and gets its funds immediately. But the importer does not have to pay the draft until ninety days hence. The acceptance is initially sold by the exporter at a discount so that the purchaser earns a return by holding it until its maturity.

The accepting bank derives its security from the fact that it typically accepts drafts only of firms with good credit risk and also that before accepting the draft it requires the shipping or ownership documents for the imports. And for providing its name and credit standing to the draft, the bank gets a commission.

Most bankers' acceptances have maturities of from thirty to 180 days. And even though most bankers' acceptances are based on international trade, some are based on domestic trade or dollar exchange between banks of different countries. The main purchasers of commercial paper—shown in Table 9–20—tend also to be the major investors in bankers' acceptances. In addition, commercial banks tend to be major purchasers of their own acceptances, as Table 9–21 indicates.

Active trading occurs in bankers' acceptances and consequently there is a well-developed secondary market for them. Because commercial paper is a short-term obligation of very credit-worthy corporations and bankers' acceptances are a short-term obligation of credit-worthy commercial banks, interest rates on these securities tend to be very similar.

CERTIFICATES OF DEPOSIT

Certificates of deposit (CDs) are depository liabilities of commercial banks. Passbook savings accounts are also depository liabilities of commercial banks but some important distinctions are apparent between them and CDs. First, CDs are negotiable; that is, the ownership of the CD can be legally transferred to another holder. Second, the CDs can be exchanged on a secondary market. And third, since mid-1973 there have been no Regulation Q interest rate ceilings on negotiable CDs of denominations of $100,000 or more and with maturities of one year or less.[10] These three characteristics make CDs a money market instrument

TABLE 9–21 HOLDINGS OF BANKERS' ACCEPTANCES, APRIL, 1977
(MILLION DOLLARS)

Total banker's acceptances	$22,544
Held by:	
Accepting banks	7,410
Own acceptances	6,032
Acceptances bought	1,378
Federal reserve banks	
Own account	881
Foreign correspondents	394
Others	13,858

Source: Federal Reserve Bulletin, June, 1977, Board of Governors of the Federal Reserve System.

---

[10] Actually, the Regulation Q ceilings on CDs with denominations of $100,000 or more and maturities of less than ninety days were suspended on June 24, 1970; the ceilings on CDs with the same denominations and maturities of ninety days or greater were suspended on May 16, 1973.

very akin to bankers' acceptances and commercial paper. And the yields on these three securities are very similar.

Prior to 1961, certificates of deposit were nonnegotiable because of the implicit agreement between the issuing bank and the depositor that the ownership of the deposit could not be legally transferred. They were nonmarketable because no secondary market existed. But in February 1961, the First National City Bank of New York began offering CDs that were negotiable. And at the same time, the Discount Corporation, a government securities dealer, started making an over-the-counter market in these securities. These actions made CDs money market instruments. However, the Regulation Q ceilings imposed on these deposits until mid-1973 (or mid-1970 for maturities less than ninety days) reduced their flexibility, particularly during times of high interest rates. When Regulation Q ceilings on them were removed, they became like other money market instruments.

CDs have maturities ranging from one month to one year, with an average of approximately ninety days. They can be issued in any denomination of $100,000 or greater, although a round lot trade on the secondary market is one million dollars and secondary trading in amounts less than $500,000 is unusual.

CDs are issued on the primary market by commercial banks that post rates, by maturity, which they are willing to pay depositors. The secondary market in CDs is an over-the-counter market conducted mostly by government securities dealers and a few large banks. If banks wish to aggressively increase their issues of CDs, they must post rates above the secondary market rates; if they wish to let some of their CDs run off, then they post rates that are lower than the secondary market rates.

There is competition among commercial banks in issuing CDs, and investors discriminate among the CDs of different banks. Within a small group of the nation's largest banks all CDs trade at about the same rate. Other banks, typically smaller and less well known, issue CDs that are traded on secondary markets but that require higher rates primarily because there are not as many investors in their CDs. Still other banks occasionally issue CDs for which no secondary market exists. This lack of homogeneity in CDs makes the secondary market in CDs less perfect than that of Treasury bills.

CDs represent a very flexible source of funds for commercial banks. During times of tight credit, banks can increase their CD rates and raise substantial levels of funds in the very large money market pool, as they did during late 1973 and 1974. When the demand for credit declines they can reduce their rates and let their CDs run off, as they did during 1975, 1976, and early 1977. Figure 9–5 illustrates these variations, and also the magnitude of CDs relative to commercial bank deposits.

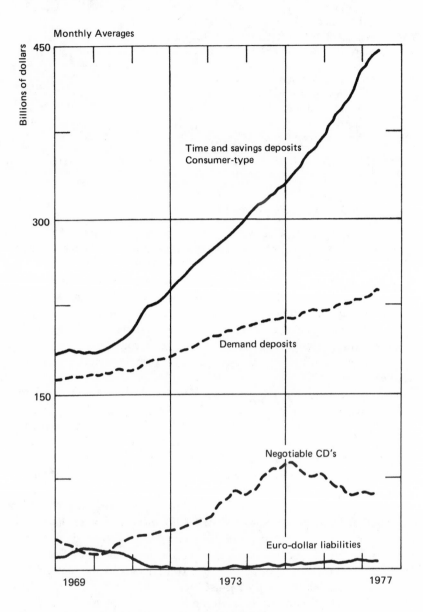

FIGURE 9–5 COMMERCIAL BANK LIABILITIES
Source: Monthly Chart Book, Federal Reserve System.

Corporations are the main holders of CDs. They hold them for short-term investments.

Table 9–22 shows that CDs are second only to Treasury bills in amount outstanding among the money market instruments. Commercial paper and bankers' acceptances are third and fourth.

TABLE 9-22 AMOUNTS OUTSTANDING FOR MONEY MARKET INSTRUMENTS, END OF YEAR, 1975 (BILLION DOLLARS)

Short-term Treasury securities	$219.0
Certificates of deposit	82.9
Commercial paper	47.7
Short-term municipal securities	16.7
Bankers' acceptances	18.7

Source: Flow of Funds Data, Board of Governors of the Federal Reserve System.

FEDERAL FUNDS (FED FUNDS)

Federal funds or Fed funds (properly Federal Reserve Funds) are funds that commercial banks have on deposit at the Federal Reserve Banks to satisfy their reserve requirements. Federal funds are traded among commercial banks when some banks have excess reserves and others have deficit reserves. The maturity of these exchanges or loans is one day (or on Friday three days, over the weekend). Essentially, one bank notifies its Federal Reserve Bank to transfer reserves from its reserve account to another bank's reserve account for one day. At times, government securities dealers also participate in the federal funds market.

Reserve requirements must be met weekly by commercial banks. According to the Fed's regulation, the average of the banks' reserves during the week divided by the average of their 'deposits must equal the reserve requirement ratio set by the Fed. For most banks, the weekly averaging period for deposits extends from Thursday morning to Wednesday morning; the weekly averaging period for reserves is from the close of business on Thursday to the close of business on Wednesday. Consequently, the bank knows on Wednesday morning what the average level of its reserves must be during the week and what its reserves must be on Wednesday to meet this average. So Wednesday is an important day in the federal funds market and the interest rate on federal funds may change substantially on this day. If most banks determine on Wednesday morning that they must increase their reserves, most banks will be borrowers and the federal funds rate will increase on Wednesday. If most banks have excess reserves, the rate will decrease on Wednesday because most banks will be lenders. For example, on Wednesday, March 23, 1977, the federal funds rate went from 4⅝ percent to 8 percent and back to 4⅞ percent the next day in response to a surge in demand. Friday is also an important day in the federal funds market because funds lent over the weekend affect reserve levels for three days.

With the exception of its volatility on Wednesday, changes in the

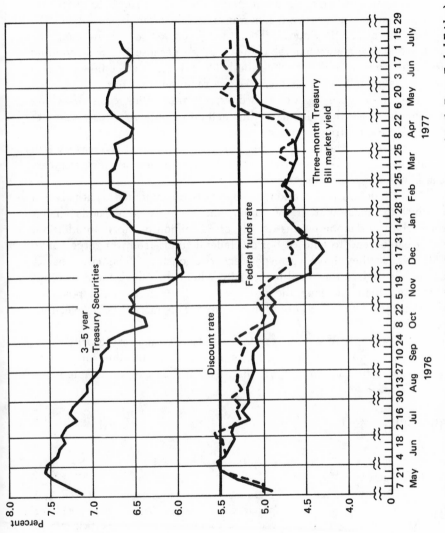

FIGURE 9–6 SELECTED SHORT-TERM INTEREST RATES (Averages of Daily Rates Ended Friday)
Source: U.S. Financial Data, Federal Reserve Bank of St. Louis.

federal funds rate tend to conform to those in the Treasury bill rate as shown in Figure 9–6. The federal funds rate is of additional importance because the Fed uses it as an indicator in implementing monetary policy. As discussed in Chapter 6, the Fed sets a range on the federal funds rate and attempts to keep the actual rate within this range through open market operations.

Commercial banks have alternatives to federal funds to obtain reserves to meet their reserve requirements. They can borrow from the Fed at the discount window. But although banks do borrow from the Fed, banks are somewhat reluctant to do so because the Fed monitors their investment behavior while the banks are indebted. Banks can also sell Treasury bills to meet their reserve requirements. But if they need the reserves for only one or two days, the transaction costs of selling and buying back the bills make this method of obtaining reserves more expensive than through one-day federal funds borrowing. But this is the main reason that the federal funds rate tends to follow the Treasury bill. Figure 9–6 shows the interest rates for the three methods that commercial banks use to obtain reserves.

The federal funds market consists of two components. Large banks conduct the main market by buying and selling federal funds among themselves in denominations usually of $1 million or more. In addition, small banks tend to lend or borrow federal funds from the large banks with which they have correspondent relationships. The large banks essentially satisfy the small banks with whom they have these relationships and then make up the discrepancies in their own net positions through the market with other large banks. This market is an over-the-counter market.

Only purely domestic capital and money market securities are discussed in this chapter. Securities in which either the supplier or demander of funds is foreign are discussed in the next two chapters.

questions

1. Discuss the nature of the primary and secondary markets for Treasury bonds and bills.

2. Discuss the nature of investment banks, how they are chosen, and the services they provide in corporate equity issues. What is the spread for this type of placement and how is it distributed among the participants in the issue?

3. Discuss the nature and the relative importance of organized exchanges and over-the-counter markets in the secondary markets for corporate bonds and stocks. Discuss the turnovers of stocks and bonds on the secondary markets.

4. Discuss what it means for a secondary market to function well and the characteristics a secondary market should have in order to function well.

5. Discuss the money markets in which commercial banks participate and how these markets are related through the commercial bank participation in them.

6. Discuss the relationship of the yields on stocks and bonds and how arbitrage affects these yields.

selected references to part III

Block, Ernest and Sametz, Arnold W. *A Modest Proposal for a National Securities Market System and its Governance.* New York: New York University, Graduate School of Business Administration, Center for the Study of Financial Institutions, 1977.

Darst, David M. *The Complete Bond Book.* New York: McGraw-Hill Book Company, 1975.

Dougall, Herbert E. and Gaumnitz, Jack E. *Capital Markets and Institutions,* 3rd ed. Englewood Cliffs, N.J.: Prentice-Hall, Inc., 1975.

Fisher, Irving. *The Theory of Interest.* Clifton: August M. Kelley, Publishers, 1974.

Friend, Irwin. *Investment Banking and the New Issues Market, Summary Volume.* Philadelphia: Securities Research Unit, Wharton School of Finance and Commerce, University of Pennsylvania, 1965.

Gup, Benton E. *Financial Intermediaries: An Introduction.* Boston: Houghton Mifflin Co., 1976.

Henning, Charles N., Pigott, William, and Scott, Robert Harvey. *Financial Markets and the Economy.* Englewood Cliffs, N.J.: Prentice-Hall, Inc., 1975.

Investment Banking Arrangements. New York: The Conference Board, 1976.

Polakoff, Murray E. et al. *Financial Institutions and Markets.* Boston: Houghton Mifflin Co., 1970.

Prochnow, Herbert and Prochnow, Herbert V. Jr., eds. *The Changing World of Banking.* New York: Harper & Row, 1974.

Ritter, Lawrence S. and Silber, William L. *Principles of Money, Banking, and Financial Markets.* New York: Basic Books, Inc., 1974.

Robinson, Roland I. and Wrightsman, Dwayne. *Financial Markets, the Accumulation and Allocation of Wealth.* New York: McGraw-Hill Book Company, 1974.

Van Horne, James C. *Function and Analysis of Capital Market Rates.* Englewood Cliffs, N.J.: Prentice-Hall, Inc., 1970.

THE INTERNATIONAL
FINANCIAL
SYSTEM

---

the international financial system

10

introduction

In the financial transactions considered in the first nine chapters, both the lender and borrower have been assumed to be United States citizens and the exchanges have been assumed to take place in dollars within the confines of the United States. In this chapter, these assumptions are relaxed and international financial transactions are considered.

To assess the need for international financial transactions, consider the historical development of firms' international operations. The early international activities of U.S. and foreign firms were confined to imports and exports. Goods produced in one country were sold to another country. This process was efficient if the producing country had a better source of raw materials, a cheaper or better labor force, more managerial expertise, a better technology, or simply if goods could be produced more cheaply in large volumes in one location (economies of large scale production). In addition to these conditions, transportation costs must be reasonably cheap for international trade to be efficient. Imports and exports have been important to U.S. business since its infancy.

More recently, businesses whose headquarters are in the United States and whose stockholders are primarily U.S. citizens have begun to establish plants in foreign countries (in the form of branches, subsidiaries, or joint ventures). There are several incentives for establishing overseas production facilities. For example, the foreign country might have the raw materials but the cost of transporting the raw materials to the U.S. is high. It might also have a cheap or well-qualified labor force. And it might have a large market for the product but the transportation costs of exporting the products from the U.S. are high. A more recent incentive for U.S. firms to establish foreign operations has been the formation of economic communities composed of foreign countries which put limitations on goods imported from countries outside the community. These limitations can be in the form of *tariffs* which are charges by the importing country on imported goods, *quotas* which are quantitative limitations on the volume of imports, and in many other forms. To avoid being put at a competitive disadvantage in these markets because of such limitations, U.S. firms can establish operations in these countries. The establishment of the European Economic Community (EEC, or the "Common Market") in 1957 and the European Free Trade Area (EFTA) in 1958 provided incentives for U.S. firms to establish operations in member European countries. The establishment of such foreign operations was the beginning of the multinational firm.

Initially, foreign operations of U.S. firms were financed with funds transferred from the United States. However, during the 1960s, because of the national concern with the U.S. balance of payments deficits, the U.S. government imposed limitations on the amounts of funds U.S. firms could transfer to their foreign operations and U.S. commercial banks could lend overseas. These restrictions made it necessary for U.S. firms to raise the funds needed to finance their foreign investments overseas and substantially increased the level of international financial transactions. It also expanded the types and sizes of the foreign financial markets. And when U.S. firms discovered that they could raise funds overseas to finance their foreign investments, they began to use funds raised overseas to finance their U.S. operations as well.

The result of this progression of international operations is the *multinational firm*. The epitome of the multinational firm is a corporation headquartered in country A and whose stockholders are primarily located in country A, purchasing raw materials from country B, transporting them to country C for fabrication in the corporation's production facilities, exporting the fabricated goods for sale in country D, and initially raising the funds needed to finance the plant construction and perhaps the accounts receivable and inventories in country E. In a world filled with such firms, international financial flows are essential and large in volume.

This chapter discusses the problems involved in international financial flows, particularly those related to changes in exchange rates and international interest rate differentials. It also discusses the institutions and markets that are important to international finance.

the international business environment

The international business environment can be approached by contrasting international business operations to domestic business operations. The production manager in a multinational environment experiences different wage rates, work habits, raw materials costs, and perhaps even different technologies than does his domestic counterpart. The multinational personnel manager has to deal with workers of different backgrounds and different financial and personal requirements. The multinational marketing manager witnesses different customs, habits, and traditions that require different advertising and other marketing techniques, and lead to the demand for different products. Different transportation modes might also be required to deliver the goods to the markets.

Multinational financial managers experience two major differences. First, different countries have financial systems with different structures. The financial institutions accept different types of deposits and make different types of loans. The financial markets deal in securities with different characteristics (different interest rates, maturities, and so forth) and which have different types of primary and secondary markets. Some of these issues are discussed in this chapter.

Perhaps an even more important difference is that different countries have different currencies. The unit of currency in the United States is the dollar, in Canada a different Canadian dollar, in Britain the pound, in Germany the mark, in Mexico the peso, and so forth. If, then, a U.S. firm exports goods to Britain, either the U.S. exporter will have to accept pounds or the British importer will have to pay in dollars for the transaction. In either case, one of the participants deals in a currency other than that of their own country and therefore must exchange currencies.

International markets for foreign exchange exist on which one currency can be exchanged for another. The number of units of one currency that can be exchanged for a given number of units of another currency is called the *exchange rate*. The exchange rate is the price of one currency in terms of another. For example, in early 1977 the dollar price of the pound was $1.70: it cost $1.70 to buy one pound. Alternatively, it cost £ 0.59 (= 1/1.70) to buy one dollar. The exchange rate between dollars and marks is $.40 per mark or equivalently 2.5 DM per dollar. Each pair of currencies has an exchange rate. Table 10–1 lists selected current exchange rates in dollars.

International financial transactions encounter problems only if exchange rates change. For example, assume that a German producer agrees to sell a Volkswagen to a U.S. importer at a time when the dollar/mark exchange rate is $.40 per mark. Assume that the sales price of the VW in Germany is 7,500 DM, and on this basis the U.S. importer agrees to pay the German exporter 7,500 DM for the VW. The U.S. importer needs $3,000 to purchase the required number of marks at the prevailing exchange rate ($3,000/$.40). Assume that the VW can be sold in the U.S. for $3,300, for a profit of $300 or 10 percent. Assume, however, that after the agreement is made and before the United States pays the German exporter, the dollar/mark exchange rate changes to $0.50 per mark (or 2 DM per dollar). In this case the dollar is said to be *devalued* with respect to the mark since it now costs more dollars to purchase a mark than it did previously ($0.50 rather than $0.40). Similarly, the mark is said to be *upvalued* with respect to the dollar, since it now takes fewer marks to buy a dollar (2 DM rather than 2.5 DM).

After the devaluation of the dollar, the U.S. importer must supply $3,750 ($0.50 per mark times 7,500 DM) to get the agreed 7,500 DM.

TABLE 10–1 SELECTED FOREIGN EXCHANGE RATES (IN DOLLARS), APRIL 6, 1977

Argentina (peso)	$ .0030
Brazil (cruzeiro)	.0760
Britain (pound)	1.7141
Canada (dollar)	.9483
Denmark (krone)	.1663
France (franc)	.2014
India (rupee)	.1145
Israel (pound)	.1105
Italy (lira)	.001128
Japan (yen)	.003662
Mexico (peso)	.0445
Saudi Arabia (riyal)	.2850
South Africa (rand)	1.1530
Spain (peseta)	.01460
Sweden (krona)	.2287
Switzerland (franc)	.3942
West Germany (mark)	.4191

Selling the VW for $3,300 then yields a $450 loss for the U.S. importer. Consequently, the devaluation of the dollar after the completion of the agreement between the exporter and the importer converts a $300 profit into a $450 loss.[1] The change in exchange rates can cause similar problems in international borrowing and lending, and is discussed below.

Such problems are not encountered if both parties in the exchange have the same currency, such as in exchanges between residents of two states within the United States. And these problems do not occur if the two parties use different currencies but the exchange rate between their currencies remains constant during the transaction. They only occur if exchange rates change during the transactions.

Between 1946 and 1973, the exchange rates between the currencies of most major countries remained fixed most of the time. Infrequently, large changes occurred in some exchange rates. But since 1973 exchange rates have fluctuated continuously. Because exchange rates are so important in international financial transactions, the factors that affect exchange rates are investigated in the following section. International financial institutions and markets are considered at the end of this chapter.

THE DETERMINANTS OF EXCHANGE RATES

Since exchange rates are prices of one currency in terms of another, the factors that affect these prices should be similar to the factors that affect any other prices—those of jelly beans, for example. If the demand for jelly beans increases and the supply remains fixed, the price of jelly beans will rise. If the supply of jelly beans increases with demand constant, the price of jelly beans will decrease. Similarly, if the demand for U.S. dollars in Britain increases, the value of the dollar should increase in terms of the pound; that is, the dollar should be upvalued, from $1.70 per pound to, say, $1.60 per pound. If the demand for pounds in the U.S. increases, the value of the pound should increase and the dollar should be devalued from $1.70 per pound to, say, $1.80 per pound.

What determines the demand for dollars in Britain and the demand for pounds in the United States? An important determinant of the demand for dollars in Britain is the British demand for imports of goods produced in the United States. And an important demand for pounds in the United States is the U.S. demand for imports of British goods. As

---

[1] If the agreement between the importer and exporter had been made in dollars, specifically at $3,000, the devaluation of the dollar would not have affected the U.S. importer. But the German exporter would be able to exchange the $3,000 received for only 6,000 DM. In this case the German exporter would lose 1,500 DM as a result of the dollar devaluation.

British imports of U.S. goods increase, the British demand for dollars increases and the dollar is upvalued relative to the pound. As U.S. imports of British goods increase, the U.S. demand for pounds increases and the dollar tends to be devalued.[2]

But the international exchange of currencies depends on more than just imports and exports. If a U.S.-based multinational firm uses dollar funds generated in the United States to build and equip a factory in Europe, this direct foreign investment by a U.S. firm will cause an outflow of dollars from the U.S. Likewise, a foreign portfolio investment by a U.S. citizen—for example, the purchase of a foreign stock or bond—will cause an outflow of dollars and will tend to devalue the dollar. Conversely, direct or portfolio investments in the United States by foreigners causes inflows of foreign currencies which tend to devalue the foreign currencies and strengthen the dollar.

In a supply-demand context, the outflows of dollars relative to the inflows of foreign currencies affect the dollar exchange rates of other currencies. The accounting framework that has been developed to keep track of international currency flows for the United States is called the U.S. *balance of payments accounts*. Table 10–2 shows one version of these accounts for the fourth quarter of 1976. If the sum of the items that generate dollar outflows (mainly U.S. imports and U.S. direct and portfolio investments abroad) exceeds the sum of items that generate dollar inflows, the balance of payments accounts are said to be *in deficit*. In the opposite case they are said to be *in surplus*.[3] Deficits tend to make the dollar decrease in value; it is devalued relative to other currencies. Surpluses tend to upvalue the dollar.

The United States balance of payments accounts measure the outflow of dollars relative to the inflow of foreign currencies. And these relative flows affect the dollar exchange rates. A more basic question, then, is what factors affect these currency flows, or more specifically, what factors affect the level of U.S. imports, exports, direct foreign investment, and portfolio investment. The major international factors that affect these types of currency flows are discussed next.

---

[2] Equivalently, imports could be viewed as causing an excess supply of the importing country's currency in the exporting country, causing the value of the importing country's currency to decrease. For example, U.S. imports of British goods could be viewed as supplying dollars in Britain which would tend to devalue the dollar; British imports of U.S. goods could be viewed as supplying pounds in the U.S. which would tend to devalue the pound.

[3] The terms *surplus* and *deficit*, with respect to the balance of payments accounts, have fallen into disfavor recently because of ambiguity about what types of outflows and inflows should be considered in balance of payments measures and which flows are the causes and which are the effects of balance of payments surpluses and deficits.

TABLE 10-2 U.S. INTERNATIONAL TRANSACTIONS (MILLIONS OF DOLLARS), FOURTH QUARTER, 1976

Merchandise exports	$29,717
Merchandise imports	33,291
Service exports	12,790
Service imports	8,989
Unilateral transfers (net)	1,139
Direct investment abroad	1,593
Direct investment in U.S.	155
Portfolio investment abroad	2,123
Portfolio investment in U.S.	21
Deposits abroad (demand, time)	701
Deposits in U.S. (demand, time)	1,509

Definitions:

I. *Merchandise exports and imports:* the current dollar value of physical goods which are exported from and imported into the United States.

II. *Service exports and imports:* receipts of earnings on U.S. investments abroad and payments of earnings on foreign investments in the United States (interest, dividends, and branch earnings), sales and purchases of military equipment, expenditures for U.S. military stations abroad, and payments and receipts associated with foreign travel and transportation.

III. *Unilateral transfers:* private transfers representing gifts and similar payments by Americans to foreign residents and government transfers representing payments associated with foreign assistance programs.

IV. *Direct investment abroad:* capital transactions of U.S. residents with foreigners in which the U.S. residents by themselves or in affiliation with others own 10 percent or more of the voting securities or other ownership interests of a foreign enterprise.

V. *Direct investment in the U.S.:* capital transactions of U.S. enterprises with foreign owners who control 25 percent or more of the voting securities or other ownership interests.

VI. *Portfolio investments:* net transactions between U.S. and foreign residents in foreign and U.S. equities and debt securities, other than U.S. Treasury issues, with no contractual maturities or with maturities of more than one year; excludes transactions recorded as Direct Investments.

VII. *Deposits abroad (demand and time):* a measure of claims on foreign banks reported by U.S. banks and large nonbanking concerns.

VIII. *Deposits in U.S. (demand and time):* a measure of the short-term liabilities to foreigners reported by U.S. banks.

Source: U.S. International Transactions and Currency Review, Federal Reserve Bank of St. Louis.

FACTORS THAT AFFECT THE BALANCE
OF PAYMENTS

Exchange rates are an important determinant of imports and exports. Extending the above example, assume that it costs $3,200 to produce a Pinto in the United States and 7,500 DM to produce a VW in Germany. At an exchange rate of $0.40 per mark, VW's will sell for $3,000 in the U.S. and Pintos for 8,000 DM in Germany, as shown in part (a) of Table 10–3. VW's are cheaper than Pintos in both the United States and Germany. Consequently, the United States will have high imports of VW's and low exports of Pintos, which tends to put the U.S. balance of payments in deficit.

But if the dollar is devalued to $0.50 per mark, Pintos will be cheaper than VW's in both the United States and Germany, as shown in part (b) of Table 10–3. And the United States will have a higher level of exports, a lower level of imports, and a tendency toward a balance of payments surplus. The conclusion is that the devaluation of a country's currency will cause its exports to increase, its imports to decrease and its balance of payments to tend toward a greater surplus. This will strengthen the country's currency.

Inflation affects a country's imports and exports in the same manner as do changes in exchange rates. If, with an exchange rate of $0.40 per mark, a 20 percent inflation in Germany causes the German mark value of the VW to increase to 9000 DM, the VW's price in the U.S. would be $3,600. If there were no inflation in the United States, the dollar and mark values of the Pinto would remain the same ($3,200 and 8,000 DM, respectively) and the Pinto would be cheaper in both countries. Consequently, U.S. imports would be small, exports large, and its balance of payments accounts in greater surplus.

Of course, if the U.S. experienced 20 percent inflation also, the dollar price of the Pinto would increase to $3,840 and the competitive positions of the VW and Pinto would remain the same as before the

TABLE 10–3   AUTOMOBILE TRADE AND EXCHANGE RATES

a. Exchange Rate = $0.40 per 1 DM

Germany	U.S.
VW: 7,500 DM ——————————————→	$3,000
8,000 DM ←——————————————	$3,200 : Pinto

b. Exchange Rate = $0.50 per 1 DM

Germany	U.S.
VW: 7,500 DM ——————————————→	$3,750
6,400 DM ←——————————————	$3,200 : Pinto

inflations occurred. The conclusion is that if a country experiences less inflation than do its competitors, it will tend to export more, import less, and its balance of payments will tend toward greater surplus. If it experiences more inflation, the opposite will occur. It is *relative* inflation that is important to balance of payments.

If a country's economic growth is more rapid than that of its competitors, its balance of payments will tend toward a greater deficit. As a country's economy grows, its demand for all goods and services, including those imported, increases. The growth of its exports depends on the economic growth of the countries that import its goods. So if a country's economy grows more quickly than that of its competitors, its imports will grow more quickly than its exports, and its balance of payments will tend toward greater deficit. Again, it is *relative* economic growth that is important to the balance of payments accounts.

The level of international interest rates affects the level of international portfolio investment. If the interest rate is 8 percent in Germany and 6 percent in the United States, U.S. funds tend to flow to Germany for portfolio investment and the U.S. balance of payments will tend toward a deficit. So high interest rates make a country's balance of payments tend toward a surplus. The relation between international portfolio investments and international interest rate differentials is discussed in detail below.

Exchange rates, inflation, economic growth, and interest rates all affect a country's balance of payments. However, tariffs and quotas, long-run economic growth potential, and political stability also affect the balance of payments. Changes in the various entries in the U.S. balance of payments accounts because of changes in these and other factors from 1951 to 1975 are shown in Table 10–4. The sum of these entries describes the total outflow of U.S. currency relative to the inflow of foreign currencies. And these relative flows, or fundamentally the supplies and demand of currencies for these purposes, represent the economic forces that determine exchange rates.

INTERNATIONAL AGREEMENTS
CONCERNING EXCHANGE RATES

Frequently throughout history, exchange rates have been regarded as too important to be determined by the pure economic forces discussed above; instead, political forces were thought important. At the end of World War II, as part of the Bretton Woods Agreement among the major Western countries, fixed exchange rates were established among these countries. How were these fixed exchange rates preserved over periods of balance of payments surpluses and deficits experienced by the countries? They were preserved by *support operations* by the coun-

TABLE 10–4 U.S. INTERNATIONAL TRANSACTIONS[1] (MILLIONS OF DOLLARS) FOURTH QUARTER, 1976

Year	Merchandise Exports	Merchandise Imports	Service Imports	Service Exports	Unilateral Transfers Abroad (Net)	Direct Investment Abroad	Direct Investment in U.S.	Portfolio Investment Abroad	Portfolio Investment in U.S.	Deposits Abroad (Demand, Time)[2]	Deposits in U.S. (Demand, Time)[3]
1951	14,200	11,200	4,600	3,900	4,954	508	90	353	126	— 149	— 122
1952	13,400	10,800	4,700	4,900	5,113	852	132	87	37	— 3	— 446
1953	12,400	11,000	4,700	5,600	6,657	735	158	— 91	70	18	304
1954	12,900	10,400	5,000	5,600	5,642	667	124	206	141	74	863
1955	14,400	11,500	5,500	6,300	5,086	823	197	— 20	181	26	13
1956	17,600	12,800	6,200	6,800	4,990	1,951	232	421	323	— 11	663
1957	19,600	13,300	7,100	7,500	4,763	2,442	155	470	237	11	663
1958	16,400	13,000	6,800	7,900	4,647	1,181	98	1,250	*	4	32
1959	16,500	15,300	7,200	8,000	4,422	1,372	238	668	449	47	1,117
1960	19,700	14,800	7,900	8,800	4,003	1,674	141	663	282	22	605
1961	20,100	14,500	8,800	8,800	3,989	1,598	73	762	324	36	1,253
1962	20,800	16,300	9,800	9,300	4,175	1,654	132	969	134	139	1,244
1963	22,300	17,000	10,400	9,800	4,316	1,976	— 5	1,105	287	9	89
1964	25,500	18,700	11,900	10,200	4,121	2,328	— 5	677	— 85	67	1,039
1965	26,500	21,500	13,100	10,900	4,490	3,468	57	759	— 358	— 88	1,711
1966	29,300	25,500	13,500	12,800	4,824	3,625	86	720	906	— 3	119
1967	30,700	26,900	14,900	14,400	5,164	3,072	258	1,308	1,016	88	2,063
1968	33,600	33,000	16,300	15,400	5,498	2,880	319	1,569	4,414	48	1,551
1969	36,400	35,800	18,300	17,900	5,604	3,190	832	1,549	3,730	1,629	2,458
1970	42,500	39,900	20,000	19,700	6,007	4,281	1,030	1,076	2,189	— 281	7,329
1971	43,300	45,600	22,300	20,300	7,247	4,738	— 175	1,113	2,289	— 312	— 5,693
1972	49,400	55,800	23,300	22,800	8,340	3,530	380	618	4,507	623	—10,902
1973	71,400	70,500	30,700	27,800	6,692	4,968	2,656	671	4,041	735	3,046
1974	98,300	103,700	46,500	37,500	9,001	7,753	2,745	1,854	378	920	4,074
1975	107,100	98,100	41,300	34,000	6,852	6,307	2,437	6,206	2,505	205	5,531
1976	114,700P	123,900P	49,500P	35,900P	5,405P	5,000P	561P	8,682P	1,250P	1,989	4,294

* Less than $500,000.

[1] The signs in this table do *not* indicate whether a particular transaction is an inflow or outflow, as is the case in standard balance-of-payments tables. In this table a negative sign indicates that there was a reduction in the stock of assets during a particular time period.

[2] Deposits Abroad of Nonbanking Concerns not available before 1968. Since the post-1968 entries do not contain deposits of nonbanking concerns, these numbers are not strictly comparable with the pre-1968 entries. Deposits Abroad of Banking Concerns only available for deposits payable in foreign currencies.

[3] Deposits in U.S. only available for deposits payable in dollars.

P — Preliminary

tries participating in the agreement. Essentially, if a country ran a balance of payments deficit which generated an excess supply of its currency on the international money markets and tended to devalue the currency, the central bank of the country "bought up" the excess supply of its currency by paying with gold, currencies of other countries, or credit provided by the International Monetary Fund. The IMF is a world central bank instituted at Bretton Woods in 1946 to maintain order in the international monetary markets.

Each participating country had a responsibility according to the Bretton Woods Agreement. The United States was obliged to keep the dollar price of gold at $35 per ounce by either supplying gold or purchasing gold in exchange for dollars in amounts sufficient to preserve this price. Each other country was obliged to keep its currency at the agreed exchange rate in terms of the dollar by either buying or selling its currency in exchange for dollars, other currencies, gold, or IMF credit. Between 1946 and 1971, this system prevailed and exchange rates changed only infrequently as the participating countries supported the fixed exchange rates.[4]

However, initially in 1971 and finally in 1973 this system of fixed exchange rates disintegrated. In addition, in 1971 the United States discontinued buying and selling gold to maintain the dollar price of gold. Now exchange rates are allowed by their countries to *fluctuate freely* and respond to the economic forces described above. However, some countries, at some times, continue to conduct some support operations on their currency either to reduce the fluctuations in its exchange rates or to keep its exchange rate from increasing or decreasing as much as it otherwise would. Nevertheless, exchange rates do fluctuate much more frequently now than they did between 1946 and 1971. Figure 10–1 shows the substantial variations in the dollar exchange rate since 1971. The autonomous devaluations of the dollar in 1971 and 1973 are evident.

The politics and economics of the choice of an optional exchange rate for a country are ambiguous. Businesses and workers in export industries do not like to see their currency upvalued because it increases the prices of the products they export to foreign markets. Therefore, they become less competitive, and their production and sales decrease. So currency upvaluation decreases profit margins and employment in export industries. Conversely, importers do not like to see their currency devalued because the domestic price of their imported goods increases and these goods become less competitive in the domestic market. And frequent tourists of other countries do not like their own currency de-

---

[4] There were infrequent changes in exchange rates. For example, France devalued its currency in 1957, 1958, and 1968, and Britain its currency in 1967. Germany upvalued its currency in 1961 and 1969.

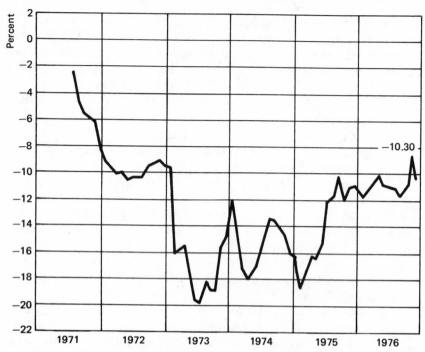

Note: Effective devaluation is measured by the appreciation of the twenty-two
currencies of OECD countries relative to the par values which prevailed as of
May 1970. The appreciation is then weighted by separate export and import
shares with the United States based on 1972 trade data.
Latest data plotted: December

FIGURE 10–1 EFFECTIVE DOLLAR DEVALUATION

Source: U.S. International Transactions and Currency Review, Federal Reserve Bank
of St. Louis.

valued because it takes more domestic currency to pay for their foreign
travels. Parts of the economy both benefit and lose from both devaluation and upvaluation. The prospect of either, therefore, is not met with
unanimity. Domestic politics have an ambiguous effect on exchange rate
determination.

International political forces on countries also attempt to support
their currencies at certain levels. Countries that conduct support operations to prevent their currencies from being upvalued, particularly if
they are also running balance of payments surpluses, are often criticized
for protecting their export industries and minimizing their imports,
thereby maintaining their domestic employment at the expense of employment in other countries. Germany and Japan have recently been
criticized for keeping their exchange rates too low. However, countries

The International Financial System

that prevent the value of their currencies from declining, particularly if they are running a balance of payments deficit, are often criticized for continually using more of another country's goods and services than they supply to the other countries (that is what a deficit relative to exports and imports signifies). The United States was criticized for this in the late 1960s, particularly because their balance of payments deficit was partially due to its support of an unpopular war.

international borrowing and lending

In the last section, the effects of exchange rates on the levels of international imports and exports were discussed. This section considers international borrowing and lending and the variables that affect these activities.

Again, exchange rates are an important determinant. Consider a U.S.-based multinational firm that wishes to build a plant, which costs 4,000 marks, in Bonn, Germany. Assume the exchange rate is $0.40 per mark. The firm has the choice of borrowing either 4,000 DM in Germany or $1,600 in the U.S. (4,000 DM × $0.40 per mark). Assume that interest rates are the same in Germany and the United States (this assumption is relaxed below). Profits to pay off the loan will be generated in marks in Bonn. If the exchange rate remains $0.40 at the maturity of the loan, there will be no difference in the cost of the two loans. It will take 4,000 DM to pay off the loan whether it was made in marks or in dollars.

Assume, however, that the dollar was devalued to $0.50 per mark at the maturity of the loan. This represents a 25 percent devaluation of the dollar [(.4 − .5)/.4 = − 25 percent].[5] With the devaluation, the final cost of the loan depends on the currency in which the loan was initially denominated. Four thousand marks would still be required to retire the mark loan. But to obtain the $1,600 needed to retire the dollar loan would require only 3,200 DM ($1,600 × $0.50 per mark). This represents a 20 percent savings (800/4,000) if the loan is in dollars. The loan is cheaper in dollars than in marks because of the devaluation of the

---

[5] Note that if the exchange rates are expressed in terms of the number of marks needed to purchase one dollar, the original exchange rates would have been 2.5 marks per dollar and the final exchange rate 2 marks per dollar, a 20 percent upvaluation of the mark in terms of the dollar [(2.5 − 2.0)/2.5 = 20 percent]. Since the percentage amount of devaluation or upvaluation depends on whether the mark value of the dollar or the dollar value of the mark is used, one must be careful about which is actually being used. In the U.S., the dollar value of other currencies is always used.

dollar. Table 10–5 summarizes the quantity of marks needed to retire the original loan (used to raise 4,000 DM) by the original denomination of the loan and by the exchange rate at the time of retirement of the loan.

It takes 20 percent fewer marks (4,000 − 3,200/4,000) to repay the loan made in dollars because of the 25 percent devaluation on the dollar (more appropriately expressed for Germany and the German plant deciding how to raise marks as a 20 percent upvaluation of the mark). Of course, the number of marks needed to retire the mark loan remains the same.

The firm would have to make similar considerations in deciding whether to borrow in marks or dollars to finance the construction of a plant in New York in which the profits would be generated in dollars. Assume that the plant will cost $1,600 and this amount has to be raised. At an initial exchange rate of $0.40 per mark, either 4,000 DM would have to be borrowed in Germany or $1,600 in the United States. If the exchange rate were still $0.40 per mark at the maturity of the loan, the cost of each loan would be the same, assuming the interest rates in the two countries were the same. However, if the dollar were devalued to $0.50 per mark at the maturity of the loan, it would cost $2,000 (4,000 DM × $0.50 per mark) to retire the mark loan but only $1,600 to retire the dollar loan. Again, it would benefit the borrower to borrow in the currency that will be devalued. Table 10–6 summarizes the quantity of dollars that must be used to retire the original loan (used to raise $1,600) by the original denomination of the loan and by the exchange rate at the time of retirement of the loan.

It costs 25 percent more dollars (400/1,600) if the loan is made in marks because of the 25 percent devaluation of the dollar. Of course, the devaluation of the dollar does not affect the number of dollars needed to retire a loan made in dollars.

Two conclusions are obvious. First, if the interest rates in two countries are equal, borrow in the currency that is most likely to be devalued. A currency that is likely to be devalued is called a *weak currency;* one that is likely to be upvalued is called a *strong currency.* So

TABLE 10–5 MARKS NEEDED TO RETIRE MARK AND DOLLAR LOANS

| | Marks Needed to Retire Loan | |
| | Original Denomination of Loan | |
Final Exchange Rate	Mark	Dollar
$0.40 per mark	4,000	4,000(= 1600/.4)
0.50 per mark	4,000	3,200(= 1600/.5)

TABLE 10–6   DOLLARS NEEDED TO RETIRE MARK AND DOLLAR LOANS

| | Dollars Needed to Retire Loan | |
| | Original Denomination | |
Final Exchange Rate	Mark	Dollar
$0.40 per mark	$1,600(= .4 × 4,000 marks)	$1,600
$0.50 per mark	$2,600(= .5 × 4,000 marks)	$1,600

borrow in a weak currency. In terms of the above examples, this means that either the German or U.S. borrowers would be better off borrowing in dollars than in marks. Second, the amount lost (gained) by borrowing in a currency that is upvalued (devalued) relative to yours, is equal to the amount of the devaluation (upvaluation) of your currency. The greater the devaluation (upvaluation) of your currency, the greater your loss (gain) if you borrow in another currency.

The two previous examples consider international borrowing. The same issues are involved in international lending or investing. Consider a German citizen who wishes to invest 4,000 DM in either a mark investment in Bonn or a dollar investment in New York. Assume that the interest rates in Bonn and New York are the same. Assume also that the initial exchange rate is $0.40 per mark. The German investor can either invest 4,000 DM in Bonn or $1,600 in New York. If at the time of liquidation of the investment the exchange rate is still $0.40 per mark, the saver will receive either 4,000 DM from the Bonn investment, or $1,600 from the New York investment which can be converted into 4,000 DM (plus accrued interest in both cases). With interest rates equal, the saver is indifferent to the two forms of savings.

Assume, however, that the exchange rate is $0.50 per mark when the saver liquidates the investment. The Bonn investment is still worth 4,000 DM plus accrued interest. But the New York investment worth $1,600 can now be converted into only 3,200 DM (1,600/.5). The German saver has lost 800 DM or 20 percent of the investment (800/4,000) by investing in a currency that was devalued relative to the saver's currency (recall that if exchange rates are expressed in terms of marks, the mark was upvalued by 20 percent relative to the dollar). Of course, the change in exchange rates does not affect the investment made in Bonn in marks. The saver is, consequently, better off saving in the strong currency, the mark.

Consider the alternative example of the New York citizen deciding whether to invest $1,600 in a dollar investment in New York or in a mark investment in Bonn. Again, if the exchange rate remains at $0.40 per mark until the liquidation of the investment, there is no difference in the returns of the two investments if the interest rates are the same. The

$1,600 New York investment returns the initial amount plus accrued interest. The initial 4,000 DM investment (made from converting $1,600 at a rate of $0.40 per mark), can be reconverted into $1,600, plus accrued interest at the liquidation of the investment.

If, however, the exchange rate is $0.50 per mark at the time of liquidation of the investment, the value of the New York investment remains $1,600 but the 4,000 DM investment can be converted into $2,000. The mark loan produces a 25 percent advantage [(2,000 − 1,600)/1,600] over the dollar loan in the case of the devaluation of the dollar.

Again, two conclusions are obvious. First, if interest rates in the two countries are equal, lend or invest in the strong currency, or the currency that is likely to be upvalued. In the examples above, both the German and U.S. savers would be better off making an investment denominated in marks rather than in dollars. So *lend or invest in a strong currency*. Second, the amount lost by investing in a weak currency is the percent devaluation of that currency, and the amount gained by investing in a strong currency is the percent upvaluation of that currency.[6]

Two basic conclusions have been developed: borrow in a weak currency, and lend in a strong currency. These conclusions are based on the assumption that interest rates in different countries are the same. But interest rates differ among countries, as Figure 10–2 illustrates. The determinants of the level of interest rates in a country are discussed in Chapter 7. The factors discussed there, however, are all domestic rather than international. But international factors also affect domestic interest rates. And the nature of the effect of these international factors is based on the principles developed above. If, initially, worldwide interest rates were equal, and worldwide borrowers tended to borrow in weak currencies and worldwide lenders tended to lend in strong currencies, as the principles indicate, interest rates in countries with weak currencies would rise, because of the borrowing in that country. And interest rates in countries with strong currencies would tend to decline because of the investing in that country. Consequently, interest rates in countries with weak currencies would be higher than in those countries with strong currencies. This is confirmed by Figure 10–2. During recent years, Germany has had a strong currency (it has been upvalued relative to other currencies) and the United Kingdom a weak one (it has been devalued). And the German interest rates have been lower than the U.K. interest rates.

The relationships among the expected strength or weakness of

---

[6] The percent devaluation or upvaluation should be expressed in terms of the value of the currency of the investor—for example, marks in the first example and dollars in the second.

The International Financial System

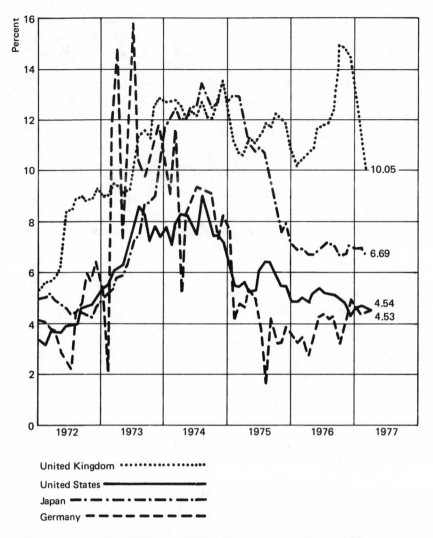

FIGURE 10–2   SHORT-TERM INTEREST RATES—INTERNATIONAL
Source: U.S. International Transactions and Currency Review, Federal Reserve Bank
of St. Louis.

another currency in terms of the dollar, the interest rate differential between the U.S. and another country, and the incentive for U.S. citizens
to lend or borrow abroad can be made more exact. Consider the following examples. Assume that the one-year interest rate is 8 percent in the
United Kingdom and 6 percent in the U.S. Assume, however that the
dollar is expected to be upvalued by 1 percent with respect to the pound
during the next year. A U.S. investor could thus get 2 percent more by

investing in the U.K. but, as discussed above, would lose 1 percent on the pound investment due to the devaluation of the pound (remember: lend strong). But there would still be a net advantage of 1 percent by investing in the pound. It would cost a U.S. borrower 2 percent more to borrow pounds under the circumstances and the borrower would save only 1 percent because of the pound devaluation. Consequently, it would be cheaper to borrow dollars.

If, alternatively, the pound is expected to be devalued by 2 percent with interest rates the same, the U.S. investor would get a 2 percent higher interest rate by investing in the pound but lose 2 percent because of the pound devaluation. The investor would, therefore, be indifferent between the pound and dollar investments. A borrower would similarly be indifferent.

If the pound is expected to be devalued by 3 percent, there would be a 3 percent loss to the U.S. investor investing in the pound, which would more than nullify the 2 percent interest rate advantage of the pound investment. The dollar investment would be preferable to the U.S. investor. But in this case the U.S. borrower would prefer the pound to the dollar for raising funds. The pound loan would cost the U.S. borrower 2 percent more but the borrower's cost of repaying the loan in terms of dollars would be reduced by 3 percent due to the 3 percent devaluation. So the borrower would be 1 percent better off borrowing in pounds rather than in dollars. These three cases are summarized in the upper half of Table 10–7.

TABLE 10–7 INTEREST RATE DIFFERENTIALS AND CURRENCY REVALUATIONS

	Foreign Interest Rate (i_f)	U.S. Interest Rate ($i_{U.S.}$)	Interest Rate Differential ($i_f - i_{U.S.}$)	Expected Change in Value of Dollar Relative to Foreign Currency (Upvaluation of \$ is +; Devaluation of \$ is −) (CV \$)	Action	NII = ($i_f - i_{U.S.}$) − CV\$		
	8%	6%	2%	1	Invest in Pounds	(2% — 1%)	=	1%
U. K.	8%	6%	2%	2	No preference	(2% — 2%)	=	0%
	8%	6%	2%	3	Borrow in Pounds	(2% — 3%)	=	−1%
	4%	6%	−2%	−1	Borrow in Marks	[− 2% — (− 1%)]	=	−1%
Germany	4%	6%	−2%	−2	No preference	[− 2% — (− 2%)]	=	0%
	4%	6%	−2%	−3	Invest in Marks	[− 2% — (− 3%)]	=	1%

Assume that the one-year interest rate is 4 percent in Germany, and 6 percent in the United States. Assume also that the dollar is expected to be devalued relative to the mark during the next year. A U.S. investor would gain 1 percent by investing in marks if the dollar were devalued by 1 percent but this would not compensate for the 2 percent interest rate disadvantage of marks. The U.S. investor should invest in dollars. But the U.S. borrower would save 2 percent in interest by borrowing in marks and lose only 1 percent due to the dollar devaluation and would, therefore, experience a net savings of 1 percent by borrowing in marks.

If the dollar is expected to be devalued by 2 percent relative to the mark, the U.S. investor would gain 2 percent by investing in the mark but this would only compensate for the 2 percent interest rate disadvantage of the mark. The U.S. investor would, therefore, be indifferent between the mark and dollar investments. The U.S. borrower would be similarly indifferent.

If the dollar is expected to be devalued by 3 percent, the U.S. investor would gain 3 percent by investing in the mark, which would more than compensate for the 2 percent interest rate disadvantage of the mark. The U.S. investor would prefer the mark investment. The U.S. borrower would experience an interest rate savings of 2 percent by borrowing in the mark but a 3 percent exchange loss due to devaluation of the dollar, for a net loss of 1 percent from borrowing in the mark. Borrowers, therefore, would borrow dollars. The lower half of Table 10–7 summarizes these three cases.

The six cases discussed can be generalized by defining the *net incentive to invest* in a foreign currency (*NII*) as shown in equation (1):

$$NII = (i_f - i_{U.S.}) - CV\$ \tag{1}$$

where i_f is the foreign interest rate, $i_{U.S.}$ is the U.S. interest rate, and $CV\$$ is the expected percent change in the value of the dollar over the maturity of the security to which the interest rate refers (upvaluations of the dollar are positive and devaluations of the dollar are negative). Table 10–7 shows the *NII* for the six cases. As shown, if *NII* is greater than zero, it is preferable to invest in the foreign currency because either the weakness of the foreign currency does not nullify the interest advantage of the foreign currency, or the strength of the foreign currency more than compensates for the interest rate disadvantage of the foreign currency. And U.S. borrowers would borrow in dollars if *NII* is greater than zero.

If *NII* equals zero, both the U.S. investor and borrower are indifferent between the foreign currency and the dollar. If *NII* is less than zero, U.S. borrowers would borrow in the foreign currency either because the devaluation of the foreign currency more than compensates for the interest rate disadvantage of the foreign currency, or the upvaluation of the foreign currency is not large enough to nullify the interest rate disadvantage of the foreign currency. And U.S. investors would invest in dollars.

The conclusions reached in this section about international borrowing and lending are based on assumptions about expectations about future changes in the value of the dollar relative to the value of foreign currencies. These expectations can be assessed by the futures markets in foreign currencies, which are discussed in more advanced texts in international finance.

The next sections discuss the financial markets and institutions through which international financial transactions, borrowing and lending, occur.

international financial markets and institutions

Purely domestic finance occurs when U.S. firms borrow dollars in the U.S. financial system and, say, German firms borrow in the German financial system. There are two types of international finance. The first type to develop was for firms to borrow in another country in the currency of that country—for example, for U.S. firms to borrow marks in Germany (and in some cases convert them into dollars) and for German firms to borrow dollars in the U.S. (and in some cases convert them into marks). Both short-term and long-term transactions of this type now occur. Long-term bond issues of this type are called foreign bonds.

In the last decade, a second type of international finance has developed. It involves the borrowing and lending of a currency outside the country of that currency. The borrowing and lending of dollars in Europe has been the most important market of this type. Short-term borrowing and lending of dollars in Europe is conducted through the so-called *Eurodollar markets*. Short-term commercial bank borrowing and lending of European currencies outside the country of that currency also occurs. These markets along with the Eurodollar market are called the *Eurocurrency markets*. Intermediate and long-term borrowing and lending of dollars in Europe are conducted through the so-called *Eurocredit and Eurobond markets*, respectively. Some other European currencies, mainly the German mark and the Swiss franc, are also borrowed and lent in Europe outside the currency's country. There is also a small European market in dollar-denominated equities, the Euroequity market, which is also considered to be part of the Euromarkets. A modest amount of dollar borrowing and lending in Asia, the so-called Asia-dollar market, also occurs. However, no borrowing and lending of any foreign currencies takes place in the United States.

Figure 10–3 shows examples of the types of financial transactions that occur today. The remainder of this chapter discusses transactions of types (2) and (3). After a general discussion, international transactions are discussed by their maturity, short-term, intermediate-term, and long-term.

SHORT-TERM INTERNATIONAL FINANCE

Substantial volumes of short-term borrowing and lending of type (2) have occurred for many years. Much of this activity consists of the purchase of marketable securities of a country by citizens and institutions of another country. United States citizens and businesses purchase the securities issued by foreign governments and foreign business (and denominated in foreign currencies). There is an active market for many foreign stocks and bonds in this country both on the over-the-counter markets and on the listed exchanges. The U.S. purchase of foreign securities has often been of concern to the U.S. government because of the effect on the U.S. balance of payments. Similarly, foreign citizens, businesses, and official institutions purchase U.S. Treasury securities and U.S. business stocks and bonds (denominated in dollars) either on the U.S. markets or on the markets for these securities in their own countries.

Type (2) transactions may also occur through U.S. and foreign commercial banks. For example, U.S. commercial banks could lend dollars to U.S. subsidiaries of foreign companies (they would use the dollars in the U.S.), to foreign companies located in foreign countries (they would probably convert the dollars into their currency), and to foreign subsidiaries of U.S. companies (the dollars would, again, probably be converted). The effects of the second and third types of loans are much

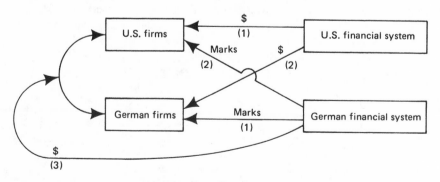

FIGURE 10–3 TYPES OF FINANCIAL TRANSACTIONS

different from that of the first because the first would not lead to a conversion of the dollar and hence not affect exchange rates and would not affect the U.S. balance of payments. Transactions of the first type could be accomplished by the U.S. locations of the U.S. commercial banks. Transactions of the second and third types might require foreign branches.

Similarly, foreign commercial banks lend their currencies to foreign subsidiaries of U.S. businesses, U.S. businesses in the United States, and U.S. subsidiaries of businesses headquartered in their country. Again, transactions of the first type do not require conversions of the currency and may be accomplished through the domestic branches of that commercial bank.

Since commercial banks are so important in international finance of type (2) and, as is discussed below, are primarily responsible for international finance of type (3), the role of U.S. commercial banks in international finance is discussed in the next section.

THE ROLE OF U.S. COMMERCIAL BANKS IN INTERNATIONAL FINANCE

Following World War II when the domestic business clients of U.S. commercial banks began establishing offices overseas, the U.S. banks found they could not serve these clients adequately from their U.S. offices. Since they did not wish to lose this business to foreign banks, they established overseas offices. This internationalization of U.S. commercial banks accelerated during the 1960s. In 1960 eight banks in the U.S. had 131 overseas branches with $3.5 billion of assets. By 1974, 129 U.S. banks has 737 foreign branches with a total of $155 billion of assets.[7] Multinational business led to multinational banking.

Making loans and accepting deposits is the core of the international banking business. But foreign branches of U.S. banks have diversified their services to offer leasing, factoring, computer services, mortgage banking, and many other services including underwriting, as discussed below.

Initially, the transactions of the foreign branches of the U.S. banks were in the currency of the country in which they were located. For example, the French branch of a U.S. corporation borrowed francs from the French branch of a U.S. bank to build a plant in France. Similarly, foreign banks established branches in the U.S. to service the U.S. branches of foreign corporations.

---

[7] Andrew F. Brimmer and Frederick R. Dahl, "Growth of American International Banking," *Journal of Finance*, May, 1975, pp. 341–63.

Table 10–8 shows the locations of the foreign subsidiaries and branches of the ten largest U.S. banks. Of course, all these countries have domestic banks that attempt to serve their domestic business and the domestic branches of U.S. businesses. The U.S. branches in these countries, then, compete with domestic banks.

Other factors increased the need or desire for U.S. banks to establish overseas branches and made it easier for them to do so. United

TABLE 10–8 INTERNATIONAL ACTIVITIES OF TEN LARGEST U.S. COMMERCIAL BANKS

	Subsidiaries				Branches			
	Total	Europe and Canada	Latin America	Africa and Australasia	Total	Europe and Canada	Latin America	Africa and Australasia
1. Bank of America NT & SA San Francisco, California	9	6	1	2	96	21	41	34
2. First National City Bank New York, New York	34	11	13	10	230	29	150	51
3. Chase Manhattan Bank NA New York, New York	4	2	2	—	81	17	46	18
4. Manufacturers Hanover Trust Co. New York, New York	3	2	1	—	4	3	—	1
5. Chemical Bank New York, New York	1	—	1	—	7	6	1	—
6. Morgan Guaranty Trust Co. New York, New York	3	3	—	—	12	10	1	1
7. Bankers Trust Co. New York, New York	3	3	—	—	4	3	1	—
8. Security Pacific National Bank Los Angeles, California	—	—	—	—	4	3	—	1
9. Continental Illinois National Bank & Trust Co. Chicago, Illinois	6	4	—	2	10	8	—	2
10. The First National Bank of Chicago Chicago, Illinois	2	1	—	1	14	9	2	3
Total	65	32	18	15	462	109	242	111

Source: Table on pp. 362–3 by Frederick Heldring in *The Changing World of Banking* edited by Herbert V. Prochnow and Herbert V. Prochnow, Jr. Copyright © 1974 by Herbert V. Prochnow and Herbert V. Prochnow, Jr. By permission of Harper & Row, Publishers, Inc.

States government regulations imposed during the early 1960s made it difficult for U.S. banks to engage in overseas lending and for U.S. firms to transfer funds to their overseas branches. To serve the growing number of foreign offices of U.S. companies, then, U.S. banks had to establish overseas offices. In addition, periods of tight credit in the U.S. during 1966 and 1969 made banks eager to establish foreign branches so they could raise funds in Europe which could be remitted to the U.S. for lending. This phenomenon, and how the Fed's change in Regulation M in 1969, which imposed reserve requirements on remittances from European branches to U.S. banks, reduced this advantage of foreign branches, are discussed below.

Many of the large U.S. banks established their own foreign branches, as Table 10–8 illustrates. Many smaller banks, however, were unable to establish their own foreign branches and instead formed a consortium with other small banks. For example, the Allied Bank International consortium has seventeen participants. Consortia permitted smaller banks both to pool their resources and to share the risks and yet participate in international banking.

Foreign branches of U.S. banks are allowed to engage in only those activities permitted to their parents in the United States. These branches are therefore at a competitive disadvantage since in most countries foreign banks are allowed considerably more latitude. However, since 1919 U.S. banks have been allowed to establish "Edge Act" subsidiaries (called Edge Act and Agreement corporations), which are allowed to engage in many other activities. Such corporations may engage in standard international banking activities, serve as holding companies which own shares of subsidiaries engaging in financial services such as commercial financing, consumer financing, export-import financing, factoring, leasing, mortgage banking, and investment banking. Edge Act and Agreement corporations are also allowed to make equity or debt investments in foreign commercial and industrial firms. Equity participation in long-term development projects has been common. The use of Edge Act and Agreement corporations increased rapidly during the 1960s. By 1973 104 such subsidiaries had total assets of $6.9 billion.

The transactions discussed so far in this chapter have been international financial transactions of type (2) where the transaction is in the currency of the country in which the transaction occurs. During the 1960s, however, conditions existed that led to the development of a market for borrowing and lending dollars in Europe. Substantial U.S. balance of payments deficits had generated large dollar balances in Europe and elsewhere. These dollars could have been converted into the currencies of the foreigners on the foreign exchange markets. But in many cases, they were not because of the perceived stability of the dollar despite these deficits, the universal acceptance of the dollar, the attractiveness of the U.S. financial system for investing these dollars, and the inability of foreign central banks to make substantial dollar conversions without undermining the dollar-based international financial system. In addition, because of U.S. government regulations preventing dollar outflows from the United States by U.S. commercial banks and corporations investing abroad, there was a demand for dollars in Europe. This dollar borrowing and lending in Europe was conducted by both European banks and European branches of U.S. banks. The market for short-term commercial bank dollar borrowing and lending in Europe is called the *Eurodollar market*. In addition, short-term borrowing and lending by commercial banks of other currencies outside the country of that currency developed, particularly in marks outside Germany and in Swiss francs outside Switzerland. The short-term bank European market in all currencies outside their country is called the *Eurocurrency market*. Most of this short-term Eurocurrency activity is in Eurodollars. The Eurocredit market refers to the intermediate-term borrowing and lending of currencies outside the country of the currency. The intermediate-term Eurocredit market is also accomplished through European commercial banks and European branches of U.S. commercial banks. The next two sections discuss the Eurodollar markets and the Eurocurrency markets, respectively.

EURODOLLAR MARKET

Strictly, Eurodollars are short-term financial assets and liabilities of commercial banks denominated in dollars but traded outside the United States.[8] Eurodollars, then, are dollar-denominated deposits and loans of commercial banks located in Europe.

Most Eurodollar deposits have maturities of less than one year. These deposits may be in the form of time deposits which may be payable on demand; deposits with one-day maturities or other short maturities; or large ($100,000 or more) certificates of deposit of longer maturities (three months or more). There are no demand deposits (with zero interest rate) in the Eurodollar system. The deposit rates are sensitive to changes in the U.S. interest rates and are discussed below.

Eurodollar loans are made in very large amounts, from $500,000 up to several million dollars. Maturities range from thirty days to several years. Loans of more than one year in maturity are considered intermediate-term loans and often have different characteristics than short-term Eurodollar loans; they are discussed in the next section. The in-

---

[8] As indicated above, although currencies other than the dollar are traded on the Eurocurrency markets, the dollar component is the largest and is treated exclusively in this section.

terest rate on these loans is usually quoted as a certain amount over the London Interbank Offer Rate (LIBO), the rate banks charge each other on Eurodollar loans.

The basis for the development of the Eurodollar market was a series of government regulations, particularly by the U.S. government. Regulation Q ceilings on the CDs of U.S. banks, which existed until 1973 on CDs with maturities greater than ninety days, made it difficult to attract these deposits during times of high interest rates. So to maintain their deposits, U.S. banks often told their potential depositors to purchase CDs in their European branches where there were no Regulation Q ceilings. In addition, before 1969 during times of tight credit in the United States, U.S. banks were able to raise Eurodollar deposits in their European branches and remit these deposits to the U.S. headquarters for domestic lending. And until 1969, there were no reserve requirements on these transfers of Eurodollars. On October 16, 1969, however, the Fed imposed reserve requirements on these transfers of Eurodollars to the United States under its Regulation M authority. Since 1969, the level of these transfers has been relatively low even though the Eurodollar market has grown substantially. Finally, three types of government regulations in effect between 1963 and 1974, designed to reduce U.S. balance of payments deficits by restricting capital outflows from the United States, generated a demand for dollars in Europe. These regulations were the interest equalization tax (imposed in 1963), a tax on the interest return of foreign securities sold in the U.S.; restrictions on U.S., bank foreign loans and investments (imposed in 1965); and, restrictions on U.S. corporations transferring funds overseas (imposed on a voluntary basis in 1965 and made mandatory in 1968). These three regulations were eliminated in January, 1974.

Eurodollar deposits are based on dollar deposits in U.S. banks. Assume that corporation A transfers its deposit from bank M in the U.S. to bank X in Europe to get a higher interest rate. Bank X usually keeps a dollar deposit of equal amount in a U.S. bank, perhaps bank M or another U.S. bank, bank N. When bank X makes a dollar loan based on its new deposit to a European corporation, the corporation typically deposits these funds in another European bank, say bank Y. Bank Y may keep its deposits with yet another U.S. bank, say bank P, so the U.S. deposits will be shifted to bank P in bank Y's name from bank M or N in bank X's name. So Eurodollar deposits are based on deposits in U.S. banks. And, as the first step in this example showed, Eurodollars are created when dollar deposits are held in Europe instead of in the U.S. And the primary incentive for this transfer is higher Eurodollar deposit rates.

Because the Eurodollar market is not regulated by any country, data on the Eurodollar market are not as available as for other markets.

Table 10–9 shows the dollar loans of foreign branches of U.S. banks. Of the total loans of $165,317 million, only $3,692 million (1.9 percent) were to the parent bank. This shows, to some extent, the effect of Regulation M. And $100,609 million ($39,816 plus $60,793) were loans to other U.S. banks, 60.8 percent of the total. These interbank loans do not create new loans but just represent churning among the Eurobanks. The LIBO is the base interest rate for these interbank loans. The net nonbank European loans of the foreign branches of the U.S. banks are the sum of the $9,853 million to official institutions and $44,460 million to nonbank foreigners.

Figure 10–4 indicates the total size of the Eurodollar market. The external foreign currency liabilities of banks in eight European countries increased from less than $25 million at the beginning of 1968 to approximately $220 million at the end of 1974. Of this, $155.7 million or 70.9 percent of the total, was in U.S. dollars. The mark and the Swiss franc are the other prominent currencies.

EURODOLLAR INTEREST RATES

From the lenders' or depositors' vantage, Eurodollar deposits offer an alternative to dollar deposits in the United States. Depositors would not accept a lower Eurodollar rate than they could get in the U.S., so Eurodollar rates must exceed U.S. rates to keep the Eurodollar market viable.

In practice, Eurodollar deposit rates are higher than U.S. CD rates and fluctuate similarly, as shown in Figure 10–5. Eurobanks are able to pay these higher rates because, due to lack of regulation, there are no reserve requirements on Eurodollar deposits. However, Figure 10–5 shows that Eurodollar deposits cost banks more than CDs, even after adjusting for reserve requirement differentials.

TABLE 10–9 DOLLAR LOANS OF FOREIGN BRANCHES OF U.S. BANKS, FEBRUARY, 1977 (MILLION DOLLARS)

Total loans payable in U.S. dollars	$165,317
Claims on United States	6,773
Parent bank	3,692
Other	3,081
Claims on foreigners	154,922
Other branches of parent bank	39,816
Other banks	60,793
Official institutions	9,853
Nonbank foreigners	44,460

Source: Federal Reserve Bulletin, Board of Governors of the Federal Reserve System.

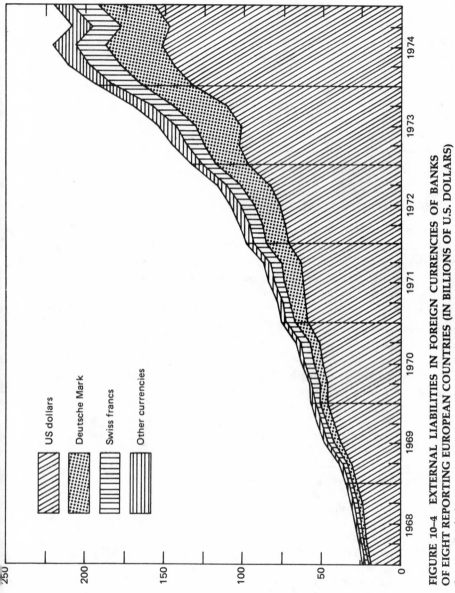

FIGURE 10–4 EXTERNAL LIABILITIES IN FOREIGN CURRENCIES OF BANKS OF EIGHT REPORTING EUROPEAN COUNTRIES (IN BILLIONS OF U.S. DOLLARS)

Source: Bank for International Settlements, Annual Report, 1975, p. 129.

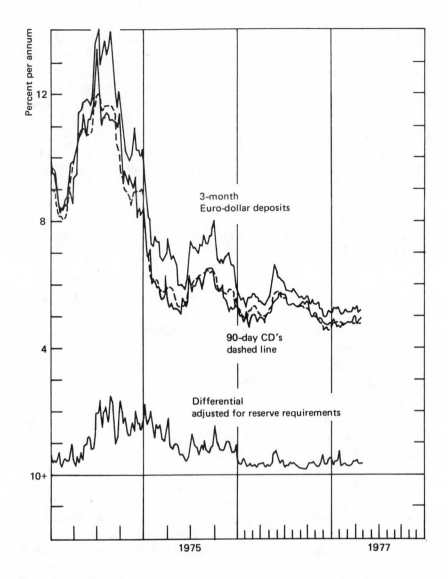

FIGURE 10-5 SELECTED INTEREST AND EXCHANGE RATES

Source: Selected Interest and Exchange Rates, Weekly Series of Charts, May 2, 1977, Board of Governors of the Federal Reserve System.

It might seem, similarly, that to remain viable, Eurodollar loan rates would have to be less than U.S. loan rates for Eurobanks to be able to make loans. However, before the U.S. restrictions on foreign lending by U.S. banks were removed in 1974, U.S. banks did not provide an option as a source of dollars for foreign use. And, as Table 10–10 shows, during 1973 and 1974 Eurobank loan rates were higher than U.S. interest rates. However, during 1975 and 1976 competition from U.S. banks has reduced Eurodollar loan rates below U.S. bank loan rates. And the effective cost of borrowing from Eurobanks rather than from U.S. banks is relatively lower than the interest rate differential indicates, because there are no corresponding compensating balances on Eurodollar loans whereas there usually are on U.S. loans.

The squeeze on Eurobanks because they are paying higher deposit rates and charging lower loan rates than U.S. banks is shown by the spreads in Table 10–10. At the end of 1975 and 1976, Eurobank spreads were substantially less than those of U.S. banks. Eurobanks were able to operate with these lower spreads because of lower costs due to the absence of reserve requirements and other regulations and because their loans were made in very large volumes to prime customers.

Figure 10–6 shows the rate premium paid on Eurodollar deposits and the similar movements of Eurodollar and CD deposit rates. Figure 10–7 shows the rate premium charged on domestic loans, adjusted for compensating balances, over Eurodollar loan rates and their similar movements. Note particularly the recent similarity between the rates on Eurodollar loans and commercial paper loans.

INTERMEDIATE-TERM INTERNATIONAL FINANCE

The intermediate-term market in international finance of type (3) is called the *Eurocredit market*. In this market European banks and European branches of U.S. banks make intermediate-term loans to corporations, governments, government agencies, international organizations, and to each other. Governments and government agencies borrow substantially in this market to finance balance of payments deficits and development projects. Often the loans are so large that single banks do not want to risk making the entire loan so *Eurocredit* loans are usually *syndicated*—that is, a group or syndicate of banks each participate

TABLE 10–10 U.S. AND EUROBANK DEPOSIT AND LOAN RATES

	Commercial Bank Deposit Rates		Prime Commercial Bank Loan Rates		Spreads (Deposit minus Loan Rate)	
End of Year	U.S.	Eurobanks	U.S.	Eurobanks	U.S.	Eurobanks
1973	9.25	10.13	9.75	10.75	.50	.62
1974	9.25	10.19	10.25	11.32	1.00	1.13
1975	5.50	5.81	7.25	6.69	1.75	0.88
1976	4.70	5.00	6.00	5.50	1.30	0.50

Source: *World Financial Markets*, Morgan Guaranty Trust Company of New York.

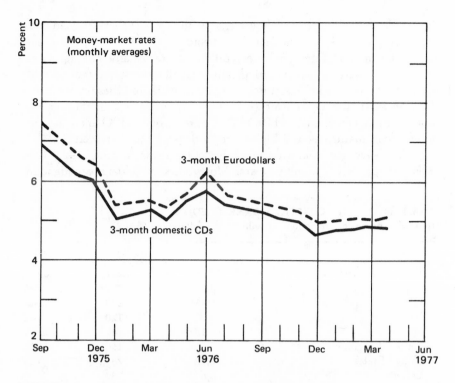

FIGURE 10–6   EURODOLLAR AND U.S. CD DEPOSIT RATES

Source: *World Financial Markets*, March, 1977, Morgan Guaranty Trust Company of New York.

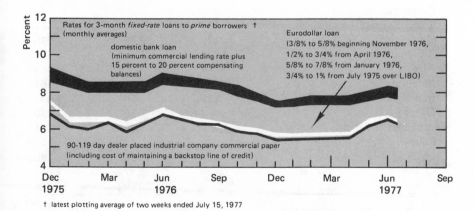

† latest plotting average of two weeks ended July 15, 1977

FIGURE 10–7   U.S. BANK LOAN AND COMMERCIAL PAPER RATES AND EURODOLLAR LOAN RATES

Source: *World Financial Markets*, July, 1977, Morgan Guaranty Trust Company of New York.

in the loan. Table 10–11 shows the volume of *Eurocredit* loans, by borrowing country, for the last three years.

The interest rates on Eurocredit loans are usually floating rates; that is, they are adjusted periodically (usually every six months) for changes in current interest rates. The benchmark for these rates is the London Interbank Offer Rate (LIBO). For example, a loan rate may be quoted as 2 percent over LIBO. This spread over LIBO increases for longer loan maturities and higher credit risks of the borrowers.

The average maturity of Eurocredit loans during 1972–1973 was between six and nine years. Most Eurocredit loans are denomi-

TABLE 10–11 EUROCURRENCY BANK CREDITS
(publicly-announced in period, in millions of dollars)

	1974	1975	1976
Industrial countries	20,683	7,231	10,918
France	3,244	719	587
Greece	419	239	323
Italy	2,322	120	355
Spain	1,151	1,147	1,977
United Kingdom	5,655	160	1,671
United States	2,221	764	677
Other[a]	5,671	4,082	5,328
Developing countries	7,342	11,164	15,243
Non-OPEC countries	6,276	8,264	11,349
Brazil	1,672	2,152	3,158
Mexico	948	2,311	1,993
Peru	443	334	395
Philippines	844	363	970
South Korea	134	347	834
Other[b]	2,235	2,757	3,999
OPEC countries	1,067	2,900	3,894
Algeria	—	500	583
Indonesia	669	1,348	461
Iran	115	265	1,400
Other	283	787	1,450
Communist countries	1,238	2,597	2,503
Poland	509	475	525
U.S.S.R.	100	650	282
Other[c]	629	1,472	1,696
TOTAL	29,263	20,992	28,664

[a] Includes multinational organizations.
[b] Includes regional development organizations.
[c] Includes COMECON institutions.
Source: *World Financial Markets*, March, 1977, Morgan Guaranty Trust Company of New York.

nated in dollars. Because the maturity of Eurocredit loans is longer than that of available forward foreign exchange contracts, these loans cannot be hedged by the borrower. Consequently, the borrower runs the risk of the dollar strengthening substantially relative to their currency.

LONG-TERM INTERNATIONAL FINANCE

The international bond market is the main instrument in long-term international finance. An *international bond* is defined as one sold outside the country of the borrower. International bonds are divided into two categories, foreign bonds and Eurobonds. *Foreign bonds* are issues underwritten by investment banks of a country, sold mainly in the country, and denominated in the currency of the country. For example, a mark-denominated bond issued in Germany by a U.S. firm and a dollar-denominated bond issued in the U.S. by a German firm would both be foreign bonds (bonds issued in the U.S. by foreign firms have been called Yankee bonds). *Eurobonds* are usually underwritten by a syndicate composed of firms from more than one country and sold mainly in countries other than the country of the currency in which the issued is denominated.[9] For example, a dollar-denominated issue sold in Germany or a mark-denominated issue sold in Britain would both be Eurobonds.[10]

International bonds are underwritten in much the same way U.S. bonds are. Table 10–12 shows the changing composition of the major underwriters in Eurobond issues. Note particularly the decline in the importance of U.S. and British investment banks.

Table 10–13 shows the volumes of issues of the various categories of international bonds by type of borrower and currency of denomination during the last three years. Foreign companies are the major borrowers on the Eurobond markets; U.S. companies have been relatively minor borrowers. Most Eurobonds are denominated in dollars although substantial amounts are also denominated in marks and Canadian dollars. Most foreign bonds issued outside the U.S. are issued in Switzerland (and denominated in Swiss francs) and Germany (and denominated in marks). Again, U.S. companies are relatively minor borrowers.

Foreign bonds issued in the U.S., Yankee bonds, have grown rapidly during the last three years. Canada has been the major borrower on this market.

Table 10–14 describes the characteristics of a selection of interna-

---

[9] These definitions are from *World Financial Markets*, Morgan Guaranty Trust Company of New York.

[10] There is also an Asian bond market, that is, the issue of dollar-denominated bonds in Asia. Euro-equities, or dollar-denominated equities, have also been issued in Europe.

tional bonds issued during February, 1977. The maturity of most of the Eurobond issues is between five and seven years but some borrowers obtained funds in the twelve- to fifteen-year range.

The volume of issues of international bonds by currency of denomination depends on international interest rate differentials and the expected strength of the various currencies. No hedging of bonds issued in currencies other than that of the borrower is possible because there are no forward markets of sufficiently long maturities. A strengthening of the currency in which the loan is denominated relative to that of the borrower's own currency can substantially increase the cost of a loan. In this case, firms tend to recall their loans where possible.

Restrictions by various governments against foreign lending and other types of currency outflows can also affect the type and volume of

TABLE 10–12 THE RANKS OF INTERNATIONAL BANKERS

(Publicly offered Eurobonds, managed and co-managed)*	
The 10 biggest in 1969 Bank	Amount Billions of dollars
Deutsche Bank (Ger.)	$2.0
S.G. Warburg (Brit.)	1.5
White Weld (U.S.)	1.3
Banca Commerciale Italiana (Italy)	1.1
Morgan & Cie. International (Fr.-U.S.)	1.1
Lehman Bros. (U.S.)	1.0
N.M. Rothschild & Sons (Brit.)	1.0
Paribas (Fr.)	0.9
Kuhn Loeb (U.S.)	0.9
Dresdner Bank (Ger.)	0.8

The 10 biggest in 1976 Bank	Amount Billions of dollars
Credit Suisse White Weld (Swiss-U.S.)	$5.9
Union Bank (Swiss)	5.5
Swiss Bank Corp. (Swiss)	5.4
Deutsche Bank (Ger.)	4.8
Westdeutsche Landesbank (Ger.)	3.2
Kredietbank Luxembourgeoise (Lux.)	3.0
Amsterdam-Rotterdam Bank (Neth.)	3.0
Paribas (Fr.)	2.9
Commerzbank (Ger.)	2.7
S.G. Warburg (Brit.)	2.6

* With full credit for each issue given to each co-manager.
Source: Business Week, March 14, 1977, p. 63.

TABLE 10–13 NEW INTERNATIONAL BOND ISSUES
(new issues in period, in millions of dollars)

	1974	1975	1976
Eurobonds, total	2,134	8,567	14,056
by category of borrower			
U.S. companies	110	268	435
Foreign companies	640	2,903	5,277
State enterprises	542	3,123	3,930
Governments	482	1,658	2,228
International organizations	360	615	2,186
by currency of denomination			
U.S. dollar	996	3,738	8,932
German mark	344	2,278	2,661
Dutch guilder	381	719	502
Canadian dollar	60	558	1,407
European unit of account	174	371	99
French franc	—	293	39
Other	179	610	416
Foreign bonds outside the United States, total	1,432	4,884	5,764
U.S. companies	77	61	28
Foreign companies	455	1,386	1,109
State enterprises	568	1,314	1,857
Governments	138	765	1,025
International organizations	194	1,358	1,745
by currency of denomination			
German mark	253	1,089	1,058
Swiss franc	911	3,297	3,822
Dutch guilder	4	182	571
Other	264	315	313
Foreign bonds in the United States, total	3,291	6,462	10,006
by category of borrower			
Canadian entities	1,962	3,074	5,716
International organizations	610	1,900	2,275
Other	719	1,488	2,015
International bonds, total of which issued by:	6,857	19,913	29,826
Industrial countries	5,090	15,213	22,025
Developing countries	603	827	1,595
International organizations	1,164	3,873	6,206

Source: *World Financial Markets*, March, 1977, Morgan Guaranty Trust Company of New York.

TABLE 10–14 NEW INTERNATIONAL BOND ISSUES

Issuer (Grantor) *(Eurobond: E; Foreign bond: outside United States—F, O; in United States—F, US)*	*Country/state of domicile*	*Amount, millions*	*Offer date*	*Coupon rate*[a]	*Maturity*	*Offer price*	*Yield*[b]
February 1977							
U.S. companies							
Gulf and Western International Finance N.V. (Gulf and Western Industries, Inc.) (E)	N. Antilles	$50	3	8¼a	1984	100	8.09
Foreign companies							
Industrial Bank of Japan Finance Co., N.V. (Industrial Bank of Japan Ltd.) (E)	N. Antilles	$50	1	*	1982	100	*
Light-Servicios de Electricidad S.A. (E)	Brazil	DM 100	2	8½a	1982	99½	8.46
C.M. Industries (F, O)	France	SwF 30	7	5¾a	1989	99	5.79
Nippon Paint Company Ltd. (F, O) c, d	Japan	DM 30	8	6	1985	100	6.00
Beneficial Finance International Corp. (Beneficial Corp.) (E)	Canada	C$50	8	9a	1984	99	9.01
Williams and Glyn's Bank Ltd. (National and Commercial Banking Group) (E)	U.K.	$40	9	**	1984	100	**
Volvo AB (E)	Sweden	$35	14	8a	1987	100	7.85
Hitachi Zosen K.K. (Sanwa Bank Limited) (E)	Japan	$30	15	7¾a	1984	99¼	7.74
Great Lakes Paper Co., Ltd. (E)	Canada	$20	18	8¾a	1984	100	8.57
Toyo Kanetsu K.K. (Fuji Bank Ltd.) (E)	Japan	$15	22	7¾a	1982	100	7.61
Solvay Finance B.V. (Solvay et Compagnie S.A.) (E)	Netherlands	$20	22	7¾a	1984	100	7.61
Saab-Scania AB (E)	Sweden	$50	22	8½a	1989	99¼	8.43
Banque Louis-Dreyfus (E)	France	$20	25	†	1983	100	†
N. V. Philips Gloeilampenfabricken (F, O)	Netherlands	SwF 80	25	5a	1992	100	4.94
Shell International Finance N.V. (E) c	Netherlands	$300	n.a.	7¾a	1987	n.a.	n.a.
Gulf Oil Canada Limited (F, US) c	Canada	$125	n.a.	8⅜	1997	n.a.	n.a.
State enterprises							
Copenhagen Telephone Co. (F, O)	Denmark	SwF 80	1	5½a	1992	100	5.43
Norsk Hydro A/S (E)	Norway	$50	3	8½a	1992	99½	8.39
Outokumpo Oy (Republic of Finland) (F, O)	Finland	SwF 50	8	5½a	1992	99	5.52

Statsforetag AB (E)	Sweden	DM 100	11	7a	1985	99½	6.96
Korea Development Bank (Republic of South Korea) (E)	Korea	$25	14	9½a	1982	99½	9.41
Canadian National Railways (E)	Canada	C$60	21	8⅞a	1987	99¼	8.75
Nippon Telegraph and Telephone Public Corp.	Japan	$100	24	7⅝	1982	100	7.63
(Government of Japan) (F, US)		$50	24	8⅛	1987	99¾	8.16
Norpipe A/S (E)	Norway	$50	28	8½a	1989	99¾	8.36
Australian Shipping Commission (E) c	Australia	$50	n.a.	8a	1985	n.a.	n.a.
Eurofima (F, O) c		DM 80	n.a	6¾a	1987	n.a.	n.a.
Governments							
Kingdom of Norway (F, US)		$150	2	7⅜	1982	99.70	7.40
Kingdom of Denmark (F, O)		FI 75	2	8½a	1992	99	8.45
Republic of Iceland (E)		$20	3	9a	1987	99½	8.88
City of Toronto (F, US)	Canada	$28	9	8	1987	100	8.00
		$55	9	8½	1997	99½	8.55
Republic of Venezuela (E)		$100	9	8a	1984	99½	7.94
Republic of Austria (F, O) c		DM 50	9	6¾a	1987	99½	6.71
City of Vienna (F, O)	Austria	SwF 70	10	5¼a	1992	100½	5.14
Government of New Zealand (E) c		FI 75	11	8a	1983	99¾	7.90
Province of Newfoundland (E)	Canada	$50	15	9a	1989	100½	8.76
City of Oslo (E)	Norway	Lux F 500	15	8½a	1987	99¼	8.44
City of Stockholm (F, US)	Sweden	$50	16	8⅞	1992	100	8.88
Republic of the Philippines (E)		BD 8	16	9a	1984	99½	8.90
Republic of Singapore (F, O)		SwF 50	16	5½a	1989	99	5.54
Province of Manitoba (F, O)	Canada	Y 12,000	18	8.60	1987	100	8.60
Copenhagen County Authority (F, O)	Denmark	SwF 50	24	5¾a	1992	100	5.67
International organizations							
European Coal and Steel Community (E)		$50	8	7¼a	1982	99	7.36
European Coal and Steel Community (E) c		$10	n.a.	8¼a	1987	n.a.	n.a.

[a] Coupon interest is payable semiannually, unless followed by an "a" which indicates an annual coupon.
b Where coupon interest is payable annually, payment is discounted semiannually for comparability in computation of yield.
c Private placement.
d Convertible into the common stock of the company after May 1, 1977. Conversion price premium over closing price of stock on day preceding offer was 7.75%.
* Interest rate is payable at ¼% over six-months Eurodollar interbank rate. Minimum interest is 6% p.a.
** Interest is payable at ¼% over six-months Eurodollar interbank rate. Minimum interest is 6½% p.a.
† Interest is payable at ⅜% over six-months Eurodollar interbank rate. Minimum interest is 6½% p.a.

Source: *World Financial Markets*, March, 1977, Morgan Guaranty Trust Company of New York.

international borrowing and lending. An instrumental factor in the growth of the Eurobond market was the set of restrictions by the U.S. government on dollar outflows to Europe in the mid-1960s. This generated a demand for dollars in Europe.

The Eurocurrency and Eurobond markets represent the second largest markets of their types. They are larger than the national markets of any country except the United States. Consequently, they fulfill an important role in international finance.

questions

1. If the spot price for the French franc is $0.20, the rate twelve months from now is expected to be $0.19 and the current French interest rate on one-year securities (in francs) is 11 percent, should U.S. investors invest in franc securities or dollar securities if the one-year interest rate in the U.S. is: a) 5 percent? b) 8 percent?

2. Assume that in 1973 the spot rate for the Swiss franc was .40 and the five-year bond rate was 7 percent. The five-year rate in the U.S. during 1973 was 10 percent. When the loan matured in 1978 the spot exchange rate was .50. If a U.S. firm had borrowed $100,000 worth of *Swiss francs* during 1973, converted them into dollars, and invested them in the U.S., what would the effective rate of interest on this loan be?

3. Discuss how exchange rates are determined by support operations and when rates are freely fluctuating.

4. What is the Eurodollar market? How do borrowing and lending rates in this market compare with similar borrowing and lending rates in the United States? What was the impact of Regulation M on the level of Eurodollar borrowing by United States banks?

5. Discuss the various types of international financial transactions that occur today. What is the role of United States banks in these transactions?

selected references to part IV

Kaufman, George G. *Money, the Financial System and the Economy,* 2nd ed. Chicago: Rand McNally, 1977, Part VI, pp. 423–490.

Kenen, Peter B. and Lubitz, Raymond. *International Economics,* 3rd ed. Englewood Cliffs, N.J.: Prentice-Hall, Inc., 1971.

Lee, Francis A. and Eng, Maximo. *International Financial Markets,* New York: Praeger Publishing, 1975.

Rodriguez, Rita M. and Carter, E. Eugene. *International Financial Management.* Englewood Cliffs, N.J.: Prentice-Hall, Inc., 1976.

THE FINANCIAL BEHAVIOR OF THE CORPORATE BUSINESS SECTOR

V

business sources
of funds:
the recent evidence

11

Chapters 8 and 9 discuss the individual domestic financial markets and institutions and provide some indication of how important they are to the business sector. This chapter examines some quantitative information of how business has raised its funds over the past several years. This information is used to describe and to investigate the business motivations for the ways in which businesses raise their funds.

the business balance sheet

A convenient way to begin this investigation is by considering the business balance sheet. The balance sheet for any entity, business or otherwise, normally consists of two columns. The left column shows the various assets of the entity and their amounts. The right column gives the various types of indebtedness (or liabilities) of the entity and their amounts and also the wealth (also called the amount of ownership or equity) of the entity. By definition, the entity's equity is the excess of the quantity of its assets over the quantity of its liabilities. Table 11–1 represents a somewhat simplified version of the balance sheet of a hypothetical business.

TABLE 11-1 BALANCE SHEET FOR CORPORATE BUSINESS SECTOR (BILLION DOLLARS)

Assets (Uses of Funds)		Liabilities + Equity (Sources of Funds)		
Current assets	$ 80	Total liabilities		$115
Cash, deposits and		Short-term liabilities	80	
marketable securities	15	Bank loans	50	
		Commercial		
Accounts receivable	25	paper	20	
		Accounts		
Inventories	40	payable	10	
		Long-term liabilities	35	
Fixed assets (plant		Bonds	25	
and equipment)	120	Mortgages	10	
Historical cost	180			
Depreciation	60	Equity		85
		New issues of		
		common stock	20	
Total assets	200	Retained earnings	65	
		Liabilities plus equity		200

The business balance sheet can also be viewed in a slightly different way. The liabilities and equity on the right side are *sources of funds* to the business. Liabilities are funds procured by borrowing; equity funds are those contributed by owners, either by buying the stock of the business or by refraining from taking the business' profits as dividends but instead letting the firm retain the earnings. On the other side of the balance sheet, assets are essentially *uses of funds* by business—assets are procured by using funds to purchase them. Consequently, the left or asset side of the balance sheet is the uses of funds by business, and the right-hand side is the sources of borrowed funds (currently outstanding) and sources of funds contributed by owners.

In considering the recent financial behavior of firms, however, it is of more interest to look at recent sources and uses of funds, such as the sources and uses of funds during the last quarter or year, rather than the sources and uses over the life of the firm as the balance sheet shows. Consequently, the data presented in this chapter are for *changes in* balance sheet entries during a year. These so-called flow of funds data show the sources and uses of funds by business during a year or quarter. This incremented balance sheet (the change in the balance sheet over a specific period of time) is formulated in Table 11–2 and is called a

TABLE 11–2 FLOW OF FUNDS STATEMENT FOR CORPORATE BUSINESS SECTOR* (INCREMENTAL BALANCE SHEET)

Uses of Funds	Sources of Funds

Increase in current assets:
  Liquid assets (cash, deposits, and
  short-term marketable securities)
  Accounts receivable (consumer
  credit and trade credit)
  Inventories
 	
Increase in fixed assets (gross) —
  Investment in plant and equipment
	Increase in short-term liabilities:
	  Bank loans
	  Commercial paper
	Increase in long-term liabilities:
	  Bonds
	  Mortgages
	Increase in equity:
	  New issues of common stock
	  Retained earnings during the year
	  (= profits after taxes — dividends)

* This statement is not complete, but incorporates all the categories that are used in this chapter.

"Flow of Funds Statement" for the corporate business sector (the sector composed of all corporate businesses combined).

Data for the categories of sources and uses of funds shown in Table 11–2 are given for each year from 1965 through 1975 in Table 11–3.

In considering how the various sources and uses of corporate business funds relate to national economic activity, recent economic and financial history should be recalled. This chapter treats business financial behavior since 1965. During this period, there was a mild slowdown during 1967 and full-fledged recessions during 1970 and late 1974–75. During 1966, 1969, 1973 and 1974, there were periods of high interest rates, tight credit (credit crunches), and strong economic activity. Table 11–4 presents data on the behavior of several interest rates during this period. Figures 11–1 and 11–2 are graphs of the interest rates.

Several types of observations about corporate financial behavior can be made from the data of Table 11–3. Most of these observations follow naturally from the discussions of previous chapters.

ACQUISITION OF ASSETS

First, the acquisition of real or physical assets, inventories and plant and equipment, follows the business cycle. That is, investment in these assets is high when the economy is strong and low when the economy is weak. During 1967 and 1970, additions to inventories were smaller than in the preceding years and in 1975 the level of inventories actually decreased. During 1967 and 1970, investment in plant and

TABLE 11–3 SOURCES AND USES OF FUNDS (BILLION DOLLARS)

Uses of Funds (Acquisition of Assets)	1965	1966	1967	1968	1969	1970	1971	1972	1973	1974	1975
1. Liquid assets	2.6	− 3.7	4.8	8.0	2.3	− 0.4	10.6	4.0	6.9	13.2	19.1
2. Accounts receivable—consumer credit	0.2	0.5	0.3	0.0	0.3	0.7	0.6	1.6	2.0	1.2	1.1
3. Accounts receivable—trade credit	14.0	12.0	8.3	18.6	22.7	8.4	5.7	20.0	24.1	20.8	10.4
4. Inventories	7.8	13.9	9.2	7.1	8.3	5.0	5.2	10.7	15.5	10.6	−14.6
5. Investment in plant and equipment	51.6	59.9	60.9	65.9	72.7	73.2	77.0	86.9	101.7	109.2	107.8
(percent change)		(16.1%)	(1.7%)	(8.2%)	(10.3%)	(0.6%)	(5.2%)	(12.9%)	(17.0%)	(7.3%)	(−1.3%)
Sources of Funds											
6. Bank loans	10.5	8.3	6.6	9.6	11.8	5.6	4.4	13.5	30.6	29.9	−13.2
7. Commercial paper	− 0.3	0.8	1.4	1.5	2.3	2.2	−1.7	−0.6	−0.2	4.1	−2.4
8. Trade debt	12.1	10.6	7.4	17.2	21.0	7.4	3.8	13.7	19.6	18.1	8.1
9. Bonds	5.4	10.2	14.7	12.9	12.0	19.8	18.8	12.2	9.2	19.7	27.2
10. Mortgages (commercial)	2.9	4.0	3.1	4.8	3.7	3.6	7.9	12.0	14.1	9.1	8.7
11. New issues of common stock	0.0	1.3	2.4	− 0.2	3.4	5.7	11.4	10.9	7.4	4.1	9.9
12. Retained earnings	20.0	21.9	18.9	17.6	14.4	8.1	13.4	20.6	28.9	30.3	27.7
Miscellaneous											
13. Profits after taxes	37.1	39.9	37.8	38.2	35.1	27.9	33.4	42.2	53.2	60.7	58.4
14. Dividends	17.1	18.0	18.9	20.6	20.7	19.8	20.0	21.6	24.3	30.4	30.7
15. Depreciation	32.6	35.5	39.1	42.8	47.5	52.7	57.7	62.0	68.1	77.6	88.6
16. Retained earnings + dep.	52.6	57.4	58.0	60.4	61.9	60.8	71.1	82.6	97.0	107.9	116.3
17. Gross internal funds	56.3	60.6	61.4	62.4	61.8	58.7	68.0	80.2	83.8	77.7	103.8
18. Net funds raised in markets	20.4	25.3	29.6	31.5	38.9	39.5	46.8	55.3	67.2	77.1	35.8

Source: Flow of Funds Data, Board of Governors of the Federal Reserve System.

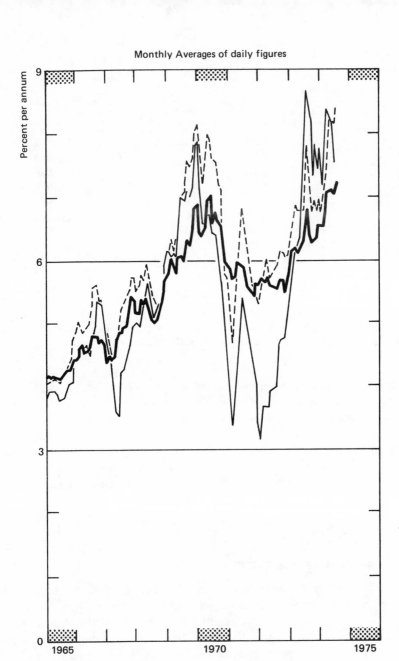

Monthly Averages of daily figures

Percent per annum

9

6

3

0

1965   1970   1975

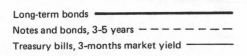

Long-term bonds ━━━━━━━━

Notes and bonds, 3-5 years ━ ━ ━ ━ ━ ━ ━

Treasury bills, 3-months market yield ━━━━━━

FIGURE 11–1 YIELDS ON U.S. GOVERNMENT SECURITIES

Source: Historical Chart Book, Board of Governors of the Federal Reserve System.

TABLE 11-4 INTEREST RATE DATA*

	Bank Prime Rate on Short-Term Business Loans	Prime Commercial Paper Rate, 4–6 months	Moody's AAA Bond Rate	Dividend to Price Ratio— Standard & Poor's Common Stocks	Price Index— Standard & Poor's Common Stocks (500)
1965	4.53	4.38	4.49	3.00	88.2
1966	5.62	5.55	5.13	3.40	85.3
1967	5.64	5.10	5.51	3.20	91.9
1968	6.29	5.90	6.18	3.07	98.7
1969	7.95	7.83	7.03	3.24	97.8
1970	7.91	7.72	8.04	3.83	83.2
1971	5.70	5.11	7.39	3.14	98.3
1972	5.25	4.69	7.21	2.84	109.2
1973	8.02	8.15	7.44	3.06	107.4
1974	10.80	9.87	8.57	4.47	82.9
1975	7.86	6.33	8.83	4.31	86.2

* All except the Standard & Poor's Price Index are in percent.
Source: The bank prime rate data are from the Federal Reserve Bulletin; the remaining data are from the Economic Report of the President.

equipment increased at very low rates, and in 1975 it decreased.[1] During years of strong economic activity, 1966, 1969, 1973 and 1974, investments in inventories and plant and equipment increased at high rates.

Accounts receivable, largely due to trade credit, follow the same pattern as investments in real assets; that is, they increase more during strong economic times and at lower rates during recessions. This pattern is due to the fact that accounts closely follow the pattern of sales.

sources of funds

INTERNAL VERSUS EXTERNAL FUNDS

This section considers how business raises the funds needed to finance the purchase of these assets. Three considerations arise: 1) whether the funds are generated internally, or within the firm, or generated externally, or outside the firm; 2) if external, whether the funds are long-term funds or short-term funds; and, 3) if long-term, what the composition is between bonds and equities; if short-term, what the com-

---

[1] These data are in nominal or current dollars; that is, they are not corrected for inflation. Consequently, the numbers increase more during inflationary years. Also a small increase in nominal terms may be a decrease in real terms during inflationary years.

The Financial Behavior of the Corporate Business Sector

position is between bank loans and commercial paper. Variations of these decisions are considered later in this chapter.

Consider first the business decision regarding the internal versus external composition of funds. Funds generated internally by business include the retained earnings of the firm (profits after taxes minus dividends) (line 12 in Table 11–3) plus depreciation expenses during the year (line 15). Depreciation expenses are a source of internal funds because even though they are subtracted as an expense on the income statement of the business sector to arrive at profits, they are not an out-of-pocket cost to the firm. Since this amount does not flow out of the firm, it should be added to retained earnings as a source of internal funds. Line 17 shows total internal funds.[2] Line 18 shows the volume of external funds raised in the financial markets.

Table 11–5 shows the ratio of gross internal funds to external funds. Two observations are clear. First, over the period shown there has been a downward trend in this ratio. The business sector has become progressively more dependent upon external funds during the last decade. Because external debt funds require future interest payments, this has added to the business requirement for funds to pay the interest expenses and has made profits less than they would have been if internal

TABLE 11–5   GROSS INTERNAL FUNDS DIVIDED BY NET FUNDS RAISED IN MARKETS

1965	2.75 (17.7%)
1966	2.39 (−13.1%)
1967	2.07 (−13.3%)
1968	1.98 (− 4.3%)
1969	1.59 (−19.7%)
1970	1.49 (− 6.3%)
1971	1.45 (− 2.7%)
1972	1.45 (− 0.0%)
1973	1.25 (−13.8%)
1974	1.01 (−19.2%)
1975	2.90 (187.1%)

Source: Calculated from data in Table 11–3.

---

[2] Gross internal funds, as shown on line 17, also include foreign branch profits and adjustments, the latter because during inflationary times it costs more to replace inventories and plant and equipment than is indicated by the costs shown on the Income Statement of producing inventories and depreciating of plant and equipment, respectively. During inflationary times, therefore, internal funds are reduced because it costs more to replace inventories and plant and equipment than was reflected on the Income Statement.

funds had been used (this reduction is mitigated somewhat because interest expenses are tax deductible). External equity funds also lead to the need (financial, not legal) for future dividend payments. Internal funds, however, require no future explicit or out-of-pocket payments. The decline in the internal to external funds ratio has, therefore, put more pressure on the business sector.

The second observation relates to changes in this ratio over the business cycle. This ratio declines more quickly during times of rapid economic growth and high interest rates ($-$ 13.1 percent during 1966, $-$ 19.7 percent during 1969, $-$ 13.8 percent during 1973, and $-$ 19.2 percent during 1974) because even though total interest payments either increase or decrease little during these times, the need for external funds increases substantially to finance the increased acquisition of assets.[3]

During times of weak economic activity this ratio either declines more slowly or increases, indicating an increased reliance on internal funds. This is because even though the generation of internal funds is not high (although such funds increased substantially in 1975 due largely to a reduction in inflation and the corresponding adjustment in profits), the need for external funds decreases (or increases less quickly) because of smaller asset increases.

During times of strong economic activity and rapid asset growth, business becomes more reliant on external funds. During recessions, the need for total funds decreases and the fraction of this that can be funded from internal sources increases.

LONG-TERM VERSUS SHORT-TERM FUNDS

How does the business sector decide whether to use long-term or short-term funds to finance its asset expansion? Two principles attempt to explain this decision. The first principle relates to the expectations hypothesis explanation of interest rates discussed in Chapter 7. According to the expectations hypothesis, business chooses the maturity of funds that minimizes its interest costs over the period it plans to have the funds outstanding. According to this principle, business therefore raises short-term funds when the level of interest rates is high so it has to pay the high rates for only a short period of time. It raises long-term funds when interest rates are low to "lock-in" the low rates for a long period of time. This principle could be called the *principle of minimum interest costs*.

The second principle is the *suitability principle*, which says that

---

[3] These times of strong economic activity are also normally times of inflation, which leads to a reduction in internal funds because of the need to replace inventories and plant and equipment at higher prices.

business should use long-term funds to finance the acquisition of long-term assets, such as plant and equipment, and short-term funds to finance the acquisition of short-term assets, such as inventories and accounts receivable. The rationale for this principle is evident. If, contrary to this principle, business used short-term funds to purchase plant and equipment, it would not have generated sufficient funds from the investment to pay back the loan at its maturity. Consequently, business would have to borrow new funds to be able to repay the original loan, which is called *rolling over* the debt. If credit were very tight at the roll-over time, some businesses might not be able to borrow new funds to repay the original loan (or could do so only at a very high interest rate). The business would be in a very illiquid, and therefore precarious, situation.[4]

If, conversely, a business financed the temporary acquisition of short-term assets with long-term funds, the funds would still be outstanding even after the firm no longer had the assets financed by the funds. The firm could certainly invest the excess funds in financial assets. But typically, the firm must pay a higher rate of interest on its loans than it earns on its financial investments. Consequently, the business would have some financial investments earning less than the interest being paid on the funds used to finance the investment. The firm would not choose to do this because it is unprofitable.

Consequently, it would not seem wise for the firm to violate the suitability principle by either financing long-term assets with short-term funds, or by financing short-term assets with long-term funds. What does the evidence on firm funding behavior say about the applicability of the minimum cost principle and the suitability principle?

The data in Table 11–3 are used to construct Table 11–6, which shows business short-term funds (for simplicity only bank loans and commercial paper are considered) and long-term funds (bonds, mortgages, and new issues of common stock), their total, and the short-term funds as a percentage of total funds (called the short-term ratio). The ratio of short to total varies considerably. The ratio is low during the recession years of 1970–1971 and 1975 (even negative during 1975 as business paid off short-term loans) and low during 1967. The ratio is very high during the tight credit years of 1973 and 1974; high during the credit crunch year of 1969 and high during 1965 and 1966. Thus, during times of low interest rates business has increased the proportion

---

[4] In Chapter 2, the liquidity of an asset was defined as the ease of converting an asset into a pre-known amount of cash. The liquidity of a business is similarly defined. It refers to the capacity for a business to pay its imminent debts (debts due within a year) with assets that will be converted into cash within one year. An illiquid business has insufficient assets that can be converted into cash to be able to pay the debts that mature within a year.

TABLE 11-6 SOURCES OF FUNDS: SHORT-TERM VERSUS LONG-TERM (BILLION DOLLARS)

	Short-Funds *Bank Loans plus Commercial Paper*	*Long-Funds* *Bonds plus Mortgages plus New Issues of Common Stock—Total*		*Short (in %)* *Total (Short-term Ratio)*
1965	10.2	8.3	18.5	55.1
1966	9.1	15.5	24.6	37.0
1967	8.0	20.2	28.2	28.4
1968	11.1	17.5	28.6	38.8
1969	14.1	19.1	33.2	42.5
1970	7.8	29.1	36.9	21.1
1971	2.7	38.1	40.8	6.6
1972	12.9	35.1	48.0	26.9
1973	30.4	30.7	61.1	49.8
1974	34.0	32.9	66.9	50.8
1975	−15.6	45.8	30.2	−51.6

Source: Calculated from data in Table 11–3.

of its long-term funds and during times of high interest rates it has increased the proportion of its short-term funds. This evidence is consistent with the minimum cost principle. The process of replacing short-term funds with long-term funds (either proportionately, or even absolutely as business did during 1975) is called *funding the debt*. As indicated, business typically funds its debt during recessions.

How would business sources of funds vary over time according to the suitability principle? As indicated in Table 11–3, both long-term business assets, investment in plant and equipment, and short-term business assets, inventories, and accounts receivable, tend to increase during years of strong economic growth and decrease during recessions. Since they tend to increase and decrease at the same times, according to the suitability principle there should be little variation in the short-term ratio.

The evidence in Table 11–6 appears much more consistent with the minimum cost principle than with the suitability principle. This is not to say that the suitability principle has no effect on business behavior, but only that the minimum cost principle apparently has a much greater effect. Typically during times of high interest rates, business increases its sources of short-term funds and during times of low interest rates and recession, business funds its debt—that is, reduces its short-term sources of funds by increasing its long-term sources. This is also

The Financial Behavior of the Corporate Business Sector

consistent with the assumptions underlying the expectations hypothesis of the term structure of interest rates.

COMPOSITION OF SHORT-TERM AND LONG-TERM FUNDS

After having considered how the fractions of total long-term and total short-term funds vary over the business cycle, changes in composition of the types of short-term funds within the short-term total and the types of long-term funds in the long-term total are considered in this section.

The short-term funds considered are bank loans and commercial paper. Each has an explicit interest rate. And since these funds represent very similar types of liabilities, the proportions of either type of short-term debt to total short-term debt should vary according to the interest rate differential between them.

The ratio of changes in bank loans to changes in total short-term debt (called the bank loan ratio) is shown in column (1) of Table 11–7; the interest rate differential between the prime bank loan rate and the commercial paper rate (prime bank rate minus commercial paper rate) is shown in column (2). The bank loan ratio and the rate differential

TABLE 11–7   COMPOSITION OF SHORT-TERM SOURCES OF FUNDS, ANNUAL

	(1) Bank Loans Divided by Bank Loans plus Commercial Paper (Bank loan ratio)	(2) Bank Prime Rate minus Commercial Paper Rate [(3)–(4)] %	(3) Bank Prime Rate on Short- term Business Loans (%)	(4) Prime Commercial Paper Rate 4–6 months (%)
1965	1.03	0.15	4.53	4.38
1966	9.1	0.07	5.62	5.55
1967	.83	0.54	5.64	5.10
1968	.86	0.39	6.29	5.90
1969	.84	0.12	7.95	7.83
1970	.72	0.19	7.91	7.72
1971	1.63	0.59	5.70	5.11
1972	1.05	0.56	5.25	4.69
1973	1.01	−0.13	8.02	8.15
1974	.88	0.93	10.80	9.87
1975	.85*	1.53	7.86	6.33

* Both bank loans and commercial paper decreased during 1975; bank loans contributed to the 85 percent of the total decrease.

Source: Calculated from data in Tables 11–3 and 11–4.

should be inversely related; that is, the greater the amount by which the bank rate exceeds the commercial paper rate, the smaller the bank loan fraction should be.

Two factors, however, may make this relationship somewhat more complex. Only the most credit-worthy corporations (AAA or better) are eligible for the commercial paper market; that is, only the paper of these firms can be sold. The bank loan category includes loans to businesses of all sizes.[5] Consequently, the bank loan category includes loans to very credit-worthy companies that have an alternative in the commercial paper market and also to less credit-worthy companies that do not. Second, the effective bank loan rate of interest depends on the level of compensating balances as well as the prime rate. At times banks require that a fraction of their loans be kept on deposit at the bank. This reduces the effective size of the loan and increases the effective rate of interest on the actual loan.

What does the evidence in Table 11–7, also plotted in Figure 11–2, indicate? Certainly since 1973 there has been an inverse relationship between the bank loan ratio and the rate differential. Before 1973, however, there was not always an inverse relationship. Between 1966 and 1968 there was an inverse relationship; during the other years before 1973 there was not. The impact of bank loans to companies not eligible for the commercial paper market may have been responsible for the discrepancies.

Because the short-term loan market is a very volatile market, annual data conceal many sharp variations. For this reason quarterly data (which may still conceal some variations) on sources of funds and the rate differential are shown in Table 11–8 for the most recent period.

The annual evidence indicates the inverse relation between the bank loan fraction and the interest rate differentials since 1973. Therefore, two specific episodes in the quarterly data are considered. Typically, the prime bank rate exceeds the commercial paper rate (and therefore the rate differential is positive). During the first three quarters of 1973, however, the commercial paper rate exceeded the prime bank rate and the rate differential became negative. During this period, the Chairman of the Federal Reserve Board put pressure on commercial banks to restrain prime rate increases for reasons associated with the wage-price controls of that period. Consequently, the commercial paper

---

[5] The prime bank interest rate used is the rate changed to the most credit-worthy firms so that the difference between the prime bank rate and the commercial paper rate is a good indication of the interest rate differential to the most credit-worthy firms. In addition, the prime bank rate is a good surrogate for the rate changed to all businesses because the rate changed less credit-worthy business varies with the prime rate.

TABLE 11-8 COMPOSITION OF SHORT-TERM SOURCES OF FUNDS, QUARTERLY (BILLION DOLLARS AT ANNUAL RATE)

	Bank Loans	Commercial Paper	Sum of Bank Loans and Commercial Paper	Bank Loans Divided by Total Short-term Funds	Bank Prime Rate minus Commercial Paper Rate
1972–1	8.2	3.0	11.2	.73	0.83
–2	5.3	4.2	9.5	.56	0.43
–3	13.4	−2.7	10.7	1.25	0.40
–4	25.7	−1.6	24.1	1.07	0.42
1973–1	47.0	−6.7	40.9	1.15	−0.18
–2	24.5	2.7	27.2	.90	−0.43
–3	28.7	−0.4	28.3	1.01	−0.74
–4	18.8	9.5	28.4	.66	0.83
1974–1	32.5	2.1	34.6	.94	0.95
–2	38.0	5.1	43.1	.88	0.48
–3	26.0	8.8	34.8	.75	0.46
–4	26.4	1.2	27.6	.96	1.95
1975–1	−26.3	5.2	−21.1	1.25	2.42
–2	−19.5	−6.7	−26.2	.74	1.40
–3	−8.1	−1.5	−9.6	.84	0.90
–4	4.1	−7.1	−3.0	−1.37	1.46
1976–1	−15.2	2.8	−12.4	1.23	1.54
Sum (1975–1 through 1976–1):	−65.0	−7.3	−72.3	.90	

Sources: Flow of Funds Data, Board of Governors of the Federal Reserve System; Federal Reserve Bulletin, Board of Governors of the Federal Reserve System; and, Economic Report of the President.

rate increased more than the prime bank rate and the rate differential became negative. During the first quarter of 1973, when the differential first became negative, corporate business increased their bank borrowing by 82.8 percent (from 25.7 percent to 47.0 percent) and increased the rate of liquidation of commercial paper by 281 percent (from 1.6 percent to 6.1 percent). This response to changed short-term interest rate conditions was prompt and massive.

During the second and third quarters of 1973, bank borrowing continued high and commercial paper borrowing low, but the differences did not remain as great as the initial response. During the fourth quarter of 1973, when the pressure on banks to restrain their prime rate increases was relieved, however, bank loans decreased sharply (from 28.7

percent to 18.8 percent) and commercial paper borrowing increased sharply (from − 0.4 percent to 9.5 percent).

The second episode occurred during the recession and postrecession period of 1975–1 through 1976–1. During this period commercial banks did not reduce their prime rate as quickly as commercial paper rates increased. Banks adopted this policy to increase their profit margins, and also to restrict their loan growth and improve their liquidity that had been impaired during 1973 and 1974. Typically, as discussed, business liquidates short-term loans during recessions. However, during the five quarters beginning 1975–1 corporate business liquidated $65.0 of bank loans and only $7.3 of commercial paper. With the large interest rate differential, bank loans were liquidated much more quickly.

Table 11–9 shows the change in the composition of external long-term funds between long-term debt funds, bonds and mortgages, and new equity issues. The fraction of long-term debt to total long-term funds (called the long-term debt ratio), as shown in column (4), ranges from a high of 101 percent to a low of 69 percent with an average of 84 percent.

The Moody's AAA bond rate can be used as a surrogate for the cost of long-term debt and the dividend to price ratio for Standard and Poor's common stocks as an indication of the cost of equity capital. These rates are shown in Figure 11–2. The difference between these

TABLE 11–9 COMPOSITION OF LONG-TERM SOURCES OF FUNDS*

	(1) Long-Term Debt (Bonds plus Mortgage)	(2) Net New Issues of Equities	(3) Total Long-term Funds (Long Debt plus Equities)	(4) Long-term Debt Divided by Total Long-term Funds (Long-term Debt Ratio)	(5) Yield Differential– Moody's AAA Bond Rate minus Stock Dividend to Price Ratio	(6) Per cent Change in Yield Differential
1965	8.3	0.0	8.3	1.00	1.49	7.2
1966	14.2	1.3	15.5	.92	1.73	16.1
1967	17.8	2.4	20.2	.88	2.31	33.5
1968	17.7	−0.2	17.5	1.01	3.11	34.6
1969	15.7	3.4	19.1	.82	3.79	21.9
1970	23.4	5.7	29.1	.80	4.21	11.1
1971	26.7	11.4	38.1	.70	4.25	1.0
1972	24.2	10.9	35.1	.69	4.37	2.8
1973	23.3	7.4	30.7	.76	4.38	2.3
1974	28.7	4.1	32.8	.88	4.10	−6.4
1975	35.9	9.9	45.8	.78	4.52	10.2
Average	—	—	—	.84	—	12.2

* Columns 1–3 are in billion dollars.

Source: Calculated from data in Tables 11–3 and 11–4.

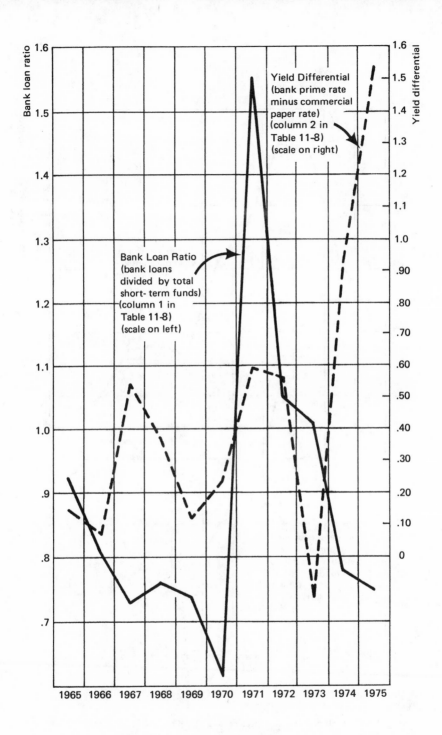

FIGURE 11–2 BANK LOANS VERSUS COMMERCIAL PAPER: AMOUNTS
AND YIELDS

Source: Data in Columns 1 and 2 in Table 11–8.

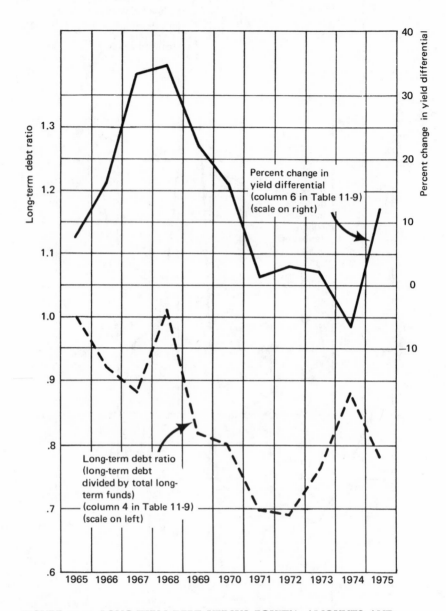

FIGURE 11-3   LONG-TERM DEBT VERSUS EQUITY: AMOUNTS AND YIELDS

Source: Data in Columns 4 and 6 in Table 11-9.

rates, their yield differential, is shown in column (5) of Table 11–9. The higher this differential is, the higher is the cost of bonds relative to equities and, therefore, bonds become less preferable and equity issues more preferable. Due to the substantial increase in bond rates in the post-1965 period, there has been a strong upward trend in the yield differential. Because of this trend, the percent change in the yield differential, rather than the yield differential itself, is calculated and shown in column (6) of Table 11–9. Again, a high (positive) percent change in the trend value means that bonds are becoming more expensive relative to equities and should lead to a lower long-term debt ratio.

The long-term debt ratio and the percent change in the bond-equity yield differential are shown in Figure 11–3. As discussed, these curves should move in opposite directions, and in most instances they do. For example, from 1974–1975 when the stock market improved and the yield differential increased, the long-term debt ratio declined. Previously when the stock market declined from 1972 through 1974, the yield differential declined and the long-term debt ratio increased substantially. During 1967 and 1968 the yield differential increased and the long-term debt ratio accordingly decreased. However, anomalously the debt ratio increased sharply in 1968 when the yield differential increased substantially and decreased from 1968 through 1971 when the percent change in the yield differential decreased. Obviously, the yield differential is an important but not the only factor that affects the composition of long-term funds between debt and equity issues. An additional factor is considered later in this chapter.

financial characteristics of the firm

LIQUIDITY

Three other characteristics that relate to firm funding decisions and that vary over the business cycle are considered in this section. The first is a specific definition of a firm's *liquidity*. As discussed above, a firm's liquidity relates to its ability to pay its debts maturing within one year, with assets that mature within one year. A firm's *current ratio* is defined as its current assets (that is, assets maturing within one year) divided by its current liabilities (liabilities due within one year) and is therefore a measure of a firm's liquidity. Obviously, a high current ratio indicates the firm is liquid; a low current ratio that the firm is illiquid.

Table 11–10 shows the changes in current assets and current lia-

TABLE 11–10   LIQUIDITY AND WORKING CAPITAL (BILLION DOLLARS)

	Change in Current Assets (CA)*	Change in Current Liabilities (CL)**	Incremental Current Ratio (CA/CL)
1965	24.6	22.3	1.103
1966	22.7	19.7	1.152
1967	22.6	15.4	1.468
1968	33.7	28.3	1.191
1969	33.6	35.1	0.957
1970	13.7	15.2	0.901
1971	22.1	6.5	3.40
1972	36.3	26.6	1.365
1973	48.5	50.0	0.970
1974	45.8	52.1	0.875
1975	16.0	− 7.4	−2.162

* Change in current assets is the sum of the lines (1) through (4) in Table 11–3; that is liquid assets, accounts receivable–consumer credit and trade credit, and inventories.
** Change in current liabilities is the sum of lines (6) through (8) in Table 11–3; banks loans, commercial paper, and trade debt. (Most, but not all, bank loans mature within one year.)
Source: Calculated from data in Table 11–3.

bilities of the business sector derived from the data in Table 11–3; their quotient is shown in the third column.[6] Note that the incremental current ratio was low during the tight credit years of 1969, 1973, and 1974: business became less liquid when interest rates were high and credit tight. Business became much more liquid during the recession years of 1967, 1970, and 1975, as indicated by the current ratio (note that the large increase in the current ratio due to the 1970 recession lagged one year and occurred during 1971; note also that in 1975 current liabilities actually decreased and the negative current ratio indicates a large increase in liquidity).

During times of tight credit, business increases its current liabilities relative to its current assets and becomes less liquid; during easy credit

---

[6] Since a firm's current ratio is defined as the quotient of its *total* current assets divided by its *total* current liabilities and the data in Tables 11–3 and 11–10 refer to *changes in* current assets and current liabilities, the quotient in the third column of Table 11–3 is not the current ratio of the business sector but an indication of the change in the current ratio during the year. It is therefore called the *incremental current ratio*.

recession years business reliquifies by replenishing its current assets relative to its current liabilities. A factor related to this behavior is implicit in the discussion of the next characteristic.

Business liquidity is closely watched by lenders to business and investors in business as an indication of financial stability. Two other indicators of financial stability are the balance between short-term and long-term debt, and the balance between debt and equity.

As indicated above, the business fund-raising decision can be viewed as a series of three decisions: 1) whether to use internal funds or to raise funds from external financial markets; 2) if raised externally, whether to raise them via long-term funds or short-term funds; and, 3) what the composition of the long-term and short-term funds should be. The two characteristics of the firm discussed below represent different groupings of the internal versus external funds and the long-term versus short-term funds, and convey something different about firm funding behavior and the resulting financial condition of the firm than the previous groupings do.

DEBT VERSUS EQUITY

The balance between a firm's debt funds and its equity funds is an important characteristic of the firm. Its new equity funds are a combination of internal funds in the form of retained earnings and external funds in the form of new equity issues. Its debt includes both long-term and short-term debt. Two very important distinctions between equity funds and debt funds are their maturity and their cost. Equity funds need never be paid back; they are with the firm forever. Debt funds have a fixed maturity at which time they must be repaid. Equity funds are thus a more flexible source of funds.

Debt funds also have a fixed cost, the interest rate agreed on at the time of the loan. The cost to the firm of its equity funds is the dividend it must pay on its common stock. But the dividend is not fixed. The firm can increase its dividends during prosperous years and decrease its dividend during years of low profits. Equity funds are more flexible also because of the fixed cost of debt and the variable cost of equity. Thus, equity funds are preferable to debt funds for the firm on the basis of longer maturity and flexible cost. Debt funds are preferable for other reasons.

Another important aspect of the composition of debt and equity in the financial structure of the firm relates to the tendency for the firm's balance between debt and equity to affect its profitability over the business cycle. The firm's total assets are financed by either debt or equity. Define a firm's *earning power* (EP) as the ratio of its earnings before interest charges and taxes are deducted (*EBIT*) to total assets (*TA*), that is $EP = EBIT/TA$. A firm's earning power normally changes with the business cycle.

The relation between a firm's earning power (*EP*), the average interest cost of its debt (*i*), and the fraction of debt divided by debt plus total assets (the debt ratio) determines how the return to the stockholders of the firm responds to changes in its earning power. The firm earns, on the average, its earning power on all its assets. It pays, on the average, the average cost of the debt on only those assets financed by debt. The remainder of the return then accrues to the stockholders.

If *EP* equals *i*, the firm earns exactly enough on its assets financed by debt to pay the interest costs on the suppliers of debt. The amount of debt has no effect on the return to stockholders. If, however, the earning power is greater than *i*, the firm is earning a surplus on the assets financed by debt. For example, if $EP = 8$ percent and $i = 6$ percent, the firm is earning a surplus of 2 percent on each dollar of assets financed by debt. This surplus can be divided up among the suppliers of equity, the stockholders. The return to stockholders will then be equal to the earning power on the assets financed by equity (8 percent) plus the surplus generated on assets financed by debt. In this case the larger the share of debt in the firm's funding structure, the larger the total surplus generated and the smaller the amount of equity over which to allocate the surplus. Consequently, the higher the debt ratio, the greater the return to equity for a given earning power, given that *EP* is greater than *i*.

If, however, *EP* is less than *i*, the firm generates a deficit on each dollar of its assets financed by debt. If, for example, $EP = 4$ percent and *i* remains at 6 percent, the firm is losing 2 percent on each dollar of assets financed by debt. This deficit must be allocated over the equity funds and reduces the remaining return to the equity funds. In this case, the firm with less debt, and which therefore generates a smaller deficit on debt-financed assets, generates a higher return for its stockholders.

To summarize, if *EP* exceeds *i*, the return to the stockholders (return on equity or ROE) of the firm will be greater, the greater is the fraction of debt. If *EP* is less than *i*, the return to the stockholders decreases as the fraction of debt increases. Consequently, the higher the fraction of debt in a firm, the more volatile is its return on equity—the return on equity is higher when *EP* is high and lower when *EP* is low.

Figure 11–4 shows that as *EP* changes over the business cycle the firm with the higher fraction of debt will show greater variations in the return on equity than will a firm with a lower fraction of debt. The debt ratio, therefore, affects how variations in *EP* are translated into greater or smaller variations in the return on stockholders' equity. For this reason, the debt ratio is referred to as *financial leverage*. The higher the fraction of debt, the greater is the financial leverage, and the greater is

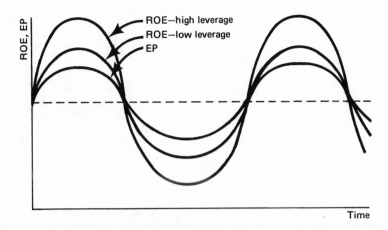

FIGURE 11-4   EARNING POWER, DEBT RATIO, AND RETURN ON EQUITY

the variability in return on stockholders' equity; that is, the greater the firm's risk. High risk, therefore, gives stockholders the potential for high and low returns. If, however, stockholders are risk averse, they will require a higher average return from high risk firms.

Consequently, a firm with a high fraction of debt has more risk than does a firm with a low fraction for three reasons: 1) it has more funds that must be repaid at a fixed maturity; 2) it has more funds with fixed costs; and, 3) it has more variation in the return on its stockholders' equity. The firm considers all of these factors when considering the debt versus equity funding decision.

Table 11–11 shows the relation between the amounts of debt and equity raised by the corporate business sector since 1965. Recently, the ratio of debt to total debt plus equity, the leverage ratio, has been very sensitive to the business cycle. From 1965 through 1970 this ratio increased as firms deliberately increased their leverage in an attempt to increase their profits even more during this fairly prosperous period. The ratio increased even during the modest stock market declines of 1966 and 1969. Since 1970, however, the ratio has fluctuated with the business cycle. The ratio declined due to the recessions of 1970 and 1975 (although the decline due to the 1970 recession was somewhat delayed) and increased during the periods of tight credit during 1973 and 1974. Firms have thus become more highly leveraged, and hence adopted a riskier posture, during times of tight credit and then reduced their leverage and risk during recessions.

During times of tight credit firms increase their debt, mainly in the form of short-term debt, even more than their equity, the retained earnings component of which is normally high during tight credit times.

TABLE 11-11 SOURCES OF FUNDS: DEBT VERSUS EQUITY (BILLION DOLLARS)

	Short-term Debt (Bank Loans plus Commercial Paper)	Long-term Debt (Bonds plus Mortgage)	Total Debt (Long-term plus Short-term)	New Equity Issues	Retained Earnings	Total Equity	Total Debt plus Equity	Total Debt Divided by Debt plus Equity (Leverage Ratio)
1965	10.2	8.3	18.5	0.0	20.0	20.0	38.5	.48
1966	9.1	14.2	23.3	1.3	21.9	23.2	46.5	.50
1967	8.0	17.8	25.8	2.4	18.9	21.3	47.1	.55
1968	11.1	17.7	28.8	— 0.2	17.6	17.4	46.2	.62
1969	14.1	15.7	29.8	3.4	14.4	17.8	46.6	.63
1970	7.8	23.4	31.2	5.7	8.1	13.8	45.0	.69
1971	2.7	26.7	29.4	11.4	13.4	24.8	54.2	.54
1972	12.9	24.2	37.1	10.9	20.6	31.5	68.6	.54
1973	30.4	23.3	53.7	7.4	28.9	36.3	90.0	.60
1974	34.0	28.7	62.7	4.1	30.3	34.4	97.1	.65
1975	−15.6	35.9	20.3	9.9	27.7	37.6	57.9	.35

Source: Calculated from data in Table 11–3.

During recessions, they reduce their debt, again mainly their short-term debt, and increase their new equity issues to replenish their equity base.

LONG-TERM DEBT VERSUS SHORT-TERM DEBT

When a firm decides to issue debt and increase its leverage, it must decide whether to issue short-term debt or long-term debt. If the funds are to be used to finance plant and equipment expenditure, long-term debt is preferable because the firm has longer to repay the loan. A firm with a large amount of short-term debt is in an inflexible and possibly precarious situation because it may need to raise new funds frequently to refinance its maturing loans and it must do so no matter how high the interest rate. In addition, if credit were very tight for the financial system as a whole or for the firm in particular, the firm may be unable to borrow to refinance its maturing loans and be forced into bankruptcy by its creditors. Firms with large volumes of short-term credit are deemed less credit-worthy by lenders. Thus the very firms that need additional credit to refinance their maturing loans find themselves less able to get credit, an undesirable situation for both the firm and its past lenders.

The interest cost motivation for a business deciding whether to borrow short-term or long-term funds is discussed in Chapter 7 in the section on the expectations hypothesis. There is a rationale to borrow short-term during times of high interest rates and long-term during times of low interest rates. Table 11–12 shows that firms do exactly this.

TABLE 11–12 SOURCES OF FUNDS: SHORT-TERM DEBT VERSUS LONG-TERM DEBT (BILLION DOLLARS)

	Short-term Debt	Long-term Debt	Total Debt	Short-term Debt Divided by Total Debt
1965	10.2	8.3	18.5	.55
1966	9.1	14.2	23.3	.39
1967	8.0	17.8	25.9	.31
1968	11.1	17.7	28.8	.39
1969	14.1	15.7	29.8	.47
1970	7.8	23.4	31.2	.25
1971	2.7	26.7	29.4	.09
1972	12.9	24.2	37.1	.35
1973	30.4	23.3	53.7	.57
1974	34.0	28.7	62.7	.54
1975	−15.6	35.9	20.3	−.76

Source: Calculated from data in Table 11–3.

Business Sources of Funds: The Recent Evidence

The ratio of short-term debt to total debt peaked during the tight credit year of 1969, declined substantially during the low interest rate years of 1970 and 1971, increased substantially during the credit crunch years of 1973 and 1974 and decreased substantially (and became negative) during the recession year of 1975.

During tight credit periods firms increase their short-term borrowing and increase their financial risk in this way. During recessions, they reduce this risk by reducing their dependency on short-term borrowing.

overview of business financing decisions

This chapter discusses three characteristics of a firm that are important to the managers of a firm, the present stockholders, and the prospective investors in and lenders to the firm. These characteristics also affect how the firm raises the funds it needs to finance its asset expansion. These characteristics are profitability, liquidity, and leverage. The profitability of a firm indicates the return to the firm's owners. Over the long-run the firm desires to be profitable. A firm's liquidity is a measure of its ability to pay its bills and other debts in the short-run and thus remain viable. It would be futile for the firm to enact policies that would make it very profitable in the long run but actually bankrupt the firm in the short run. A firm's leverage relates to the variability in the return on the stockholders' investment over the business cycle. High leverage along with low liquidity both contribute to the risk of the firm.

These three characteristics affect the way in which the firm raises its funds. The firm's decision concerning how it will raise funds can be divided into three parts. First, will the funds be internally generated or raised externally? The firm's internal funds consist of its retained earnings and depreciation expenses. Given the level of its profits after taxes, the firm can vary the level of its retained earnings by varying its dividend payments. Second, if the firm needs external funds to finance its asset expansion, it must decide whether to raise its external funds for a long-term or a short-term. Finally, if long-term, the firm must decide among new equity issues, bonds, and mortgages. And if short-term it must decide among bank loans and commercial paper. These choices are depicted in Table 11–13.

But in addition to these considerations, two other factors cut across the categories shown in Table 11–13. The first is the choice between equity funds and debt funds. This choice determines the firm's leverage. Equity funds include both internal retained earnings and external new equity issues. Debt funds include both long-term and short-term debt. If debt is chosen, it must be decided whether the debt will be

The Financial Behavior of the Corporate Business Sector

TABLE 11–13   FUND-RAISING DECISIONS

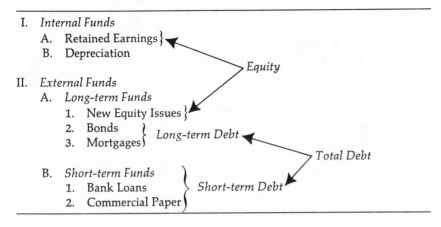

I. *Internal Funds*
   A. Retained Earnings
   B. Depreciation

              Equity

II. *External Funds*
   A. *Long-term Funds*
      1. New Equity Issues
      2. Bonds
      3. Mortgages   *Long-term Debt*

                       Total Debt

   B. *Short-term Funds*
      1. Bank Loans   *Short-term Debt*
      2. Commercial Paper

long-term or short-term debt. This choice is important because it affects the liquidity of the firm—short-term debt reduces the current ratio, long-term debt does not affect it. The debt versus equity and long-term versus short-term debt decisions, which cut across the categories in Table 11–13, must be considered in the firm's funding decision.

summary of data

In this chapter the corporate flow of funds data were used together with various rate of return data to investigate changes in business sources of funds over the business cycle. These results are summarized in this section.

During times of strong economic growth, business assets, particularly plant and equipment and inventories, expand quickly. During recessions, assets expand more slowly. Therefore, business needs a greater source of funds during economic growth. Normally, profits, and hence retained earnings, grow more quickly during times of strong economic growth than during recessions. But assets expand even more quickly than do retained earnings during times of strong economic growth, and consequently more external funds are needed during times of economic growth. During recessions, internal funds, even though retained earnings are lower, come closer to satisfying needs for asset expansion and so the need for external funds is less during recessions.

The composition of funds raised differs between times of economic growth and recessions. During times of economic growth, interest rates are high and, as expected from the expectations hypothesis, business tends to raise short-term debt rather than long-term debt. The increase in short-term debt reduces business liquidity. In addition, during recent periods of high interest rates, both the stock market and the bond market have been weak and business has reduced its stock issues as well as its bond issues. Reduced stock issues, along with high levels of increases in short-term debt, have tended to increase business leverage. Consequently, during times of high interest rates and economc growth, business raises predominately short-term funds and decreases its liquidity and increases its leverage—both indications of added risk.

During recessions with their accompanying low interest rates, business typically refunds its debt—that is, issues long-term debt and reduces its short-term debt—and also issues more new equities. Therefore, during recessions business *reliquifies*—that is, increases its liquidity by reducing its short-term debt—and increases its leverage due to increased equity issues and a reduced need for external funds. During recessions businesses reduce their risk. The business financing decision depends very much on the external financial and economic environment of the firm.

questions

1. Discuss the significance of the balance sheet and the flow of funds statement for the corporate business sector.

2. Discuss how the relation between the levels of long-term funds and short-term funds raised by the corporate business sector varies over the business cycle. How does this variation relate to the discussion of the expectations hypothesis in Chapter 7?

3. How does the concept of arbitrage relate to changes in the composition of short-term funds raised by the corporate business sector? How does it relate to the composition of long-term funds?

4. Discuss how the liquidity and the leverage of the corporate business sector vary over the business cycle. What effect should these changes have on stock prices?

5. How does the relation of the level of internal funds to external funds of the corporate business sector vary over the business cycle?

selected references to part V

Brigham, Eugene F. *Financial Management, Theory and Practice.* Hinsdale, Ill.: The Dryden Press, 1977.

Christy, George A. and Roden, Peyton Foster. *Finance: Environment and Decisions.* New York: Canfield Press, 1976.

Higgins, Robert C. *Financial Management: Theory and Applications.* Chicago: Science Research Associates, Inc., 1977.

Schall, Lawrence D. and Haley, Charles W. *Introduction to Financial Management.* New York: McGraw-Hill Book Company, 1977.

Solomon, Ezra and Pringle, John J. *An Introduction to Financial Management.* Santa Monica, Cal.: Goodyear Publishing Company, Inc., 1977.

Van Horne, James C. *Financial Management and Policy,* 4th ed. Englewood Cliffs, N.J.: Prentice-Hall, Inc., 1977.

Van Horne, James C. *Fundamentals of Financial Management.* Englewood Cliffs, N.J.: Prentice-Hall, Inc., 1977.

Weston, J. Fred and Brigham, Eugene F. *Essentials of Managerial Finance,* 4th ed. Hinsdale, Ill.: The Dryden Press, 1977.

summary and overview

The role of the financial system is to channel funds from surplus sectors, savers, to deficit sectors, borrowers. On a national level, facilitating such flows of funds increases the level of the aggregate demand for goods and services in the economy, thus generating higher employment, and increases the level of investment thus accelerating economic growth. For individual savers, the financial system enables them to earn a return on their surplus funds but maintain a degree of liquidity. The financial system enables individual borrowers to spend in excess of their currently generated funds. Specifically, businesses attempt to add to their profits by borrowing to finance increases in their capacity to produce output.

The financial system determines not only the total amount of funds available and their cost, the interest rate, but also how the funds are allocated to individual financial institutions and financial markets and the costs of the funds flowing through these individual channels. Borrowers and lenders should understand the specific financial institutions and markets and the terms, including return and liquidity, of their transactions to optimize their behavior.

Forecasting interest rates and the amounts of funds available in different forms is particularly important for business borrowers who borrow large amounts and have several borrowing options. Issuing long-term corporate bonds when interest rates are very high, for example, could be very costly.

The financial system, however, is not isolated from the overall economy. The economy affects the financial system in several ways. Consequently, to understand and forecast changes in the financial system, the economic system must be considered. For example, fiscal policy enacted to cure unemployment could increase interest rates. Monetary policy enacted to combat inflation could cause a severe credit crunch with high interest rates and low levels of credit. To forecast changes in the financial system, one has to understand how economic policies affect the financial system, and why these policies are enacted. The effects of decisions in the private sector on the financial system must also be considered.

This book discusses in detail the individual financial institutions and markets. It also discusses the specific parts of the economic system. But, perhaps more importantly, it presents an integrated view of the interrelations among various parts of the financial and economic systems. Presenting this integrated view is accomplished both by presenting explicit conceptual frameworks, or theories, and also by the extensive use of data for the purpose of illustrating past changes and relationships. Having such an integrated view is critical to understanding past changes in the financial system and forecasting future changes.

And being able to understand past changes and forecast future changes in the financial system is essential to the role of the financial manager in the firm.

GLOSSARY

Action Lag   The time between when the need for an economic policy change is recognized and when the change is implemented.

Advance Refunding   A method used by the U.S. Treasury to issue new securities whereby the Treasury offers new longer maturing Treasury securities to holders of outstanding shorter maturity Treasury securities in exchange for the latter.

Agency Securities   Debt securities of agencies that are either part of the U.S. federal government or sponsored by the U.S. federal government—the former are government guaranteed, the latter are not. Although some short-term agency securities are issued, most are long-term agency bonds.

Allocational Efficiency   How well financial markets allocate funds to borrowers with the greatest needs for funds.

American Stock Exchange (AMEX)   A national organized stock exchange. Some bonds are also traded.

Arbitrage   The simultaneous buying and selling of identical or similar securities at different prices to make a profit—the effect of arbitrage is to remove or reduce the price differential between the securities.

Automatic Stabilizers   Components of policy, particularly fiscal policy, that tend to stabilize automatically (that is, with no discretionary actions required) the economy, for example, to provide expansionary forces when a recession begins. Unemployment compensation is an automatic stabilizer. In contrast to discretionary stabilizers.

Balance of Payments   An accounting system for recording the outflow of a country's currency to other countries and the inflow of the currencies of other countries.

Banker's Acceptance   A security that is a promise by a corporation to pay the bearer of the acceptance a specified amount at maturity that is backed (or accepted) by a commercial bank. These securities are usually based on international trade (whereby the importer, the issuer of the security, promises to pay the exporter) and can be sold on a secondary market.

Bank Holding Companies   Corporations that own (hold the stock of) one or more commercial banks. Bank holding companies may or may not also own certain other nonbank companies.

Basis Point   One one-hundredth of one percent of interest. For example, the difference between 6.25 percent and 6.26 percent is one basis point.

Bearer Form Security Security for which the owner is not registered with the issuer. The security can be traded without notifying the issuer.

Best-Effort Arrangement An agreement between an investment bank and a corporation according to which the investment bank does not underwrite the new issue of a security but only sells as many of the securities as it can. The investment bank receives a fee for selling these securities.

Bonds Securities that are statements of indebtedness. The maturity date, maturity value, and the coupon payment are always stated in the bond contract. Other characteristics of the particular bond may also be stated.

Bottleneck An inadequate level of supply that cannot be increased in the short run due to constraints on production.

Breadth A characteristic of a secondary market that indicates how many different types of participants are buying and selling a given security.

Broker An agent who arranges for the exchange of an asset between buyers and sellers. The agent does not take possession of the asset but receives a commission for facilitating the exchange.

Callable A characteristic of some bonds that permits the issuer to retire the bonds before their maturity. The call price or price the issuer must pay the bond holder to retire it before its maturity is usually above its maturity value. A noncallable bond cannot be retired by the issuer for any reason. Some new bonds are noncallable for a specified period and then become callable. The date at which they become callable is the call date.

Call Date *See* Callable

Call Loans Loans by commercial banks to security dealers for which securities are used as collateral. These loans can be called by the banks, usually on twenty-four hours notice.

Call Price *See* Callable

Capacity Utilization The fraction of the nation's capital stock that is currently being used for production.

Capital Markets The markets on which marketable securities with a maturity of more than one year are traded.

Cap Loan A bank term loan (typically for more than one year) in which the interest rate change varies with the bank prime rate, but upon which a maximum rate that can be charged is set.

Central Bank A national institution with the primary functions of controlling the nation's money supply and regulating its commercial banks.

Certificate of Deposit (CD) A large (denomination of $100,000 or more) short-term (one year or less) commercial bank deposit that can be sold on a secondary market. There are no Regulation Q interest rate ceilings on these deposits. Also called Negotiable Certificates of Deposit (NCDs).

Closed-end Investment Company An investment-type financial intermediary similar to a mutual fund in many ways but that can issue only a fixed, specified number of shares that are not redeemable by the company.

Collateral Trust Bond A corporate bond with marketable securities as collateral.

Commercial and Industrial Loans Loans made by commercial banks to businesses —they must have maturities of greater than or less than one year.

Commercial Banks Deposit-type financial institutions whose main source of funds is time and demand deposits and whose main use of funds is business and consumer loans.

Commercial Paper Short-term (270 days or less) unsecured securities of large corporations. Only the "paper" of the most credit-worthy corporations is salable.

Compensating Balances The specified fraction of a business loan that must be kept in a demand deposit at the bank rather than withdrawn by the business —a requirement imposed in some commercial bank loans.

Competitive Underwriting The selection of an investment bank by a corporation to underwrite its security issue by soliciting competitive price bids on the security issue from investment banks and selecting the investment bank with the highest bid. In contrast to negotiated underwriting.

Contractionary Policy A policy that tends to make GNP decrease or increase at a slower rate. Sometimes called tight policy.

Contractual-type Financial Institutions Financial institutions whose liabilities are mainly commitments for future payments under conditions specified in a contract, such as insurance companies and pension funds.

Conventional Mortgage A mortgage that is neither insured by the FHA nor guaranteed by the VA.

Convertible Bonds Bonds that can be converted into common stock of the issuing company at the option of the bond holder. The number of shares of stock into which the bond can be converted is specified in the convertible bond (specified by either the conversion price or conversion ratio).

Cost-Push Inflation An increase in the overall price level caused by an increase in the prices of production inputs. This type of inflation may be caused by an increase in wage rates, profit levels (the cost of ownership capital), or raw materials. When increases in wages and profits are responsible for this type of inflation, it is sometimes called a wage-price spiral.

Coupon Periodic payment on a bond (usually every six months) the amount of which is agreed upon at the time the bond is issued and remains fixed over the life of the bond. It represents the interest on the bond.

Coupon Security Securities for which a coupon payment is periodically paid by the issuer to the security holder—the coupon represents the interest. In contrast to discount securities. Corporate and Treasury bonds are coupon securities.

Coupon Yield *See* Current Yield

Credit Risk The risk that a borrower will not be able to make interest or principal payments when due. Also called endogenous risk. In contrast to market risk.

Credit Union A deposit-type financial institution whose distinguishing feature is a "common bond" among its members for which it receives an exemption from federal taxes. It raises depository-type funds from its members and grants consumer loans to its members.

Crowding Out The phenomenon whereby government borrowing and spending crowds out or replaces private sector borrowing and spending, respectively.

Current Ratio A measure of business liquidity equal to its level of current assets divided by its level of current liabilities.

Current Yield (Coupon Yield) The annual coupon as a bond divided by its current price, expressed as a percentage.

Cyclical Unemployment The unemployment caused when, due to low levels of demand for their products, suppliers lay off employees in order to reduce their level of production. These employees would be rehired when demand increased.

Dealer An agent who "makes" the over-the-counter secondary markets in securities by supplying bid-ask (buy-sell) quotes, that is, offering to buy at their bid price and sell at their ask price. Dealers actually buy for their own portfolios and sell from their portfolios—their profits are the difference between their bid-ask prices and the capital gains or losses on their portfolio holdings.

Debenture An unsecured corporate bond.

Demand Deposit (Checking Account) A deposit at a commercial bank that can be withdrawn on demand and that can be used as a means of payment (by writing checks on the deposit). Demand deposits are part of the money supply and are commonly called checking accounts.

Demand-Pull Inflation An increase in prices caused by an excess level of demand or a level of demand greater than that which can be met at constant costs.

Deposit-type Financial Institutions Financial institutions whose liabilities are mainly in the form of deposits, such as commercial banks and savings and loan associations.

Depth A characteristic of a secondary market that indicates how closely grouped buy and orders for securities are around the last transaction price. Depth indicates how much the price will change before a transaction occurs that reverses the last price movement.

Devaluation A decrease in value of a currency relative to other currencies (or often gold), that is a decrease in its exchange rate.

Direct Finance Finance in which the funds flow directly from the lender to the ultimate borrower. For example, when an investor purchases a new issue of a corporate bond.

Direct Placement *See* Private Placement

Dirty Float An international system for determining exchange rates intermediate between fixed exchange rates and freely fluctuating exchange rates. With the dirty float, there is no international agreement among countries to keep their exchange rates fixed; but countries do conduct some support operations which, although they may not keep their exchange rates fixed, do affect the level of the exchange rates.

Discount Security (1) The security on which there is no coupon payment—the security is initially issued or sold at a price less than its maturity value, and the capital appreciation over its life represents the interest. In contrast to coupon securities. Treasury bills and commercial paper are discount securities. (2) A security selling at a price less than its maturity value. In contrast to premium security.

Discretionary Stabilizers Components of monetary and fiscal policies that require conscious, discretionary actions to implement. In contrast to automatic stabilizers.

Disintermediation The withdrawal of deposits from financial intermediaries such as savings and loan associations and commercial banks and the use of these funds to purchase marketable securities such as Treasury bills.

Distribution The act of selling (or marketing) a new issue of securities by underwriters and related brokerage houses.

Dividend Yield The annual dividend on stock divided by its current market price.

Earning Power The ratio of a firm's earnings (before interest and taxes) to its total assets. This is a measure of its return on assets.

Endogenous Risk *See* Credit Risk

Equipment Trust Certificate A corporate bond with rolling stock, such as railroad cars or airplanes, as collateral.

Equities (Stocks) Securities issued by corporations that represent ownership in the corporation. The equities (stocks) receive dividend payments and have no maturity date, that is, they never have to be retired by the issuing corporation.

Eurobond A bond underwritten by a syndicate of investment banks from more than one country and sold mainly in countries other than the country of the currency in which the issue is denominated. Dollar-denominated bonds issued by U.S. companies in Switzerland and mark-denominated bonds issued by German firms in Britain are Eurobonds.

Eurocredits Medium-term loans by commercial banks denominated in currencies other than the currency of the country in which the bank resides. These loans are usually syndicated, that is, several banks participate in the loan. Medium-term, dollar-denominated loans by British banks are Eurocredits.

Eurocurrencies Short-term deposits and loans by commercial banks denominated in currencies other than the currency of the country in which the bank resides. Short-term mark-denominated deposits in British banks and short-term Swiss-franc–denominated deposits in German banks are Eurocurrency deposits.

Eurodollars Dollar-denominated short-term deposits and loans by commercial banks in Europe. Short-term dollar-denominated deposits and loans by British banks are Eurodollars. Eurodollars are one form of Eurocurrency.

Excess Reserves Reserves held by commercial banks in excess of the level of required reserves.

Exchange Rate The rate at which one currency can be converted into another, or the price of one currency in terms of another. For example, if the price of the German mark were $0.25 per mark, it would require $0.25 to purchase one mark or four marks to purchase one dollar.

Exchange Refunding A method used by the U.S. Treasury to issue new securities whereby the Treasury offers a new treasury security to holders of maturing treasury securities in exchange for the latter.

Exogenous Risk *See* Market Risk

Expansionary Policy A policy that tends to make GNP increase or increase at a faster rate. Sometimes called loose policy.

Expectations Hypothesis The hypothesis that asserts that the relationship between long-term interest rates and short-term interest rates is such that the long-term interest rate equals the average (compounded) of the observed short-term interest rate and expected future short-term interest rates (where the long-term period is the same as the series of short-term periods).

External Funds Corporate funds generated outside the corporation by borrowing externally or by issuing and selling securities to external investors and lenders.

Federal Financing Bank (FFB) A federal government agency created in 1973 to coordinate the borrowing of other federal government agencies with that of the U.S. Treasury and to reduce the interest rates paid by agencies on their borrowing. Currently the FFB raises funds by borrowing from the Treasury and relending to federal government agencies that have the authority to borrow.

Federal Funds (Fed Funds) Loans of reserve funds on deposit at the Federal Reserve Banks by one commercial bank to another. They are short-term loans normally of one day's duration.

Federal Home Loan Banks Regional banks of the Federal Home Loan Bank System. These banks make loans to member savings and loan associations that indirectly support the mortgage markets.

Federal Home Loan Bank System An organization whose primary functions are to regulate and support nationally chartered savings and loan associations. Composed of the Federal Home Loan Bank Board and the regional Federal Home Loan Banks.

Federal Home Loan Mortgage Corporation (FHLMC or Freddie Mae) A corporation owned by the Federal Home Loan Banks that issues securities and uses the proceeds to purchase mortgages, mostly from savings and loan associations.

Federal Housing Administration (FHA) Federal government administration that insures mortgages, mainly for low- and middle-income housing.

Federal National Mortgage Association (FNMA or Fannie Mae) A privately owned corporation that makes a secondary market in mortgages by making advance commitments on an auction basis to buy and sell mortgages.

Federal Open Market Committee The part of the Federal Reserve System that is responsible for determining open market operation policy. It is composed of the seven members of the Board of Governors of the Federal Reserve System, the president of the Federal Reserve Bank of New York, and four of the other eleven Federal Reserve Bank presidents on a revolving basis.

Federal Reserve System The central bank of the United States established in 1913 to control the money supply and regulate U.S. commercial banks. It is composed of the Board of Governors of the Federal Reserve System (the Fed) in Washington, D.C. and twelve regional Federal Reserve Banks.

Glossary

Finance Companies Financial institutions whose liabilities are mainly debt and equity securities and that make consumer and business loans.

Financial Intermediaries Institutions that mediate in finance by borrowing from some agents and lending to others. Also called financial institutions.

Financial Markets Markets to conduct the issuing and trading of securities. Include both primary and secondary markets.

Fiscal Policy Policy enacted by changes in the government budget, that is, changes in government expenditures and tax policies.

Fixed Exchange Rates An international agreement whereby several countries agree to keep the exchange rates among their currencies fixed or constant. They do so by support operations.

Foreign Bond A bond that is underwritten by investment banks of a country, sold mainly in the country, and denominated in the currency of the country but the issuer of which is from another country. Bonds issued by U.S. companies that are denominated in marks and sold in Germany and bonds issued by British companies that are denominated in dollars and sold in the U.S. are foreign bonds.

Forward Markets in Foreign Exchange *See* Futures Markets in Foreign Exchange

Fourth Market Direct trading of equities between institutions without the service of dealers or brokers.

Freely Fluctuating Exchange Rates (Freely Floating Exchange Rates) An international monetary system whereby countries do not conduct any support operations to influence their exchange rates but instead let economic forces determine the exchange rates.

Frictional Unemployment Unemployment caused by workers voluntarily terminating their employment and looking for different employment opportunities.

Full Employment Budget The federal budget calculated on the basis of what federal expenditures and tax revenues would be if full employment (4 percent unemployment) prevailed in the economy.

Funding Debt Issuing long-term debt and using the funds to retire short-term debt.

Futures Markets in Foreign Exchange Markets in which contracts can be bought or sold that obligate the transactor to accept or supply respectively a specified amount of foreign currency at a specified time in the future at a price (in dollars) that is specified today. Current agreements are made for future currency exchanges. Futures and forwards markets for foreign exchange differ in the following ways: futures markets are organized exchanges, and the contracts are of fixed denominations (specified in the amount of the foreign currency) and of fixed maturities. The International Monetary Market of the Chicago Mercantile Exchange is a futures market in foreign exchange. Forwards markets are over-the-counter markets where the denominations and maturities are negotiable. The foreign exchange market conducted by large commercial banks is a forwards market.

General Obligation Bond A municipal bond for which the coupon and maturity payments are backed by the "full faith and credit" of the issuing municipality. In practice this means they are backed by the taxing authority of the issuing government. In contrast to a revenue bond.

Government National Mortgage Association (GNMA or Ginnie Mae) An entity in the Department of Housing and Urban Development that makes mortgage investment more attractive to a broad range of investors by guaranteeing mortgage-backed securities issued by mortgage banks, savings and loan associations, and commercial banks.

Gross National Product (GNP) The total monetary value of all final goods and services produced in the economy during a period.

Hedge To take an action to remove or reduce an exposure or a position. Hedging can be accomplished by the use of the futures or forward markets in foreign exchange.

Incomes Policy   A policy that affects the relative levels of wages and prices in the economy.

Indirect Finance   Finance in which funds flow from the lender to the ultimate borrower indirectly through a financial intermediary, for example when an individual deposits in a bank money that is relent to a business.

Inside Lag   Time between when an economic policy change is needed and when it is implemented.

Internal Funds   Corporate funds generated internal to the corporation by profits and depreciation reserves.

International Bond   A bond sold outside the country of the borrower. An international bond can be either a foreign bond or a Eurobond.

Investment Bank   A financial institution that provides several types of financial services to corporations, the most important of which is assistance in placing new issues of stocks and bonds with investors.

Investment-type Financial Institutions   Financial institutions whose liabilities are mainly shares of a common interest in a portfolio of securities, such as mutual funds and trust funds.

Keynesians   Economists who, following the writings of John Maynard Keynes, believe that the economy is basically unstable and that the government should implement both fiscal and monetary policies, particularly the former, to achieve high employment and stable prices.

Leverage   The balance between a firm's debt sources of funds and its equity sources of funds, often measured by the ratio of debt to equity or the ratio of debt to debt plus equity. The higher either of these ratios, the more leveraged the firm is said to be. High leverage causes high volatility in profits.

Liability Management   The commercial bank activity by which the level and the composition of their total sources of funds are determined. Deposits and purchased funds, such as Federal funds and commercial paper, are their main sources of funds.

Life Insurance Companies   Contractual-type financial institutions characterized by regular inflows of funds under a long-term contract. These funds are used to hold a portfolio of securities that provide the wherewithal for payments under specified conditions, usually payments to beneficiaries upon death of the insured. The insurance may be either term insurance or savings-type insurance. *See* Term Insurance and Savings-type Insurance.

Liquidity   A characteristic of a security that refers to its risk, both credit risk and market risk, and its marketability. High liquidity requires low risk and high marketability.

Liquidity Hypothesis   The hypothesis that asserts that the yield curve is influenced by the liquidity of the security. Since long-term securities have more market risk and less liquidity, the liquidity hypothesis says that interest rates on securities increase as their maturities increase.

Liquidity Preference   The hypothesis that asserts the rate of interest is determined by the supply of and demand for money.

Loanable Funds   The hypothesis that asserts that the rate of interest is determined by the supply of and demand for loanable funds or credit.

Loose Policy   *See* Expansionary Policy

M1   A measure of the money supply equal to currency plus demand deposits.

M2   A measure of the money supply equal to M1 plus time deposits at commercial banks (except for certificates of deposit).

M3   A measure of the money supply equal to M2 plus savings accounts at savings and loan associations and mutual savings banks.

Marketability   The time and cost it takes to sell a security, or other asset, for its market price.

Market Risk   The risk that the market price of a marketable security will rise or fall between the time the security is purchased and sold. Refers to potential for capital gain or loss. Also called exogenous risk.

Maturity   The time at which a borrower must repay a loan as specified at the time the loan was made.

Maturity Value   The amount that must be repaid to retire a security or loan at the maturity of the security or loan.

Model   A set of relationships among relevant variables or quantities. A model may be a series of mathematical equations or a diagram.

Monetarists   Economists who believe that the economy is basically stable; that fiscal policy is ineffectual as a stabilization policy; that monetary policy has a large impact on the economy, but because of its long lag tends to destabilize rather than stabilize the economy; and therefore that there should be no discretionary use of fiscal and monetary policies to stabilize the economy but that the economy will stabilize itself.

Monetary Policy   A policy involving a change in the money supply, such as open market operations.

Money   Whatever is commonly accepted as a means of payment or a medium of exchange in a society.

Money Market Mutual Fund   A mutual fund whose portfolio consists mainly of money market securities such as Treasury bills, commercial paper, and certificates of deposit.

Money Markets   The markets on which marketable securities with a maturity of one year or less are traded.

Mortgage   A loan with real estate and structures as collateral. A mortgage may be a nonmarketable loan made by institutions to individuals and organizations to purchase property and structures, or a marketable security issued by corporations called a mortgage bond.

Mortgage Bond   A corporate bond secured by plant and equipment.

Mortgage Broker   An institution that serves as an intermediary and sometimes as an interim financier in the mortgage market. Mortgage brokers locate prospective mortgage borrowers and lenders and bring them together. They also sometimes continue to service the loan, that is collect the payments, for the lender. Sometimes called mortgage companies.

Municipals (Municipal Securities)   Debt securities issued by state, county, town, city, and district governments. The interest (coupon) on these securities is exempt from the federal income tax.

Mutual Fund (Open End Investment Company)   Investment-type financial institution that raises funds by selling shares in a common portfolio of securities. Their funds are used to purchase these securities. Mutual funds specialize by the types of securities they hold. Mutual funds are called "open end" because they are unlimited in the number of shares they can sell. Mutual fund shareholders can redeem their shares with the mutual fund at the asset value of the share.

Mutual Savings Bank   Financial institution, much like a savings and loan association, whose main sources of funds are time and savings deposits and whose main use of funds is the mortgage. They are all mutual organizations and are concentrated in the northeast part of the United States.

Negotiable Certificate of Deposit (NCD)   *See* Certificate of Deposit

Negotiable Order of Withdrawal (NOW; NOW Account)   Similar to a checking account with the exception that it pays interest; that is, it is an interest-paying, third-party payment account. NOW accounts erode the traditional differences between demand deposits and savings accounts. MSBs in Massachusetts have offered NOW accounts since late 1972; all depository institutions in these two states have been allowed to offer them since January, 1974; and, as of March, 1976 depository institutions in all New England states have been allowed to issue NOW accounts.

Negotiated Underwriting The selection of an investment bank by a corporation to underwrite its security issue by negotiation between the issuing corporation and the investment bank rather than by formal price competition among investment banks. In contrast to competitive underwriting.

Net Borrowed Reserves *See* Net Free Reserves

Net Free Reserves The net reserve (free or borrowed) position of all commercial banks. When the excess reserves of surplus banks are greater than the deficit reserves of deficit banks, the difference is called net free reserves. If the deficits exceed the excesses, the difference is called net borrowed reserves.

New York Stock Exchange (NYSE) The largest organized stock exchange. Some bonds are also traded.

Nominal Rate of Interest The observed rate of interest, uncorrected for inflation.

Noncallable *See* Callable

Okun's Law A relationship between the unemployment rate and the GNP gap (the gap between actual GNP and the potential level of GNP). Okun's law states that for each 1 percent increase in the unemployment rate above 4 percent, actual GNP is an additional 3 percent less than potential GNP.

Open End Investment Company *See* Mutual Fund

Open Market Operations The purchase or sale of Treasury securities (occasionally government agency securities) by the Federal Reserve System enacted to change the money supply.

Operational Efficiency The costs incurred in the operation of the financial markets in allocating funds—the lower the costs, the more operationally efficient the markets.

Organized Exchanges Secondary markets that are physical locations at which representatives of buyers and sellers of securities participate in an auction for the securities. In contrast to over-the-counter markets.

Origination The initial step between an investment bank and a corporation in issuing the corporation's securities in which the investment bank assists in designing the characteristics and timing of the securities to be issued.

Outside Lag Time between when an economic policy change is implemented and when it has an impact on the economy.

Over-the-Counter Markets Secondary markets that are conducted by dealers who supply bid-ask (buy-sell) quotes on the securities in which they deal—customers can buy or sell securities through these dealers. In contrast to organized exchanges.

Pension Fund A contractual-type financial institution that is essentially a retirement fund. Raises funds by contributions from participating employers and employees and invests these funds in a portfolio of securities that provides the wherewithal for payments to participants under specified conditions, usually retirement.

Phillips Curve A curve that reflects an inverse relationship between the unemployment rate and the rate of inflation.

Preferred Stock A corporate security with some characteristics of bonds and some of equities. Has a fixed dividend but no maturity. Nonpayment of dividends is not cause for default, but dividends on common stock cannot be paid when preferred dividend payments are in arrears.

Premium Security A security selling at a price greater than its maturity value. In contrast to discount security.

Primary Security Security being issued or sold for its first time (markets on which primary securities are sold are called primary markets).

Private Placement Selling an entire new issue of a corporate security to one buyer, usually a life insurance company, instead of marketing it to the public. An investment bank is often involved as a mediary. Also called a direct placement.

Quantity Theory of Money The quantity theory of money is a combination of the identity or truism that the product of the money supply and the velocity of money equals the product of the price level and real gross national product and the assumption that the velocity of money is "stable" over time.

Real Estate Investment Trust (REIT) An institution whose assets are primarily related to real estate—both financial assets, such as mortgage loans, and real assets, property they have purchased. They raise funds by equity and commercial paper issues, bank borrowing, and mortgage borrowing. REITs are exempt from corporate income taxes if 75 percent of their assets are in real estate, cash, and government securities and 90 percent of their income is paid in dividends.

Real Rate of Interest The nominal rate of interest minus the rate of inflation.

Recognition Lag Time between when an economic policy change is needed and when its need is recognized.

Refundable A characteristic of a bond that permits the issuer of the bond to retire the bond before its maturity to reissue new bonds, presumably at lower interest rates. The refunding price, the price which the issuer must pay the bond holder to retire the bond, is usually higher than the maturity value. Nonrefundable bonds cannot be retired for the purpose of reissuing new bonds, although they may be retired by the issuer for other reasons. Some bonds are nonrefundable for a specified period and after that become refundable.

Regional Exchanges Organized exchanges for stocks and bonds other than the two national organized exchanges, the New York Stock Exchange and the American Stock Exchange.

Registered Security A security that is registered or recorded by the issuer in the holder's name. Only the holder of record can sell the security.

Regulation Q The regulation by which the Board of Governors of the Federal Reserve System can set maximum interest rates that member commercial banks can pay on their deposits.

Reserve Requirement A requirement imposed by the Federal Reserve System on member commercial banks to keep a specified fraction of their deposits as cash either in their vaults or on deposit at their Federal Reserve Bank. This fraction is called the reserve requirement.

Reserves Funds held by commercial banks either in the form of deposits at their Federal Reserve Bank or cash in their vaults.

Resiliancy A characteristic of a secondary market that indicates the tendency for new buyers or sellers to place orders for a security in response to price decreases or increases, respectively, thus tending to reverse the price change.

Return on Equity (ROE) The ratio of a firm's earnings after taxes to its total equity.

Revaluation *See* Upvaluation

Revenue Bond A municipal bond for which the coupon and maturity payments are paid from revenues from a specific revenue-generating project, such as a toll road or a water project. In contrast to a general obligation bond.

Rights Offering Distribution of "rights" by a corporation to its stockholders in proportion to their stock holdings, which entitle them to purchase additional shares of common stock, usually at a price below the current market price of the stock.

Rolling Over Debt At the maturity of one debt issue, issuing new securities to retire the original maturing debt.

Savings Accounts Deposits at commercial banks, savings and loan associations, mutual savings banks, and credit unions upon which interest is paid and which can be withdrawn at any time without any interest penalty.

Savings and Loan Association A deposit-type financial institution whose main source of funds is time deposits and whose main use of funds is mortgage loans. It receives a tax advantage for specializing in mortgage lending and may be a stock or mutual organization.

Savings-type Insurance Whole life, limited life, or endowment types of life insurance in which payments are made by the insured over a specified period of time (which may be the insured's entire life). This type of policy has a cash value that may be withdrawn at any time or used to purchase a smaller amount of completely paid insurance that requires no further premiums. This type of insurance has a savings component in addition to pure insurance.

Secondary Reserves Commercial bank holdings of very liquid securities, particularly Treasury Bills, which can be readily converted into cash.

Secondary Security After a security's initial sale by its issuer, it is called a secondary security; secondary securities are transferred among security holders on the secondary markets.

Security An IOU or statement of indebtedness. Formally, a contract stating the terms of a loan. An equity, or statement of ownership, is also a security.

Segmentation Hypothesis The hypothesis that asserts that the interest rates on securities of different maturities are essentially unrelated because the markets for securities with different maturities are segmented; that is, there is no shifting among securities of different maturities by buyers and sellers of securities.

Serial Bond A bond issue in which different parts of the issue (specified by serial number) have different maturities.

Sinking Fund The provision in some corporate bonds according to which the issuer has to deposit specified amounts of funds periodically that are used to retire the bonds at their maturity.

Specialists Members of organized exchanges who conduct the auction in certain securities and may also buy and sell for their own account.

Spread The difference between the level of interest rates on two different securities.

Stand-by Agreement An agreement between an investment bank and a corporation according to which the investment bank underwrites any securities a corporation does not successfully sell by other attempted means, usually by rights offerings.

Strong Currency A currency whose value is expected to increase in the future, that is, which is expected to be upvalued.

Structural Unemployment Unemployment caused by workers whose skills are no longer needed by producers. This type of unemployment may be long term and may require retraining or relocation.

Suitability Principle The principle that says that the purchase of long-term assets should be financed with long-term funds and the purchase of short-term assets should be financed with short-term funds.

Support Operation The purchase or sale of its currency by the currency's government for the purpose of keeping the value (or exchange rate) of its currency from decreasing or increasing, respectively. (Similarly the government could sell or purchase, respectively, a foreign currency with its own.)

Syndicate A group of investment banks that collaborate in the underwriting and/or distribution phases of a particular security issue. Brokerage houses may also be included in the syndicate for the distribution phase.

System Open Market Account (SOMA) The account of the Federal Reserve System composed of its holdings of Treasury (and some agency) securities that is either expanded or depleted by open-market operations. The manager of the System Open Market Account is responsible for the actual conduct of the open-market operations.

Tax Anticipation Bill (TAB)   A short-term (one year or less) debt issue by a state or local government that will be repaid out of anticipated tax revenues.

Tax Anticipation Note (TAN)   An intermediate-term (one to five years) debt issue by a state or local government that will be repaid out of anticipated tax revenues.

Term Insurance   A type of life insurance that has no savings component. Insurance is purchased for a specified term. If the insured dies during this term, payment is made to the beneficiary; if not, the insurance lapses at the end of the term and has no value. This is pure insurance.

Term Loans   Loans with a maturity of greater than one year made by commercial banks to businesses.

Term Structure of Interest Rates   *See* Yield Curve

Third Market   Over-the-counter trading of securities that are listed on organized exchanges.

Tight Policy   *See* Contractionary Policy

Time Deposit   Time deposits include saving accounts or deposits and also deposits (sometimes also called time deposits) that earn a higher interest than savings accounts, but which must be left on deposit for a specified period of time (their maturity) and on which a minimum deposit may be required. If these deposits are withdrawn before their maturity, an interest rate penalty is imposed. Deposits of commercial banks, savings and loan associations, mutual savings banks, and credit unions.

Transactions Costs   The costs (including the cost of the required time) of buying or selling a security.

Treasury Bills   Short-term (one year or less) securities issued by the U.S. Treasury. "T-Bills" are issued at a discount and pay no coupon.

Treasury Bonds   Long-term (over seven years) securities issued by the U.S. Treasury. Bond holders receive coupon payments.

Treasury Notes   Medium-term (one to seven years) securities issued by the U.S. Treasury. Note holders receive coupon payments.

Underwriting   The purchase of a new issue of securities from the issuing corporation by one or a group of investment banks. After the underwriting, the investment bank(s) rather than the corporation bear the risk of the security issue. Underwriters can be selected by either negotiation or competition.

Upvaluation (Revaluation)   An increase in the value of a currency, that is, an increase in its exchange rate.

Velocity of Money   The average number of times each dollar in the money supply is spent during a year. Equals nominal GNP divided by the average money supply during a year.

Veterans Administration (VA)   Federal government administration, one of whose functions is to guaranty the mortgage loans of veterans.

Wage-Price Controls or Guidelines   Government policies intended in influence the relative levels of wages and prices.

Wage-Price Spiral   *See* Cost-Push Inflation

Weak Currency   A currency whose value is expected to decrease in the future, that is, which is expected to be devalued.

Yield Curve   A curve showing the interest rates on securities of varying maturities of the same issuer (also called the term structure of interest rates).

Yield to Maturity   The annual return on a bond that represents both the coupon yield and the capital gain or loss if the bond were held until its maturity.

INDEX

Eurodollars, 143, 150, 242, 247–52, 254
Euromarkets, 242, 252–55
European Economic Community (EEC), 224
European Free Trade Area (EFTA), 224
Exchange rate, 225–27. *See also* Money
  determinants, 227–29
  effects, 230, 233–42
  international agreements, 231–35
  Expectations hypothesis, 118–23

Federal agency securities, 124, 185–88, 209
Federal budget, 9, 10, 51–77, 78–79, 186. *See also* Fiscal policies
  deficit, 24–25, 177–79
Federal Deposit Insurance Corporation (FDIC), 150
Federal financing bank, 187–88
Federal government. *See also* Federal budget; Fiscal policies
  balance with private sector, 32, 37
  as deficit sector, 24–25, 177–79
  expenditure, 51–77
  mortgage insurance, 191
  regulations, 248, 260
  and unemployment, 51
Federal Home Loan Bank System (FHLBS), 153–55
Federal Home Loan Mortgage Company (FHLMC), 193
Federal National Mortgage Association (FNMA), 192–93
Federal Open Market Committee (FOMC), 80–81, 83
Federal Reserve System, 79–80, 83, 89, 179–82, 216–17
  role in money supply, 39–44
Finance. *See also* Funds
  nonbank, 25
  direct and indirect, 14
Finance companies, 166–67
Financial institutions, types, 140–66
Financial managers, 3–6
  multinational, 225
Financial systems, 4, 10–14, 24–25, 104
Firms. *See* Business
Fiscal policies, 38, 76–79, 87–91
  and federal budget, 32, 77–79
  Keynesian vs. monetarist, 95–98
  to reduce unemployment, 51–52, 63–64, 78–79
Fixed-price securities, 16, 18
Foreign bonds, 255
Foreign exchange, 225. *See also* Exchange rate
Full employment. *See* Employment, full
Funds. *See also* Business, funds; Commercial banks, funds; Money

aggregate supply and demand, 105
borrowed, 102-5
loanable, 107–8, 129–33
nonbank, 25

General obligation bond, 188
General Theory of Employment Interest and Money (John Maynard Keynes), 91
Geographic mobility, 63–64
GNP. *See* Gross National Product
Goods, 7–9, 11, 35–36. *See also* Production
Government National Mortgage Association (GNMA), 193
Gross National Product (GNP), 34–38
  relation to quantity theory of money, 92–93

Household sector, 8–9, 13, 198
  savings, 57–61
  surplus budget, 10, 24–25
Housing market, 54, 90

Import-export business, 212, 230–31, 233–34
Income
  distribution, 32, 34, 36–37, 53, 55, 68
  household, 8–9
  tax, 115
Indexing, as cure for inflation, 70
Inflation. *See also* Recession
  effects, 34, 68–70, 230–31
  and employment, 34, 65–66, 72–74
  indexing, 70
  and interest rate, 108–14, 134
  and level of demand, 50–52, 65–66
  and production, 66–70
  and resource scarcities, 66–72
  types, 65–70
Interest rate
  business loans, 145–46
  corporate bonds, 19–20, 106
  determinants, 106–14
  effects, 12, 19–22, 53, 54, 104, 236–42, 270
  Euromarket, 249–52, 254
  forecasting, 127–35
  and inflation, 108–14, 134
  international, 231
  interrelations among, 135–38
  and liquidity preference, 106–7, 127–29
  and loanable funds, 107–9, 129–33
  long- and short-term, 22